Ethics for the Coming Storm

Ethics for the Coming Storm

Climate Change and Jewish Thought

LAURIE ZOLOTH

Oxford University Press is a department of the University of Oxford. It furthers
the University's objective of excellence in research, scholarship, and education
by publishing worldwide. Oxford is a registered trade mark of Oxford University
Press in the UK and certain other countries.

Published in the United States of America by Oxford University Press
198 Madison Avenue, New York, NY 10016, United States of America.

© Oxford University Press 2023

All rights reserved. No part of this publication may be reproduced, stored in
a retrieval system, or transmitted, in any form or by any means, without the
prior permission in writing of Oxford University Press, or as expressly permitted
by law, by license, or under terms agreed with the appropriate reproduction
rights organization. Inquiries concerning reproduction outside the scope of the
above should be sent to the Rights Department, Oxford University Press, at the
address above.

You must not circulate this work in any other form
and you must impose this same condition on any acquirer.

CIP data is on file at the Library of Congress
ISBN 978–0–19–766135–2 (pbk.)
ISBN 978–0–19–766134–5 (hbk.)

DOI: 10.1093/oso/9780197661345.001.0001

יוֹמָא חַד הֲוָה אָזֵל בְּאוֹרְחָא, חַזְיֵיהּ לְהַהוּא גַּבְרָא דַּהֲוָה נָטַע חָרוּבָא, אֲמַר לֵיהּ: הַאי, עַד כַּמָּה שְׁנִין טָעֵין? אֲמַר לֵיהּ: עַד שִׁבְעִין שְׁנִין. אֲמַר לֵיהּ: פְּשִׁיטָא לָךְ דְּחָיֵית שִׁבְעִין שְׁנִין? אֲמַר לֵיהּ הַאי גַּבְרָא: עָלְמָא בְּחָרוּבָא אַשְׁכַּחְתֵּיהּ. כִּי הֵיכִי דִּשְׁתַלוּ לִי אֲבָהָתִי — שְׁתַלִי נָמֵי לִבְרָאי.

Talmud, Bavli, Taanit 23a

To my grandchildren, in love and in hope:
Temima, Saadya, Salo, Emuna, Ezra, Zohar, Lola, and Ada.
May you live in a world where you, too, can plant trees for your children.

Contents

Acknowledgments	ix
Introduction: Lightning from a Distant Storm	1
1. The Coming Storm: An Introduction to Our Situation	11
2. The Promises of Exiles: Diaspora as Ontology	32
3. Making a Place: Lisbon and the Narrative of Disaster	69
4. Risky Hospitality: Ordinal Ethics and the Duties of Abundance	88
5. At the Last Well on Earth: Climate Change as a Feminist Issue	107
6. Strangers on a Train: Climate Change and the Problem of Responsibility	129
7. Bad Guys: Amalek and the Production of Doubt	149
8. You Must Interrupt Your Life	178
Conclusion	206
Notes	225
Index	245

Acknowledgments

My assistant editor, Paloma Escovedo, wrote to me just before the press started production on the book you have in your hands. "Do you want to make any changes?," she asked. Now, usually, one thinks of climate change as a very slow process, incremental, and book publishing as a relatively faster one, a matter of a few years, from submission, review, acceptance, to production and distribution. Yet one of the most deeply disturbing aspects of writing this book has been that climate change has actually been much faster than book production, so that every time I turn to the manuscript, I have to write a worsening narrative, add details about heat waves and drying rivers and water rationing and deadly, sudden floods. Every year, the air is warmer and warmer, every year, worsening weather and another mayor or governor on camera, saying, horrified "I have lived here all my life and never seen a storm like this." And every year, we continue to release more climate changing gases into the air above us, and every year, the extraction companies make more and more profit: in 2022, it was 22 billion, their most lucrative year ever, despite wars, inflation, supply chain collapses. So, yes, I returned to these essays to add yet another summer of reportage, and I knew that by the time this book was printed and distributed, a year from that writing, it would be a bit out of date as well, for there will be more desperate dispatches to record. Things got far worse quite quickly in the next year. And the summer of 2023, when I got the manuscript back for the last few corrections, there had already been record breaking heat in the American Southwest for weeks, well over 117 F; then skies thickened with smoke from the burning of the boreal forests of Canada; then there were torrential rains and floods in New England. In my city, Chicago, the choking air made it impossible to be outside; the next, tornado warnings meant heading to the basement. And finally, the horror of the fires in Hawaii. Yet: It is my hope in writing this that we are still capable of making a future together. While it looks like nothing can change, writing a book is a promise that it can, that reading and writing and making a public argument is what can make enduring change happen.

Many thanks are due in any academic book, for one acquires many debts—nothing is written alone. I came late to the conversation about global warming, in 2013, when my eldest son handed me a book, by Matt Ridley, about the topic. It is now a decade later, and the book turned from speculative reportage to the ordinary description of the ordinal crisis we now face, the first small signs, then the larger, tragic disasters. So, first, thank you to Rabbi Matthew Natan Zoloth Levy, PhD, and to Mr. Ridley for the serious attention to this issue, and thank you as well to the colleagues and friends, the 10,000 scholars who are the members of the American Academy of Religion, who, when I called for climate change to be the focus of our research and our conference theme for 2014, turned their serious attention toward the crisis as well. Many have continued that work, and many took up my call that year, a sabbatical year in the Jewish liturgic cycle, for a sabbatical change in how we would gather, meet, and teach. I want to thank former president Jimmy Carter, Charles Kennel, Bill McKibben, Naomi Oreskes, and the IPCC for all coming to speak to that gathering in person that year; and to Mark Oppenhimer,[1] of the *New York Times*, who wrote such a fine story about why this was important. Many others—in particular the colleagues at Yale University, led by Mary Evelyn Tucker and John Grim— have been working in this field for decades. I owe them a tremendous debt, as I do Sarah Fredricks, my colleague at the University of Chicago, who also has been researching and teaching about climate change and religious ethics. Both Erik Owens and Jim Keenen invited me to Boston College to give lectures that ended up at chapters in this book, and Peter Ochs invited me to the University of Virginia to give another. The Society for Scriptural Reasoning University Group has always been eager to think with me about this topic, including Stephen Kepnes, Miriam Feldman, Bob Gibbs, Hanoch Ben Pazi, Susannah Ticcati, David Ford, Nick Adams, Tom Greggs, Rachel Muers, and Jim Foder. *The Journal of Feminist Studies in Religion* encouraged me to think about the impact of climate change on women, which lead to a fourth chapter. Jeffrey Bishop, Helle Haker, Vincent Lloyd, and Gaymon Bennet heard early versions of the chapter on Hospitality and the one on Bad Guys, and their comments were very important as always. I am grateful for all of these opportunities to think aloud with these fine scholars. Thank you, as always, to the wonderful editors at Oxford University Press, Theodore Calderara for attention and encouragement, and to Hemalatha Arumugam, copy edit manager for her careful work.

This book would not have been finished, however, without a generous sabbatical year, granted from the University of Chicago, and without the lovely academic home that Clare Hall creates for its member scholars to think and write together at the University of Cambridge. The other home that year was my parents' house by the sea in California, where I slept and wrote in the loft at night, and in the day, walked on the beach and swam at the cove, where I had spent my childhood. I did not know then that it would be the last year I would see my mother, and the last time I would live on that fragile and vanishing curve of coast, but thinking about the rapidity of its loss, already so apparent, was largely the reason for the urgency in these pages. It is my hope that my parents, Helen and Arthur Zoloth, of blessed memory, who so loved that coast, and so deeply believed in the power of democracy to save the world, would like this book very much.

One depends not only on one's colleagues in writing a book but on one's friends. So thank you to the Berkeley Consortium: Erica Citret Roberts, Judy Kennedy, Pamela Doolan, Susie Jepsen, and Ann Nemer, who cheer me on every week and have for the last fifty years. Even longer: my friends and interlocutors from BHHS. It is a wonderful privilege to be a member of a group who have been my high school buddies since 1964 and remarkably, still love to think and argue fiercely together, including about climate change, and who are so generous with their time as extremely busy grown-ups. Thank you as always to my colleagues at the University of Chicago Divinity School, and in the Society for Jewish Ethics, all at the heart of the conversations about religion and ethics. Thank you to Roberta Glick Unterman, Kent Osband, Pinchas Giller, Willemein Otten, Dwight Hopkins, Jim Robinson, David Edelstein, Michael Balinsky, Myra Rappaport, Lauren and Seth Greenberg, and Marc Berkson, for good advice, patience, and honesty, and for all the gifts of friendship, whether you were virtual or not, during the long days of a pandemic, when this book was completed.

My children, Matty, Noah, Benjamin, Joshua, and Sarah, and the lovely people that they love and have brought to our family, Saskia, Margaux, Reby, and Josh, are always my first audience for my work. You have brought me such joy and love, without which nothing else is possible.

This book is dedicated to my grandchildren: Temima, Saadya, Salo, Emuna, Ezra, Zohar, Lola, and Ada. I have tried my hardest in this book to give voice to the warnings, and to raise the alarm, and to create ways to find solutions to the crisis of global warming and climate change. I wanted you to remember that we stood with all those who rose to the challenge, and who understood what we were facing, and who did not turn away.

Introduction

Lightning from a Distant Storm

You can see the lightning on the underbelly of clouds before you hear the thunder, and you can feel the storm in the air of the world before the rain falls. It is still distant; it may pass you by, and in the flat plains of the Midwest, in the flat city of Chicago, where the horizon is obscured by the built environment, you need to look up against the clouds for the faint blur of light. My father taught me to count, one, one thousand, between the flash and the sound, a count for each mile away, to know when to take cover, to know how much time until the storm came in full. This is a book about that moment. This is a book about climate change, about living in the counting between seeing the distant storm and being surrounded by its thunder. It is a book about how one should act when you know that the storm is inevitable, and what you will do with the time you have. It is also a book about religious ethics, using the language and the syntax and the texts of Jewish thought.

Why write such a book? In part, I wrote this book to think aloud about what I believe to be the most pressing ethical issue of our time. I work as an ethicist and I live as a citizen, and I study the texts of Jewish thought, and I argue in this book that these roles present inescapable and role-specific duties: in the face of a crisis, one must act with all that one has. I also write because, honestly, nothing else, no other language has worked to change human behavior or challenge political and economic structures that it will be necessary to challenge, and it is my hope and intention that the language of Scripture, the Talmud, and philosophy of Judaism may offer a different kind of argument and a different sort of language for such a change. I argue that the traditions, histories, and text of Jewish thought address precisely the sort of existential crisis that we face now, and thus deepen and enrich our public discourse about what to do, how to live, and who to be in our fraught time. Finally, I wrote this book because of the quickening of the air, the shift in the light, that tells us that we are running out of time to make a difference, and I want to be able to say that I did every last thing—every last thing—I could

Ethics for the Coming Storm. Laurie Zoloth, Oxford University Press. © Oxford University Press 2023.
DOI: 10.1093/oso/9780197661345.003.0001

think to do to convince my friends, my neighbors, and my community to address the global warming and the consumptive patterns that drive a disastrously changing climate.

It is impossible to begin a book about climate change without attending to the pandemic crisis of this moment. I finished the penultimate draft of the book you are holding now in England, during the hottest summer on record, day after day so hot that British people felt betrayed somehow, so hot that the land shrank to disclose ancient village walls, and the long, formal lawns turned copper. And in the year that followed, before I returned to write this introduction, things became so immeasurably worse for humans on the planet that reporters began to refer, wistfully, to that time six months ago as "the Before Time." And even though I had written a book about the dangerous way we were living and about how the increasing risks of climate destabilization, ecological greed, and habitat destruction would inevitably lead to an increase in epidemic infectious disease, I was stunned along with everyone else when the coronavirus SARS-Cov2 blazed around the world, and the systems of government were unable to protect us, and in my own country, the promise of human solidarity faltered so completely.

I should not have been. Hadn't I explained the way that scientific thought was rejected, and scientific data denied? Didn't I write about the capacity for oil companies, for example, to hide data or lie about its effects? Surely, I should have understood that powerful interests would pit "the economy" against public health in this case as they do in the case of global warming. COVID-19 was not caused by global warming, but the twin motives of greed and fear that allowed the first local officials in Wuhan, to subvert the carefully organized surveillance project of the Chinese health authorities, or the collapse of any prospect of a collective action response in the United States, or the constant street protests in country after country demanding an end to even minor public health interventions, are the same as the ones I document here. COVID-19 is not directly caused by a changing climate, but it is potentiated by the way we, the big, lovely, lurching human mammals, so very many of us, live in the world: careless, heedless, consuming everything, flying about regardless of the social cost, creating a society structured by race and class, and linking health care to that structure, measuring worth by money alone. It was made worse by politicians who ignored scientists, who thought they could somehow save economies by pretending the physical realities of the natural world could be ignored or temporalized, and who considered sickened and dying people as so many "externalities." The rhetoric of denial as the first impulse, the magical thinking, the making of every single gesture (even wearing a face mask) politically charged—all of this was disturbingly, heart sickeningly, familiar for anyone who had studied the problem of climate change. COVID-19, it was said, "exposed" the realities of health care disparities, as the poorest, oldest, and darkest of our cities died in greater numbers, but this disparity had been known for decades, because it had already happened in heat waves in Chicago, in Paris, in Mumbai. For millions of people, COVID-19 was the first intimation of a changed climate and a changed world, but for Black and Brown communities, and poor white rural communities, it was not unexpected that a catastrophe would affect them differently, for climate change has long affected the most vulnerable more profoundly.

And as I sent this last draft to the publisher, it was after a summer of such intense heat and flooding, such deep and desperate awareness of our situation, so many displaced by global warming, that I took a final look at what I had written and thought: it is already worse than I had told you.

The new news was not only terrifying, though; it was also somewhat hopeful, for it finally spurred some policy action in the U.S. Congress, who passed a formidable bill to fund climate research and support alternative energy in what was described as the most far-reaching climate legislation ever crafted, carefully labeled "The Inflation Reduction Act," which promises several critical incentives to reduce our carbon use. For all who doubt that political change is possible, it was a critical achievement.

In writing this book, however, I am attempting to do more than lament, and more than scold, and even though the warnings in this book seem prescient, more than say, *I told you so.* This book is about how to respond. Herein I describe why the textual, historical, and philosophical resources of religion, in particular Jewish thought, offer a rich and robust language that addresses our situation. This is a book in which I ask you, as reader, to think along with me in these eight linked chapters about global warming and the way it will change our world. I argue that if we do not attend to this issue, it will change the world far more profoundly than even one terrible pandemic. In these chapters, I will argue that Jewish theological and philosophical traditions allow an ethics for this time of counting down and give a grammar of inquiry to the debates about what to do about global warming. I will argue that such a grammar can be in the imperative, can be decisive, and could make you stop how you are living and think seriously about changing our fate. And while this will seem grandiose, unthinkable, it is our fate to live in unthinkable times, to need to act in unthinkable times.

One does not have to act alone, but one does have to act in the first person. One is not alone because we live in communities of meaning, memory, and history. For people of faith, one lives in awareness of God's presence, or in the presence of the staggeringly gorgeous natural world, or in the richly humming silence of meditative practices, or the cacophonous narrative of Scriptural texts. Theology, in the words of theologian Benjamin Quash, is "found" in every place. For Jews, who consider themselves as members of a reception community that observes Jewish law, or that studies the classic texts of Jewish law, in the Torah and the Talmud, this means one reflects on the questions of ethics within a profound complexity of discourse, complete with rabbis from the first century, nudging and interrupting at your elbow as you read. In this book, I also bring Emmanuel Levinas and Hannah Arendt to join the discussion, so to speak, for speaking and thinking is how we begin to live ethically. This is the puzzle of Jewish moral agency, in the writing of both these philosophers (which is why it is only right that they join us), for while you are responsible, as an individual, you are not really alone in that responsibility, for you are not without the presence of the Other, for both thinking and acting are impossible without her. Further, as a Jewish philosopher, one is never without the presence of one's teachers and their books. The act of ethics, for Levinas, is the moment of recognition of the plight of the Other, and it is the phenomenological event of this recognition that he teaches. The act of ethics, for Arendt, is the moment of thinking and judging. You will see both arguments in this book.

Here let me make a note about the methodology in this book. One way to recognize the Other and thus to think about ethics in a Levinasian way is with the narratives that have been held and saved over generations in the Hebrew Scripture, and in the Mishnah and Gemorah that make up the Talmud, the central corpus of classical Jewish thought. Let me make a note here at the outset about this method.

First, I am not a scholar of rabbinics, but an ethicist. This means that while I turn to the legal and narrative texts of the classic Jewish corpus, I do so to consider the moral puzzles about which the rabbis are arguing, and there is much more that needs to be said—and scholars far better than I do say it—about the linguistics, the syntax, and cultural history, and the intricate rules of rabbinic literature. I have had the great opportunity to study with brilliant text scholars, like David Winston, Daniel Boyarin, Michael Balinsky, Joseph

Liebowitz, and Herbert Basser, and I know how limited my knowledge is relative to my good teachers!

Levinas, when he turns to a "Jewish reading of Scriptures," makes a similar explanation about his method:

> Our more modest intention is to illustrate, by example, certain ways of reading. We shall do this by presenting a Talmudic extract which produces, in the form of arguments, the exegesis of Biblical verses. Nevertheless, in doing this we shall find ourselves being led to some propositions of a more general character . . . exegesis of the exegesis, a privileged text, even if it does not exclude different insights into the same subject. This is in keeping with the characteristic pluralism of rabbinic thought . . . this reading of the Talmud would not be possible to us without recourse to a modern language—in other words, without touching on the problems of today. Admittedly, it is not the only possible reading, but it has the value of a testimony. It testifies to at least one of the ways in which the contemporary Jews understand traditional hermeneutics.[1]

Second, when I study the Talmud, I am interested in the way in which a society is described where the most vulnerable—widows, orphans, and strangers—are central to the outworking of the theological promise. I argue in this book that this is how Jewish ethics works: as a long interpretive argument about how Scripture is understood by the reception community as divinely commanded words: Law. This, I argue, is made into a socially pragmatic system by the rabbinic authorities, involving a legal code system that they describe as having 613 commanded acts, *halachah*. It is my contention that it is in this system that ethical behavior unfolds, using a language that powerfully challenges the brutal logic of the marketplace and the imperial system of state power. Other readers of the Talmud surely will disagree or will see different aspects of rabbinic ethical thought. But you, as the reader, are both invited and cautioned. Invited, because the textual accounts I am using to understand our situation, (that task of philosophy) are interpreted with your insights; and cautioned, because broad sweeping claims about Jewish ethics or rabbinic thought are bound to be oversimplifying. These are nuanced claims, particular, and meant for contestation, and while I do make normative statements, they are meant as the beginning of a discourse, one among many other important aspects of the texts.

Third, this will not be a book with a reductive turn to texts that tell the reader what to do, for the logic of textual arguments in ethics is more complex. Levinas, here too, reminds us that "there is a danger of sporadic explanations, the danger of a premature good conscience." In my reading, the Hebrew Scripture is a set of stories, speeches, and interrupted tales. At times, arguments and failure seem to be at the center of the story. The patriarchal figures are querulous, the matriarchs sometimes lie, and the people are full of doubt and dissent. In the Promised Land, the people stray, and the glittering idols are set up. At other times, grace is possible, the people are chosen, and they have the strength to stand up from slavery and terrible plagues to make a world overflowing with abundant love and God's favor. But it is here, in the narratives of Scripture and the commentaries on their complexities, that we find language equipped to deal with the enormity of fatal choice, of nature seemingly held in the hand of God, and of a revolt of the poor against unwinnable odds, pharaohs, and chariots. This is why I turn to the exegetical narrative method I will use in the book, because it is my contention that we will need these rich and abundant languages to adequately address the enormity of a changing climate, for frankly, the language of politics has proved too contentious, the language of the marketplace too easily seductive, the language of science too technical, and the language of policy too arid.

The pandemic is, like climate change, a worldwide phenomenon, a "hyperobject,"[2] a revelation, a flood. It is of biblical proportions, and yet experienced personally, and its largeness makes it overwhelming and close. We feel the weight of history; we are aware of the momentous nature of our daily lives.

Consider the pandemic a preview of advanced climate change. What is happening in months: economic despair, disease, dislocations, flight from cities—are things scientists foretell unfolding in years. Can we learn some lessons from this pandemic? Perhaps in the way we need to respond? I will argue that we can. In thinking about the plague we face, and how it is related to climate change, and thus ends up in the introduction to this book, I have been considering the concept of sacrifice. And while it is naïve to essentialize religions or make broad sweeping claims about "religious values," I can defend the idea that sacrifice is a religious concept, and that sacrifice plays a central role in many religions. Let us turn to explore this.

One of the puzzles of climate change denial and pandemic refusals is how differently the polity—not only in America—is responding from how an earlier generation responded to the threat of fascism in World War II. Why is it so very hard to wear a mask? To give up eating or drinking in large, closely packed groups? To make the mildest of sacrifices, especially when health care workers are sacrificing so much? To accept vaccines? This is important because the essays in this book call for far more impactful and radical sacrifices, such as giving up meat, walking instead of driving, living in smaller spaces, and using fewer resources. If wearing a mask is so difficult, how will it go when these more difficult choices need to be made?

It is my contention that the call for sacrifice of self needs religious or strong communal justification, and in America in particular, where social justification is quite weak, where individualism is valorized, where we are relentlessly sold the idea that a drive in a car is not just transport, but an ontologically liberatory experience, where we are constantly told to care first for oneself, and where religion is often a cheery event promising personal satisfaction or therapeutic renewal, it is not at all surprising that the concept of radical sacrifice is so problematic. Even tiny radical sacrifice, much less what we will need to do to change how we burn fuel into the air, is considered a terrible imposition.

The sort of sacrifice I am imagining involves figuring out the perimeters of the self, and accepting upon oneself the constancy of the call of the Other as exactly that which makes us human in the first place. We find this in Scriptural terms, where we learn that what we think we possess is a fiction, for what we "have" in the Lockean sense, that soil, water, and sun which we have mixed our labor power with to create a crop, not even that, is fully ours. But my reading of the biblical and Talmudic texts reveals another possibility.

It is the cycle and shape of the harvest that teach us best about tithing or sacrificing a tenth of one's crop. In the commentary on both Ruth and in Leviticus, the farmer-readers of the text of the Hebrew Bible are reminded that the harvest is always more abundant than can be gathered in one's own hands, that the field's corners are always out of reach of the plow, that the grain will always fall behind you as you gather it in. This is not clumsiness; it is simply the way that human persons and the natural world are so constructed, with error, loss, and leavings left behind, for we are made as persons like the Torah text is written: with gaps, and silences, to be filled in with talk. Every human work is like this. When we tithe the crop, it is because not all of it belongs to us in the first place; it is simply held by us in keeping for the poor. In this deepest sense then, 10% of your work, and 10% of your life, is simply not yours: it is kept, stored, only for the moment when the poor come to call for it. Aquinas will remind Christians of this, when he notes that the clothes in your possession that you are not wearing, the food you are not eating, the gold you are not holding, all of this belongs to the poor. And it does not matter how poor you are in this most Jewish of systems, this theo-political economy, for even the poorest must also give their tenth.

A small narrative: Teaching in the wake of the destruction of the Second Temple, we are told that Johanon b. Zakkai considers what to do. At stake was how to exist without the centrality of sacrifice. Without the moaning of the animals, the pools of blood, the loss of the most perfect lamb, without the priest dipping his hands in the blood and the blood on the gold of the Temple, without the expiation of the scapegoat: how to be religious? How to act as a faithful Jew outside the Second Temple walls, walking ever deeper into exile, trying to live in the new empire of glitzy road projects and the military might of Rome. One way the narratives of the Talmud work is to tell us carefully that the answer will be a complicated set of substitutions, using speech ritual to restate the activities of the sacrifice; to replace it with structured prayers and to give *tzedakah*-charity. Giving tzedakah is elevated to the level of Temple service and the reception of the Divine Presence.[3]

This is a most serious sort of rethinking about how sacrifice works, for it is what philosophers call an ontological issue, as opposed to a normative issue. It is where one asks *Who am I?* and not only *What do I do?* One must ask:

Who you are, answers, Emmanuel Levinas, the Lithuanian, French philosopher, is the one who must respond: I am the one who will come up with what you need, naked, hungry stranger, I will find in myself the resources that you need. Levinas makes the "inconvertible demand for justice the equivalent of the spirituality of the Spirit and the proximity of God."[4]

As you have already seen in this introduction, Levinas will be important to every essay in this book, for he insists that prior to the recognition of the Other, the self is not fully constituted or called into being. This is not merely a liturgical gesture, for sacrifice is not a transactional bargain. He repeatedly writes to remind us that the central text of Isaiah 58, read on the central day of the liturgy of Yom Kippur, is about precisely this point: the pious ones ask of God: "Why have we fasted, and why have we humbled ourselves, and thou takest no knowledge of it?"

Levinas tells us that the answer of the prophet is that the ordinary economic life, the normative brutality and casual domination must in some way be broken, not only by faith expressed in ritual, but by something far harder—by interrupting one's life with the ethical, with the personal risky demand to share your bread with the hungry, and bring the homeless poor into your house, to see nakedness, and see that it is just like your own nakedness. Then, and only then, can the healing of justice begin. The Isaiah text continues, switching from admonition to reconciliation. The language of the vision is one of a curious reversal: if this is done, says the text:

> Your righteousness (tzaddik) shall go before you, and the glory of the Lord shall be your rear guard. Then you shall call, and the Lord will answer you; you shall cry, and he will say "Here I am." (Isaiah 58)

Who I am is tied to what I must do, for the self is incomplete as a self, enwrapped, clothed, in itself, until one hears the call of the Other and there finds the divine. Levinas notes:

> Ethics is not the corollary of the vision of God, it is that very vision. Ethics is an optic, such that everything I know of God and everything I can hear of his word and reasonably say to Him must find an ethical expression.[5]

There is a strong school of thought that argues that in the rabbinic imaginary, the Torah is a narrative of God's search for a person that can finally answer "Hineni"—here I am. To be present ethically is to accept God's reality and authority, difficult in modernity, to be sure, and then to find courage to act in the face of that responsibility. The biblical narrative begins with men and women who cannot utter that word: Adam, Eve, Cain, and Noah, and if after them, Abraham finally can answer in this way, then the great reversal in this verse from Isaiah is even more striking. Your own deeds of justice go first, then the self, then the Lord in the rear guard, and this time, it will be God who answers "Hinini," a presence only possible if the obligation to the Other, if the ceaseless cry of the Other to you, is heard and answered first.[6]

So here is my appeal to you, reader: my appeal-meaning entreaty, petition, invocation, prayer. The world we live in, the world I describe in this book, has become, because of our actions, balanced on the black granite edge of all that we know as steady and stable. We now know this danger because we have lived in the years of pandemic and plague, fire and flood. It is not the only time the Jewish people have been at that edge, and because of that, I believe that the Jewish tradition carries some good answers, a logic map, and narrative tools for how we might respond now only as Jews, but at participants in humanity's great moral trials. Climate change is coming, and we must think now about how to be the people that will come up with what is needed for our planet, its animals, waters, forests, air, and our precious neighbors to survive.

In these chapters, I consider how these narrative and metaphors and commands allow a better way to talk to one another, to talk as Jews and as human beings, about this present moment. This is not a how-to book. It is a book about why-to, a book of essays about the worth of our lives, and about how to act with decency when faced with the tragic, enormous consequences of choices we did not make. I reflect on our situation and suggest that attention to our scientific plight means we cannot *not* act; and that attention to our moral plight means understanding that part of us is claimed by and owed to the Other, kept until the poor come for it, a constancy of our very being.

The summer of 2020 ended with the report that it was the warmest since records had been kept in my city of Chicago, and that the permafrost in Siberia was melting at a rate 600 times faster that it would be due to natural causes. The year 2021 only brought more news of disasters. A huge sinkhole opened in the Arctic, and the methane trapped in it unfurled into the air, which will accelerate the warming of the earth exponentially. Glaciers melted at a record pace. Hurricanes swept into the Gulf of Mexico and slammed into the coasts of Texas, Louisiana, and Costa Rica, and it was still August. Tornados obliterated towns in the South in the winter of 2021, after Texas froze and Portland sweltered under a heat dome—everything unprecedented. A ring of fires surrounded the cities of the California Bay Area as the old growth redwood that had stood long before human habitation burst into flame when lightning storms raked the summer skies and torched the forests and the air thickened with heat and smoke. The fire season started early, fiercer than in a hundred years and the mountains on the coast burned, facing the sea. The Big Basin redwoods that shaded hidden streams with deep green pools, the water cold and dark, redwood bark dusting the air when the gold shafts of light broke through the lacy leaves, all burned, and the mustard hills of the East Bay burned. Here is where I had taken my children to swim, where we had camped and found wood iris and miner's lettuce, all of it gone, and it will not be the last loss. In 2022, smoke from the fires of the West rose into space, blurring the stars, the worst year for fires, floods yet seen in the world.

We are counting now, one, one thousand, two, one thousand, waiting to see what comes next.

1
The Coming Storm

An Introduction to Our Situation

When I first wrote an essay about the environment, it was late in the game, 1996. I wrote it for an interfaith group of scholars of religion, gathered to consider the relationship among consumption, reproduction, and the environment. We did not discuss global warming, nor did we mention climate change, and most of us did not know about the data that were already alarming scientists. We were concerned about pollution, food scarcity, the destruction of habitats, and the irreparable damage to a fragile ecosystem—ecological issues. I had just finished my graduate school training and had completed a book about health care ethics. My training in bioethics had focused on the dilemmas of the clinical encounter: one doctor, one patient, the dramas of death, life, and intimate choices, raising important ethical conflicts, questions, and competing moral appeals in medicine. National debates in bioethics were emerging about end-of-life care and reproductive technology but also increasingly about theoretical questions, such as "What would happen if a technology that doesn't exist (human cloning) became globally popular and fundamentally changed the nature of our species?" or "What if brain scans could be done from afar and governments could use fMRIs to know your thoughts?" Bioethicists in later decades were already beginning to focus their concern about the most arcane of issues, or the rarest of human conditions, fantastic and philosophically interesting.

But I was already looking elsewhere, beyond the world of the bedside. Medical treatments, medical science research, public policy, and health care are issues that, while they occur in the ordinary terms of a personal life, are inexorably set in a context of a far larger world, a fragile and beset environment. Far from the ethical dilemmas that academic bioethics considered were the lives of millions of people whose health status was bound up in their environment, increasingly an environment that had been degraded by exploitation of resources, or the use of chemicals, or the desertification of farmland. In this, I knew, the world's poor face faced different choices and far different dilemmas

Ethics for the Coming Storm. Laurie Zoloth, Oxford University Press. © Oxford University Press 2023.
DOI: 10.1093/oso/9780197661345.003.0002

than we in the West confronted or that were the central subject of my field. I saw this in the long stories of illness that the migrant families brought to the pediatric hospital where I worked and in the ways that children's bodies bore the fates they had fled. I saw this when I read of lead exposure in the neighborhoods where our patients lived, in the way that the few parks filled with trash, and in the way the lakes and rivers of my California childhood had become so polluted that they were closed for swimming. When I was asked to join a group that was going to research environmental issues and consider how population and consumption created pressures on the environment, I was eager to begin making the links between health care and the larger social world. If you read the first published version of this essay, published twenty-two years ago, you would see how odd it was that our project gave no thought to global warming, knew no specifics about the parts per million (ppm) of global CO_2, nor understood that sea-level rise was inevitable. It was written a year after what is still America's worst heat-related catastrophe, the Chicago heat wave of 1995, where in that steaming city, the dead bodies of the poor and the elderly were taken out to the curbs because the city ran out of spaces at the morgue. By 1996, NASA scientist James Hansen had already testified before Congress about global warming; and a decade of obfuscation by the energy industry had already blocked three treaties and U.S. legislation to take action, and despite an early consensus that action was immediately needed, the proposed legislation had already had its first defeats.[1] All of this occurred, but we at our meetings somehow did not notice or speak of it. We did not fully have an understanding of the threat that would not only potentiate but also outweigh every other environmental issue was to come.

For this book, I return to the problem I raised in that original essay. We are born into a world that we did not make, that is a free gift to us, so ordinary a gift that we think it barely worthy of notice. (Our entrance may be the last moment we are all essentially equal in our reception of this gift.) How can we come to understand our situation as beings on an earth, surrounded by air and light and water, who are living in a place that we both deliberately and carelessly abuse, where resources are becoming scarce, and where the well-being and basic health of our neighbors on this earth are threatened? It was my contention then, as it is now, that when we make moral choices about our behavior, we also make ontological decisions—they define our character, our "excellences" or virtues, which we learn from Maimonides, who as he learned it in turn from Aristotle, are the sum of our actions. Who we became as Americans was inexorably shaped by the decisions we made, both action and inaction. For I turned away from the issue of the environment as well, and for the next two decades thought about other things, raised children, worked and prayed, and thought I knew the world.

A World Connected

By 1996, we understood, or rather, had remembered, the power of epidemic infectious disease. AIDS, the epidemic which at that moment had so altered health care in American hospitals, was linked to American lives via a vast and intricate web that included dozens of disparate elements: global trade, hunger in West African villages and the need to eat bush meat to survive, the trucking industry barreling along the new roads across that continent, discriminatory anti-gay policies in Haiti, a culture of secrecy and yet suddenly changing sexual practices, and forestry use policies that allow human habitation in previously untouched areas. All of these global politics, all those large, international economic and social forces, and it came down to a young man dying of pneumonia, with his shocked family by his side.

This insight that clinical ethics, the personal dramas each family faces, was deeply connected to issues of larger global injustice also led me to reflect on why the field of bioethics needed to take into account the problem of our relationship to the environment. The relationship exists in both directions. Not only did I come to see that personal clinical choices were taken in the context of the larger world, and that all of the research and policy would in fact impact that world, but I began to see that the issues raised by theorists from the other discourse of environmentalism had important implications for the way that individuals made their personal choices about clinical medicine. AIDS, birth control, and animal research were only the most obvious issues, the ones that were most clearly understood from popular accounts. Far less obvious was that the steady accumulation of carbon dioxide (CO_2), which had begun with the first machine, was increasing the total amount of carbon in the atmosphere. This would alter the climate of the earth in ways that would have a direct and worsening effect on human health. It was a special sort of paradox that the very technology and the increasingly complex machinery of modern ICUs and NICUs that so revolutionized health care and extended so many lives was also a driver of the increased need in modernity for more and more energy, which then created a crisis that would come to endanger those lives.

But this was only one way the connection between climate change and health was expressed. The pandemic would make it clear that we actually knew very little about human epidemics and remind us again that no act in the clinic takes place in isolation. Every single choice—every one—that we made as social creatures, how to use the land, how to structure and marginalize populations, how to fund health care, how to regard aging—all cascaded upon us in bioethics as we tried to sort out a good course in the pandemic, and this made me certain that bioethics could not afford to again turn from the larger issues of how our environment was changing. Thus, the turn to the issues of this book, ever more urgently.

The Scientific History: What We Should Have Known

Let us take a condensed look at the history of the science that is behind this statement. In this first chapter, I am going to walk us briefly through the history and some of the science needed to understand our moral situation. This will prepare us to return to the question of how religion, and Jewish thought in particular, enables us to respond more coherently to this urgent moral problem of global warming. This history is condensed because there are excellent books that rehearse this in great detail, but it is included because it is important to understand how we arrived at this place and into what world we were thrown. In bioethics, we always were taught that "good ethics starts with good medicine,"[2] and here, too, good ethics starts with good science. It is one of many ways I am going to think with you about our problem.

By 1996, when we in the group of scholars were writing that book about ecology, the major oil and gas extraction and refining companies already knew that the problem of global warming did indeed have global health implications. Their own scientists told them, because their own scientists knew their history: the effect of burning coal and petroleum had been studied for years. In fact, scientists were curious about it in the eighteenth century as coal began to blacken the sky above Europe—wouldn't it affect the air in some fundamental way, they wondered, this black sky?

The awareness of how gases generated by human activity are trapped by the stratosphere, and then the awareness of the global impact on temperature of these gases largely emerged in the study of two unrelated fields. First was the nineteenth-century curiosity about glaciation, origins, and Ice

Ages, and the next was the urgency of the task facing the naval weathermen in World War II. The first of these research fields was necessarily speculative, for measurements of past events was still difficult. However, in 1824, the French physicist Joseph Fourier speculated that the reason that the glaciers had once seemed to have covered larger areas of the planet, and that, conversely, the seas had risen to levels not seen in human history, was the fluctuation of the climate. We live on Earth as if in a greenhouse, Fourier wrote:

> The temperature [of the Earth] can be augmented by the interposition of the atmosphere, because heat in the state of light finds less resistance in penetrating the air, than in re-passing into the air when converted into non-luminous heat.[3]

Louis Agassiz,[4] meanwhile, was interest in the history of fish. In 1829, he moved from an exhaustive study of the history of newly discovered Brazilian fish, to the fish of his own region, Switzerland. And he began to publish what would be a five-volume treatise on the fossil fish in the region of Neuchâtel. Now famous, he journeyed to England and Scotland, again, looking at fish fossils. It was clear to him that the earth must have been warmer in the past, a world that was tropical, but that the climate had changed, and the tropical creatures must have died and sunk into mud, and then must have been covered by earth, and then ice, over unimaginable time periods until they turned to fossilized stone.

In 1837, Agassiz proposed that the Earth had been subjected to a past ice age. He presented the theory to the Helvetic Society that ancient glaciers had not only flowed outward from the Alps, but also even larger glaciers had covered the plains and mountains of Europe, Asia, and North America, smothering the entire Northern Hemisphere in a prolonged ice age.

But how can a climate change so dramatically, and what could force such a change? Scientists in America were just as curious about the fossils they were finding, because they, too, could clearly see the existence of glaciers, and rocks that showed tropical fossil life, and the evidence of dinosaur bones, first found in 1842. How to explain these observations?

The basic scientific hypothesis behind global warming was first proposed in 1856 when Eunice Newton Foote, an American inventor and what would come to be called a "scientist," became curious about how the sun's heat affected the air, then the temperature of the air, and thus, the climate at different stages of the world's history. Foote was interested in testing one hypothesis, that the mix of molecules in the air had been different at different geological time periods and noted that:

> (A)n atmosphere of that gas would give to our earth a high temperature ... (A)t one point in history the air had mixed with it a larger proportion than at present, and an increased temperature from its own action as well as from increased weight must have necessarily resulted.[5]

The sun's rays were constant and had not changed, but the air that wrapped the earth must have changed. Foote the inventor constructed an elaborate apparatus to test this idea.

Foote conducted a series of experiments that demonstrated the interactions of the sun's rays on different gases. She used an air pump, four thermometers, and two glass cylinders. First she placed two thermometers in each cylinder, and then, by using the air pump, she removed the air from one cylinder and condensed it in the other. Allowing both cylinders to reach the same temperature, she placed the cylinders in the sunlight to measure their temperature variance once heated by the sun, but under different moisture conditions. She performed this experiment on CO_2, common air, and hydrogen. Of the gases she tested, Foote concluded that carbonic acid trapped the most heat, reaching a temperature of 125°F.

Foote illustrated her findings in a paper entitled "Circumstances Affecting the Heat of Sun's Rays," which was accepted at the eighth annual American Association for the Advancement of Science meeting on August 23, 1856. It is not clear why Foote did not present her own work at the conference, as women were in principle allowed to speak, but it was given instead by Prof. John Henry of the Smithsonian Institution. Before reading Foote's work, Henry introduced the findings by stating:

> Science was of no country and of no sex. The sphere of woman embraces not only the beautiful and the useful, but the true.

Foote's paper was published later the same year under her own name in the *American Journal of Arts and Science*. That same edition of the journal held a paper by Irish physicist John Tyndall on color blindness.[6]

Tyndall, who in histories of global warming is usually credited with first testing and characterizing how CO_2 and other gases may heat the atmosphere differently, makes no mention of Foote. Tyndall began doing experiments with gases as well, a practice made popular by Humphrey Davy, and Joseph Priestly of the British Royal Society. Like Foote, Tyndall was interested in the action of "radiant energy" or infrared radiation from the sun on the difference gas molecules being characterized as making up "air." It had been understood by others that a blanket of air surrounded the planet, and that the sun's rays were both able to penetrate it and were themselves reflected back upward. Tyndall wondered how each gas differed in absorbing and perhaps reflecting the energy of the sun. Tyndall then constructed a device that measured relative adsorption of differing gases and noted that water vapor was the most absorbent, with CO_2 close behind. In the "greenhouse" this was important.

> This aqueous vapour is a blanket more necessary to the vegetable life of England than clothing is to man.[7]

Tyndall and Foote understood that as the composition of the gases changed, more and more sunlight would be absorbed and not reflected back, disrupting the balance and leading to increased heating of the planet. This is the essential concept, and it has not changed: CO_2 molecules adsorbed heat and did not reflect it, so changing the amount of CO_2 in the air made the climate warmer or cooler within the blanket of air that encircled the earth.

And the gases in the air were changing. The Industrial Age had begun, in 1712, when the British inventor Thomas Newcomen made the first widely used steam engine to use coal. The atmosphere had already changed in the 150 years since machines had become widespread and Foote and Tyndell began their measurements.

Forty years later, this effect could precisely (and obsessively) be measured by Svante Arrhenius, a scientist, alone, during a long Swedish winter. Arrhenius measured the amount of energy reaching the top of Earth's atmosphere. He calculated that each second, on a surface area of one square meter of the earth that faced the sun during daytime, exactly how much sunlight is absorbed, and then he estimated how much of the sunlight that reaches the top of the atmosphere is reflected back into space by clouds (and later, as it turned out, by aerosols or tiny particles, which were only present in small amounts in his era but are more common today). This accounted for about one-third of the sunlight. Light-colored areas of Earth's surface—mainly snow, ice, and deserts—reflect the remaining two-thirds of the sunlight back into space. This meant that the conditions were more or less stable, with the sunlight that shone on the Earth reflected back, keeping the overall climate predictable, year after year, with the Earth's temperature generally in balance. But Arrhenius was also interested in how the Industrial Revolution functioned as the driver of atmospheric change.

Arrhenius calculated the baseline presence of CO_2 and extrapolated out the likely impact that the new Industrial Revolution would have, for as petroleum and coal were burned, carbon molecules would be released into the atmosphere. This is because all living beings—all plants, insects, birds, fish, mammals, from mice to people—have carbon molecules as a key component of their biology that exist in a precarious balance, which he worried would be disrupted.

Arrhenius knew, of course, dinosaurs are carbon-based as well. When millions of dinosaurs died over millions and millions of years, their bodies decomposed and were intensely concentrated into seams of coal, gas, and oil—animals, plants, fish, pressured into the earth, and then dug up and burned. This was coal, the first and most important driver of the Industrial Revolution. This was such an efficient source of energy it replaced the human labor, and water and wind power of earlier centuries, allowing most human beings to use their energy in nearly creative ways, and allowing a burst of human production of physical goods that had once required endless hours of labor. However, as he knew even then, significant amounts of CO_2—the carbon molecules bonded to oxygen—were given off as a by-product of the burning. CO_2 adsorbed and did not reflect sunlight; instead, it kept it in the atmospheric greenhouse. This was a new feature of the Industrial Age, this capacity to create and retain vast amounts of chemical waste in our water, our land, and CO_2 in our air, disrupting natural processes. He was aware of a quickening cycle: more carbon sources dug up and burned, the more CO_2 released, and the more absorbed radiant energy would be produced. This led Arrhenius to calculate when the warming caused by increased CO_2 would begin to be noticeable. He thought it would be apparent only over centuries, but that its effects would inexorably continue to mount.[8] If the amount of CO_2 doubled, he speculated, the global temperature would rise by 3°C–4°C. It seemed both unlikely and perhaps salutary to him, sitting in his freezing cabin in December, buried under several feet of snow. A warmer world would be abundant and fecund, he believed.

What Arrhenius did not anticipate was the rapidity and the volume of carbon fuel consumption. As machines begun to take over every aspect of human endeavor, the race to power the railroads, factories, steamships, and mills, more and more deposits of stored carbon deposits were found, petroleum for example, and the search for them shaped our geography, politics, and our history. Nations with lots of carbon sources—the U.S., the British, French, and German colonies of the Middle East—were in play, deserts and wastelands suddenly valuable because of the carbon resources beneath them.

By 1927, the carbon emissions from fossil fuel burning and industry reached 1 billion tons per year, and by 1930, the population reached 2 billion people and emissions increased to 3.92 billion tons. As the human population grew, and the use of machine and industrial coal production increased, the amount of CO_2 grew as well.

In 1938, a British engineer, curious about Arrhenius's work, began keeping records from 147 weather stations around the world. Guy Callendar showed that temperatures had risen over the previous century. He also showed that CO_2 concentrations had increased over the same period and, based on his close reading of Arrhenius, suggested this caused the warming, but it was far faster than Arrhenius had suspected.

Largely the science that warned of consequences was ignored, and the "Callendar effect" was widely dismissed by meteorologists. Weather seemed far more important and more immediate than climate; there were other pressing scientific questions to be solved; and the Industrial Age promised such a good and happy future. Predicting weather patterns was important for two reasons: planning in agriculture, and planning in war. And because weather in the nineteenth and twentieth centuries was relatively uneventful,[9] farmers tended to depend on folk wisdom, secure in its predictability.

War was another matter. The story told at this point in the history of climate research is the narrative of D-Day, where the entire victory is said to have rested on the weather experts who predicted a several-hour lull in a long storm front. The fact that the Allied scientists predicted the lull and the Axis scientists did not is a central theme of the narrative. In war, weather really matters. And this meant that for the first time, weather and climate science could be funded as a serious enterprise. During the Cold War, meteorologists quietly began collecting data about temperature change. But collection was difficult, measures varied between discipline and countries, and little was known in the West about the weather in Eastern Bloc countries or large parts of Asia and Africa. It was thought that the oceans might adsorb some of the excess carbon, but it was not clear—there were very few collection devices on the world's oceans.

It was not just the lack of instruments. Additionally, there was no one academic field to study the problem Callendar had stumbled upon, and agree on how to measure the amount of carbon being produced by all the industrial sources, or to record temperature at various locations, or to document sea-level rise or surface temperature over land masses, or to study desertification. Journals were specific for one field or another. There were no dedicated and targeted funding sources, nor an agency that would organize research. In the end, it was a field unrelated to earth sciences that began to use a technical methodology that would end up becoming critical to the search for climate data.

Off in the distant field of fossil collection, at the Oriental Institute at the University of Chicago, scientists began to experiment with an isotope of carbon (carbon 14) to date fossils and other artifacts. This technology, "carbon dating," which used measurement of carbon 14 as it degrades, meant that the scientists were able to estimate, with greatly improved accuracy, the age of specimens, based on the rate of decay of the carbon. The same instruments that measured carbon in fossils could also measure carbon in the atmosphere. This was an interest of the military, which also solved the problem with finding funding:

> (A) substantial part of the support (for climate measurement) was indirectly related to the Cold War. Libby (the head researcher) acknowledged that he was "also indebted to the Air Force . . . for a contract for the development of low-level counting techniques during 1949 . . . " The Air Force had negligible interest in the dates of Egyptian mummies, but it had a hearty concern for delicate radioactivity measurements (one likely use was detecting residues from Soviet nuclear bomb tests). As Libby discreetly remarked, Chicago people built up expertise in measuring radioactivity "in other connections." The separation of isotopes was likewise under investigation for military as well as civilian uses.[10]

In the mid-1950s, scientists had nearly forgotten questions about the relationship between an increasing industrial carbon burden—the burning of oil and gas, releasing CO_2—and a warming climate. It was the height of the Cold War, and funding was shifting toward projects that could be of more immediate interest to the military. Scientists argued that gas was ephemeral, and any extra CO_2 would not stay around in the atmosphere but would be taken up by the oceans and sink. "Most of the CO_2 on the surface of the planet was not in the tenuous atmosphere but dissolved in the huge mass of water in the oceans. Obviously, no matter how much more gas human activities might pour into the atmosphere, nearly all of it would wind up safely buried in the ocean depths."[11]

But not all scientists were as sanguine. Consider Gilbert Plass, a researcher at the University of Colorado. In 1953, Plass and colleagues James Rodger Fleming and Gavin Schmidt decided to return to Arrhenius and to measure the amount of CO_2 and the average earth temperature, and found a direct correlation. The paper, "Carbon Dioxide and the Climate," argued, alarmingly, that based on the evidence, a doubling of the carbon in the atmosphere would lead to a 3.6°F rise in average global temperatures. Very few scientists were convinced—even if that was true, ran the standard scientific response, any extra carbon would be harmlessly absorbed by the oceans.[12]

In 1957, the American oceanographer Roger Revelle decided to study the problem and actually test the theory that the ocean would absorb any additional carbon. Revelle discovered that the peculiar chemistry of sea water prevents that from happening and wrote about it in a 1957 paper with colleague Hans Suess, of the U.S. Geological Survey. This paper, in part because of Revelle's prominence as the leader of the newly established University of California Scripps Research Center, was taken more seriously. Revelle and Suess were surprised to discover that seawater would have an absorption limit, which meant that oceans could not absorb all the additional CO_2 entering the atmosphere, despite the widespread speculations of most scientists. Revelle wrote that releasing increasing tons of CO_2 into the air was unprecedented and dangerous: "Human beings are now carrying out a large-scale geophysical experiment of a kind that could not have happened in the past nor be reproduced in the future."[13]

The year 1957 had already been declared the International Geophysical Year,[14] a year devoted to collaboration between international scientific bodies to coordinate the increasing body of research about earth sciences across different fields. Sixty-seven countries participated, the United States through the National Academy of Sciences and Engineering (NAS). One of the results of that year was that researchers became aware that if CO_2 concentrations were important, someone needed to keep track of them. That person was Charles David Keeling. Keeling understood that the concentrations had to be measured away from coal-burning plants or refineries, and so chose Mount Moana Lea in the Hawaiian Islands for his station and began to take measurement there and, as a control, also at a research station in Antarctica.[15]

Moana Lea is a cold, harsh, moonlike place, with hardened volcanic ash surrounding the top of the dormant volcano—visitors (and I was one) are struck by how quickly one rises from the jungles of the lush Hawaiian shore to the stark silence of the summit. Within five years, Keeling had data: the CO_2 concentrations on Earth were steadily rising, every year a bit more. This curve, called the Keeling curve, has steady gone up, with variations for seasons, showing the accelerating concentrations of CO_2. Each year, the total amount of carbon that human beings burn into the atmosphere—even now, knowing all that we know—steadily increases.

Concerned by his findings, the National Academy of Science convened a panel on the issue, published a report, and on its advice, President Johnson convened a presidential committee to explore the policies the NAS had suggested. By 1970, the first Environmental Protection Agency (EPA) was established, Congress began to be interested in policy options, and the first Earth Day was celebrated. Global warming was not seen as especially problematic, and Earth Day focused on other sorts of concerns—human beings, through industrial farming, smelting, producing, driving, and refining were already polluting habitats. In 1973, a major piece of environment legislation was proposed and enacted in the United States. Under Nixon, the Endangered Species Act committed America to protect environments to protect species, a meaningful step in blocking oil drilling in the Western National Parks, but again, it was largely thought of as prohibiting pollution and protecting forests from clear-cutting, and the question of climate was not then a driver of the policy. In 1972, the first United Nations meeting on the environment was held and it was not on the agenda.

In 1977, then President Jimmy Carter's advisers Jim Schlesinger and Stu Eizenstat warned President Carter that the energy problem should be understood broadly, for CO_2 got "worse every year." Carter famously put solar panels on the White House roof and strengthened the EPA.

> His concern with the global environment led him to become the first president to think in terms of interconnected climate systems. When Carter assumed the presidency, he was ready to initiate measures to protect both the domestic and the global environment. During his first year in office, President Carter announced to the Congress in an environmental message that it was his intention to organize the first comprehensive study of the global environment. As the president indicated: "Environmental problems do not stop at national boundaries. In the past decade, we and other nations have to recognize the urgency of international efforts to protect our

common environment."[16] He then asked the Council on Environmental Quality, the Department of State, the Environmental Protection Agency, and the National Science Foundation National, Oceanic and Atmospheric Administration to create a year-by-year study (that would extend through the year 2000) that would take account of the changes in the world's population, in its natural resources, and in the environment.[17]

Carter, in later discussions,[18] remembers his growing alarm, and after reading the NAS report, understood the implications and the urgent need to act.

The Global 2000 Report devoted an entire chapter to climate change.[19] Carter himself, concerned by what the scientists were telling him, began to think of climate change and energy consumption as related problems with international policy implications.[20]

> The Study went on to warn that "[s]ome human activities, especially those resulting in releases of carbon dioxide into the atmosphere, are known to have the potential to affect the world's climate." Further, the *Report* concluded that "[m]any experts . . . feel that changes on a scale likely to affect the environment and the economy of large regions of the world are not only possible but probable in the next 25–50 years."[21]

Carter warned of climate change, calling it by that name:

> In his "Science and Technology Message to the Congress," for example, he indicated that "[a]dvances that can be made in understanding climate change, in predicting it—and perhaps in influencing it beneficially—will be of enormous help to us and the rest of the world."[22]

Of course, Ronald Reagan removed the panels from the roof as soon as he was elected. Yet his advisors told him that there was new information to consider:

> Research from White House advisers and federal experts—a group called the "ad hoc sub-working group on climate change"—soon warned that there was a dangerous "buildup of carbon dioxide" and other gases in the atmosphere. "The continuing buildup of these 'greenhouse gases' are likely to be the most important cause of climate change over the next century," a draft report from the group said in 1986.[23]

While Reagan largely ignored this, George H. W. Bush famously boasted during his election campaign that, as a Republican, committed to conservation, he would take on climate change:

> The problem, however, is international in scope; unilateral action by the United States alone will not solve it. In fact, some say that the problem is just too big to be solved. That the world is growing too much and too fast. I say they are wrong! Those who say we are powerless to do anything about "the greenhouse effect," are forgetting about "the White House effect." As president, I intend to do something about it. In my first year in office I will convene a global conference on the environment at the White House. It will include the Soviets, the Chinese, the developing world as well as the developed world. All nations will be welcome. Indeed, all nations will be needed. The agenda will be clear. We will talk about global warming. We will talk about acid rain. We will talk about saving our oceans and preventing the loss of tropical forests. And we will act.

While campaigning, this was in his stump speech. The promised meeting, the promised action, never took place. However, it is very important to note this moment, for there was a time when the science behind climate change was both clearly understood, tested by dozens, then hundreds of scientists, and not seen as a political issue. It was not only politicians in the United States. In Britain, Prime Minister Margaret Thatcher, who had studied chemistry at Somerville College, Oxford, and worked briefly as a research chemist, before becoming a lawyer and then a politician, told the United Nations:

> We are seeing a vast increase in the amount of carbon dioxide reaching the atmosphere. . . . The result is that change in future is likely to be more fundamental and more widespread than anything we have known hitherto.[24]

In 1988, the United Nations decided that global warming indeed needed to be studied, and they created the Intergovernmental Panel on Climate Change (IPCC) to collate and assess evidence on climate change. It was a pivotal decision.

The committee was made up of scientists from all member nations of the United Nations. It was originally a joint project of the World Meteorological Organization (WMO), who had organized the first meeting in Colorado a decade earlier, and the United Nations Environment Programme (UNEP), which had focused on pollution and land use, and was increasingly interested in global warming. Later, the General Assembly voted to support its work and offer an international forum for its reports. Its charge was to:

> Prepare a comprehensive review and recommendations with respect to the state of knowledge of the science of climate change; the social and economic impact of climate change, and potential response strategies and elements for inclusion in a possible future international convention on climate.[25]

The Committee had 120 members, including leading researchers from a variety of scientific disciplines, thousands more who participated in data collection, and thousands of scientists who read and reviewed the data it presented. Two years later, they issued their first report, and two years after that, they convened the first global meeting on the climate, the Rio Earth Summit, one that Thatcher herself had called for. At the Summit,

> Governments [agreed to] the United Framework Convention on Climate Change. Its key objective is "stabilization of greenhouse gas concentrations in the atmosphere at a level that would prevent dangerous anthropogenic interference with the climate system." Developed countries agree to return their emissions to 1990 levels.[26]

From their first report until the most recent, nothing has essentially changed from the essential hypothesis.[27] Every American president since John Kennedy had advisors who warned them about climate change.[28] Every report, including the one written in November of 2018 under Trump's own administration, despite his personal disbelief, confirmed this reality and it was reinforced by the Biden administration. Every report has made the problem clear, and the only variant that has changed is the speed of the warming trend and all its worsening consequences.[29] In 1819, when Foote was born, there were about 1 billion people on the planet. By the time Callendar was measuring temperature, there were twice as many people and there was 1 billion tons of new carbon in the air. By the time the IPCC was formed, there were 5 billion people and 22.76 billion metric tons of carbon were released in the air that year. It was at this point, as Nathaniel Rich has documented,[30] that the consensus about the urgency for action fell apart, hardening into inaction, hardening into divisions along increasingly polarized political lines. From that point until now, despite treaty after treaty, we are still unable to stop emitting carbon. In 2018, there was an all-time record set for the most carbon ever emitted: 37.1 billion tons. A new record was set in 2019. And even with the pandemic, when industries shuddered to a halt and car and plane travel plummeted, emissions barely altered, dropping only by 6.4%.[31] Carbon levels rapidly returned to pre-pandemic levels, and then begin another steady climb upward.

How Did We Get Here?

I will return to this history in my final chapter. Clearly, even the bluntest scientific language had somehow failed, and the political process, which was theoretically to be informed by factual data, acquired knowledge, and mature wisdom, had failed. In part, this book is a reflection on why, and on what sort of language we might need to have a serious discussion about our human future and how we should think and act, given this historical narrative. In the next chapter, now readied with the history and the science one needs to think clearly about the competing moral appeals and the ethical analysis, we will consider another set of arguments.

Does history matter? Our present is shaped by the opportunities and constraints of our culture. The recognition that our climate was changing came slowly, in a newly industrialized age largely oblivious even to the issue of air pollution (it took a century to address coal dust, for example). Modernity would be marked by a sense that petroleum and natural gas was cleaner and more efficient than older means of production. And, of course, it seemed correct. A world of horses, of punishing human labor, a world in which, if you left your village for America, you would never return, was a world of extraordinary difficulty, and treacherous human tasks. My grandmother remembered the mud, most vividly in a world without paved roads, making clothes by hand, before sewing machines came. Years later, she would still look up when she saw an airplane. "Marvelous!" she would nudge me, "Look."

I live in the climate of the world my grandparents made, when they got their first machines to sew, to drive, when they wore the cheap cotton clothes made in the spinning mills, the cheap leather shoes made in the new factories. They came to America on steamships, burning their new carbon trails behind them. It was very little, in the scope of things, nothing like the carbon I have burnt into the atmosphere to make the climate of the world for my grandchildren.

I wanted to begin with the history of the scientific effort to understand how climate changes, from the first fascination with the Ice Ages, from Agassi and Foote and Tyndell to the IPCC, not only because we are creatures in time, but also because it demonstrates the iterative quality of science, an epistemology based on thousands of data points, thousands of research hours and experiment after experiment, computer modeling and old-fashioned field work over decades.

In 2019, when I first returned to this essay to write this chapter, the impact of global warming had become obvious. I was in Cambridge, England, the very hottest place in that country, on the very hottest day ever recorded in British history. Across Europe, people sat outside, and in every patch of shade and public fountain, because despite years and years of warnings, little had been done to prepare the cities for temperatures in the 100s. The long arc of our story that begins with the Industrial Revolution and a few curious scientists looking at the British sky, darkened by coal smoke, is an arc of accumulation and the waste of our abundance. And that day, it was perfectly clear that we had changed the very air.

We now knew more about the full scope of the crisis, far more than we did even five years before: the warmer climate, the melting of the sea ice and the ice of the North and South polar regions, the rise in sea level, the possible disruption of the North Atlantic currents that moderate the climate of England, the chaotic nature of weather, with more severe and longer lasting droughts and torrential rains leading to catastrophic flooding, the expanding range of vector-borne diseases, the disruption of the monsoon cycle, the raging fires in the American West, the likelihood of hurricanes, the fact that "100-year storms" happen with increasing frequency, and the catastrophic spread of infectious diseases that reveal how hard collective-action problems will be to address. We began to realize that this was also about us, our habits and our consumption, and that the complex discourse about global warming comes down to the dilemmas of necessity and desire from which there is no easy personal escape. It is not only large global systems that are altered; it was something that each person in that summer of 2019 could see—the wild berries sizzled brown that year, and the lakes thickened with algae. It was already clear that to attend to the resources and systems we shared in common was not going to be enough, but that we would have to address the details of obligation and hospitality and debt, the problem of greed and oppression. It was at once personal and yet enmeshed in the deepest complexities of religious, political, and economic citizenship.

All that we knew about the worth of a life, how to live well and how to be a decent moral agent, was formulated and debated in the long period of climate stability,[32] every single piece of art and music, statecraft, or medicine, every institution, every Scriptural text—all that we knew, read, and thought.

But why, it is fair to ask, given the long history of climate science research and the remarkable consensus among international experts, did this one aspect of modern science fail to drive democratic action? To some extent, it is not only the seduction of the marketplace, or even the deliberate lying about the problem by the big energy companies, which is the subject of the final chapter in this book. To some extent, the awareness that something you cannot fully see or touch, something that in 1989 had not affected local communities, was a danger, took a great deal of trust in scientists. And trust in science had been shaken: thalidomide, given to pregnant women, caused terrible limb shortening in their babies; DES, another medication given to women in pregnancy, caused cancer in their daughters; the Three Mile Island nuclear power plant had exploded, and after that, the plant in Chernobyl. DDT, which had saved millions from malaria, turned out to be harmful to the environment. Radiation and poisoning, two of the Cold War's worst anxieties, had been loosed on the American public, *by their own scientists.*

Why this was so fundamental was that many people in modernity had shifted their faith commitment from religion to science; in fact, for many, the wonders of science, antibiotics, surgery, and vaccinations, were figurative miracles; scientists, the white-garbed priests. And of course, scientists began to use the language of faith, promising redemption, promising a life free of suffering, and an outwitting of aging and befallenness. The social goods of societies flowed toward science: prizes, money, and prestige. People increasingly gave donations—both the wealthy and the ordinary person—to scientific ventures in the way that they had given donations to the Church, and for the sake of bodily salvation, instead of the salvation of the soul.

But while faith in science's infallibility had been heartfelt, it turned out to have been misplaced. And just as people were beginning to mistrust expertise, a new sort of problem potentiated the trend: the spread of false news and the growth of the Internet. The growth of the Internet and other social forms of communication meant that all the social forces that pull toward individualism and radical autonomy were clustered by the way that computers made every single person a distributer of her own private knowledge. In this way, these forces came together at the worse possible moment for the reality of global warming to be addressed: a loss of faith in science, a distrust of governments and of expertise, a capacity for anyone to fiercely chose their facts off of an unregulated Internet stream, a divided economy with most people worried about the loss of jobs, and a growing populist movement that saw concerns about energy use as threatening.

But how to cope with the unjust impact of global warming, or the dislocation that the loss of faith presents, are not entirely new problems. Far from it. The necessity for justice in an unjust world has long been central to the vision of many religions,[33] and those issues of obligation, debt, hospitality, and greed have long been the subject of theological conversation. The problem of scarcity, the reality of loss, and the sense that it is difficult to find something to trust—these are the subjects of scripture, not really politics or geology. To speak of the deeper issues that are true for us, as surely as the scientific trends are true, is to speak in the language of theology. This language was the language of Scriptures that ordered the theo-political reality of human communities for generations, but it is a language that is now barely spoken in the policy discourse, where arguments for the poor and the inescapable duty to them are faint amid the vocal seductions of the marketplace.

It is my essential contention that this can be changed. Far beyond our failure to recognize the problem of the rising ocean in our own American cities, far beyond the ultimate failure to challenge even one aspect of food production, is the deeper failure of our leadership to raise essential questions of the outworking and meaning of justice in the larger world. Far more intractable is this loss of the sense that one can trust the truth. Far more important is the confrontation with the work that will need to be done in order to change the future, a task that would seem impossible, except that theology has changed history so powerfully before.

Why theology? In part, because theology has often been used to justify policy, particularly in population policy, and in part, because it is often by theological warrants that people are moved to substantial citizenship response. When the political, public, and secular conversation has faltered, or has been silenced by the cacophony of the marketplace, the effort to seek a new religious conversation to quicken and to challenge the traditional, even entrenched positions, with texts and praxis of a faith perspective becomes imperative. It is, really, a matter of life and death, a search for language that will allow reason to be heard. It is also because it is my contention in this book that theological language and prophetic call is the only language of justice left to counter the language of the market. That language of *noblesse oblige*? Gone, except for a glimmer on early *Downton Abbey* episodes. The language of socialism? Gone with the collapse of the Soviet Union. For make no mistake: the language of the market structures our moral sense every day. It is not only that libertarian ideas about individual rights are foregrounded, or even that universities, charities, and hospitals anxiously talk about the bottom line, pleasing wealthy donors, and the cost-benefit ratio incessantly. It is also the way the victors in the marketplace are given such power, and how the poorest are excluded and further marginalized.[34]

But in theological language, in many faith traditions we find that it is the poor who are central to the redemption of all. I would claim that it is here, in the understanding that the margins of the city are where justice must be enacted, that allows us to see more clearly the nature of global warming not only as a scientific issue but a profoundly moral one. For the core *ethical* issue of global warming is that the citizens of the nations of the West have consumed most of the energy that drives the problem, and released most of the carbon that now haunts our atmosphere, far more per capita, and that every single year we release more and more, and yet the ones who suffer the most from a changing climate have been the poorest, most vulnerable Others, often living without any electricity or commodities at all. In 2015, this question was raised by Pope Francis in his encyclical *Laudito Si* (In Praise of Creation). It has been apparent for decades.

Because I am a Jewish bioethicist, I am asked about how one ought to think about global warming as a Jew, and I recommend that my interlocutor reads this Catholic encyclical for it is a powerful statement about how faithful attention can clearly analyze a problem and call for moral action, and how Catholic moral theology can speak to a broader global community. But it is a serious question. My interlocutor wants to know how Jewish thought can speak in the same, powerful way. It is certain that Jewish tradition has never turned from the problems we call the political. In fact, Jewish discourse has taken as subjects topics both political and social, and Jewish law is responsive to new problems, new scientific realities, and shifting political powers. There is a close, even obsessive attention to the problems of *derekh eretz*, meaning literally, "the way of the land," but which implies larger moral action, the problem of how to act ethically, decently, in one's society. In this book, I reflected on how one could think carefully about this question, for the land we walk on is the global terrain. For while global warming is a problem for Jews, too, of course, and for our communities, and for the State of Israel, with which our fate is so closely tied, I also wanted to make strong arguments that can speak to people outside of the Jewish community, in the way that good arguments from Buddhist or Christian traditions have shaped the debate. Indeed, some of the first readers of this manuscript pointed out its similarities in goal with books from other specific traditions, and it is my hope that this book can be read as if in conversation with these other authors.

But I have a larger claim as well, for the long history of Jewish thought brings a distinctive theo-political argument to our problem.[35] If what is critical to theology is not might, and not power, then what Jewish thought brings to the arguments about global warming is the particular history, the particular language, and the narratives that locate the Jews as central actors in the shared moral imaginary that arcs above so much of Western philosophy. Always in exile, and from the beginning of the Common Era to 1948, always without state power, repeatedly making philosophy under conditions of precarity, Jewish philosophers always had a double task, answering the question about how Jewish people should act, and seeking something beyond, holding the responsibility that is making an argument for the world.

We all live in awareness of a series of interlocking catastrophes. We know the severity of emerging microorganisms, as outbreaks of new epidemics sweep into the food and the air, COVID-19 inevitably only the first pandemic. We see the seeming inexorability of shifts in climate, as the dead are taken from the Chicago heat, or record floods in China and Germany destroy towns that have stood for a thousand years, streets that medieval Jews walked on turned into rivers. We record the loss of frogs, of migratory birds, insects, and of entire fragile species. This is not new: we witnessed the poisoning of whole regions, as Eastern Europe was opened to public view, or Brazil was first deforested. We have been given warnings about the melting ice at both poles for decades. We know that a global warming in which we are implicated is the driver behind many of these threats. We know now we cannot turn away from this. Global warning, so long foreseen, is terrible, but it is not yet inevitable as the end of history. But, for Jewish thinkers, it is not the first time the world darkened, or famine loomed, or emigration seemed the only choice—it is the story of the Hebrew Bible, in the book of Ruth, in the wanderings of Genesis, it is in the Talmud, in the sound of the soldiers just outside the door of the study hall, it is something that Maimonides knows, reading the letters from the desperate Jews of Yemen in a hushed library in Egypt, and of course, the sense of a darkened world came most forcefully to the Jews of Europe in the 1930s, who still wrote and thought and believed that their texts and traditions had meaning and power. There is always the chance to think; there is always the choice to act.

Here are some ways to think, in Jewish terms, about what we must do and who we must be. I will explore these in the chapters that follow.

2
The Promises of Exiles
Diaspora as Ontology

How should an ethicist write about our situation in a world that is walking forward as the air, water, and land slowly but steadily change? When I began to think about this problem, it did seem as if the main catastrophes of global warming would affect my grandchildren, and so I worried on their behalf. But this year, the sky above Los Angeles and San Francisco darkened with smoke, and there were not enough face masks to go around as the hills and mountains burst into terrible flame, not then, but now. My in-laws lived in a Florida apartment—lovely, we thought, between the canal and the sea—that is now regularly flooded, not at some future time, but now. Corn prices rose in Chicago, because the spring rains had left the Midwestern states of Illinois, Iowa, and Missouri flooded, the black soil soaked and heavy into early summer. Not some future summer, this one. There is a quickening of the imperative to act, to write about how we ought to live right now.

Part I: Thinking Theologically about the Natural World

In the last chapter, I describe how we came to our present situation. In this chapter, I will turn to ways we can respond to it, and I make the argument that we might respond more thoughtfully using the language of theology and in the case of this book, and my particular area of scholarship, in the language of Jewish thought. There are some caveats to this claim. Much of the writing about religion and climate change has been about innocence betrayed, a virginal natural world despoiled. In these narratives, the problem is described as an essentialist one. Nature, in this writing (often gendered as female), has been harmed by a relentless techno-market mastery, a thoughtless sort of evil. This is understandable for many reasons.

First, because much of the literature in the early ecology movement took issue with the narrative of Genesis, objecting to the concept of "mastery" or subjection of the earth to the needs of human persons. Consider Lynn White's seminal work, "The Historical Roots of Our Ecologic Crisis," written in 1967[1]:

> By the end of the 15th century the technological superiority of Europe was such that its small, mutually hostile nations could spill out over all the rest of the world, conquering, looting, and colonizing.[2]

White believed that there was something inherently problematic about science itself, once it became Western, and lost its connection to earlier Arabic roots. It was the mastery of technology that was linked to imperial conquest, and imperial conquest, we are to understand, always and everywhere meant "conquering and looting." Moreover, White lamented a lost past in which human persons were somehow at one with the forest—happy vegetarians, gathering verdant abundance. The tragic turn from the past was the invention of the plow, which White believes (incorrectly) was unique to northern Europe. He argued:

> Man's relation to the soil was profoundly changed. Formerly man had been part of nature; now he was the exploiter of nature. Nowhere else in the world did farmers develop any analogous agricultural implement. Is it coincidence that modern technology, with its ruthlessness toward nature, has so largely been produced by descendants of these peasants of northern Europe?[3]

This tragic turn was linked, for him, in the defeat of paganism (in White's language) by Christianity, for before the Christians came, he claims:

> Every spring, every stream, every hill had its own genius loci, its guardian spirit. These spirits were accessible to men, but were very unlike men; centaurs, fauns, and mermaids show their ambivalence. Before one cut a tree, mined a mountain, or dammed a brook, it was important to placate the spirit in charge of that particular situation, and to keep it placated. By destroying pagan animism, Christianity made it possible to exploit nature in a mood of indifference to the feelings of natural objects.[4]

And it is Christianity that bears "a huge burden of guilt" for this turn, he continues:

> Since both science and technology are blessed words in our contemporary vocabulary, some may be happy at the notions, first, that, viewed historically, modern science is an extrapolation of natural theology and, second, that modern technology is at least partly to be explained as an Occidental, voluntarist realization of the Christian dogma of man's transcendence of, and rightful mastery over, nature. But, as we now recognize, somewhat over a century ago science and technology—hitherto quite separate activities—joined to give mankind powers which, to judge by many of the ecologic effects, are out of control. If so, Christianity bears a huge burden of guilt.[5]

White's view, that science and technology are necessary and inevitable outworkings of natural theology and the Christian, or perhaps the biblical, view of nature is now widely held. I will return to explore how this has become a part of the eco-feminist literature in a later chapter. Here, I will add that the consideration of nature and of nature's working and nature's law within Christianity does form a distinctive aspect of writing in climate change literatures.

It is not only White. A view of nature as normative is the starting point for much of Christian ethics. This is because some of my Catholic colleagues write out of a "natural law" tradition, and a view of nature, as colleague Willemein Otten writes, has long been important in Catholic moral theology, even as it changes over time.[6] Derived from Thomas Aquinas, who further developed Aristotle's idea of "natural kinds" to support his concept that standards of morality can be derived from the fixed or intrinsic nature of the world and the nature of human beings, many subsequent writers then consider the telos of natural objects or entities as central to a proper understanding of our role in the world. On the one hand, since human beings, in Aquinas's view, are rational, they must behave, if they are to behave morally, in a way that conforms to their rational nature—rationally choosing to do good and avoid evil: "the rule and measure of human acts is reason, which is the first principle of human acts." Alertness to the nature of things allows anyone to know the precepts of the natural law. "The precepts of the natural law are also knowable by nature. All human beings possess a basic knowledge of the principles of the natural law."[7,8] Linked to this view of human nature is the concept that morality derives from two sources: Scripture and the Book of Nature. As Catholic theologian James Keenen has noted,[9] the concept that there is meaning and order in nature is linked to the idea that human persons are rational stewards of this order, and to disrupt this order has disturbing consequences.

Secondly, it was not only Christian theologians that saw human stewardship over the natural world as rational and morally appropriate, but who were worried that a prideful mastery might corrupt it, for much of Anglo-American philosophy in the tradition of John Locke saw "America" as a second Eden.

> Thus, in the beginning all the World was America, and more so than that is now; for no such thing as Money was anywhere known.[10]

Humans were, then, no longer expelled from Eden; we were back! This idea of wilderness as virginal was left in the very names of places: Virginia once was the entire east coast, from South Carolina to Newfoundland. Locke's America was a model of goodness and possibility. (Of course, he did not mean African slaves. But he did allow, at least that Native Americans were a part of this good world.)[11] And this affection for wildness, a place left to itself, was of course, behind the original idea of conservation—the first environmental movement—that allowed for National Parks. The further one gets into "nature," meaning the beautiful, wild places in the world with no or few humans, the really real sort of nature, the better. This sort of nature then, is not only better than, say, cities, it is morally normative as well, with an order understood, even by secular thinkers, as divine.[12] However, humans have clearly violated this order, with our pollution, our messiness, our destruction. Here is how this is linked back to Scripture: If the natural world is given to humans to order first, theologically, in the Hebrew Bible and the Quran, and then, by the philosophers who value rationality, using empiricism and logic, and if despite this, the world seems spoiled, then if rationality itself, mastery itself, Scripture itself is questioned, and then White's critique follows.

I have sympathy with this understanding of nature as inherently morally good. The wild world is so very beautiful, so of course we learn to think of it as good. And for many, these arguments are persuasive and ground a subsequent argument for the restoration of the Natural.

However, in Jewish ethics it is clear that the natural world is not morally good, and its beauty does not make it so, any more than its terrible violence makes it evil. As Jewish ethicist Elliot Dorff notes, in Jewish thought, Nature is morally neutral.[13] It generally does not teach or carry sacred messages, and human nature is not always rational, nor intuition the driver of morality. Most of all, the natural world is imagined as farmland, not Yosemite. It is to be used, not exploited, and used, largely used for growing crops, or for grazing animals, not for hiking. This is a premodern order of things, where the "wilderness" meant a dry, difficult desert landscape, where nothing could grow, and the paths were covered in sand and the threat of dying of thirst drove even the devotee quietly mad. Even in the medieval period, Jews lived in settlements, for in many areas, Jews were not allowed to own land. Here, too, untilled land was uncivilized land, dangerous and difficult to traverse. Jewish communities needed a certain level of organization for a place to be considered fit for habitation, and this was usually found in towns and in cities, where the trades and crafts they were allowed could be exchanged. The view toward the natural world—has little in common with White's or Locke's elegiac descriptions.

This presents a problem for the modern Jewish ethicist writing within the general literary frame of ecological ethics. Consider Jeremy Bernstein, writing plaintively about his search for Jewish texts that support his view of nature, or the rejection of technology:

> Being a Jew with strong environmental concerns, one is often led to study the Sources with an eye for those particular teachings that are inspirational for—or at least compatible with—one's own predetermined "green" positions, and thus avoid challenging oneself with texts that don't fit current environmental wisdom.[14]

It is the intent of this chapter to explain why Bernstein is having a difficult time, and to suggest another way of thinking theologically with Jewish sources. Let us welcome the challenge of Jewish texts. To respond honestly to the question of the Jewish view of nature, and thus to global warming as a threat to the natural world, requires clarity about how narrative sources and law are used to build social order.

Part II: Thinking in Jewish Terms

This requires a brief introduction to Jewish ethics in general. Of course, that is a very large—perhaps impossible—task. As I noted in our last chapter about the scientific history of climate change, the brief introductions to grand topics in these chapters are clearly neither definitive nor complete. In my case, in all humility, it is necessarily limited as well. I am not a scholar of rabbinics. I am a bioethicist, who reads the rabbinic sources carefully, and who thinks with them about contemporary ethical dilemmas, and that is a different sort of task, so this is an introduction that is intended to allow the reader to think with me. It is my intention that such an introduction will allow the reader who is unfamiliar with Jewish thought a way into understanding the next chapters. However, as I noted in my introduction, any broad statements about "what Jewish law says" are usually incomplete, for this rich and complicated system requires much specialized knowledge to approach. Yet some general framing is in order. What follows is my particular understanding of the categories of Jewish thought in general terms.

Turning to Jewish Thought: Some Notes on Method and Context

Ethicists ask: what is the right act and what makes it so? And then they turn to categorize and define the methods by which a justifying argument proceeds, and say, in general terms, that the arguments are usually deontological, consequentialist, or based in virtue theory. Jewish ethics is harder to categorize (much less in three paragraphs). Judaism is both a deontological and a casuistic religious system, rooted in rules, duties, and normative conduct. But it is unlike a purely deontological system because it also is concerned about both virtues and, to a certain extent, outcomes which are reconsidered in a reflexive equilibrium as the consequences are retold as narratives that are considered in future decisions. As I noted in the introduction, Jewish thought is structured around the Hebrew Bible, the Torah, and the Mishnah, a collection of commentaries and interpretations of the Torah. Additionally, it includes the Gemara, which comments on the Mishnah and together with it is collectively referred to as the Talmud, or the by the larger term "rabbinic literature,"[15] and this also includes the various collections of narratives, called the midrash, and the corpus of debates from the 2nd century BCE to the 6th century CE, which is a term which would be, as Charlotte Fonrobert and Martin Jaffee note, foreign to the rabbis of antiquity but useful as a scholarly category.

There are centuries of continued commentary and theological reflections, a vast collection of case law, called "responsa" literature, and ancient, medieval, and modern philosophic texts. Much of the activity of traditional

Jewish life is centered on the reading, studying, and enacting the behaviors described in the Talmud or in the larger corpus of rabbinic writings.

As I have come to think about the law, I am aware of its complex origins. The law is largely based on cases brought to rabbinic authorities, which provide a testing ground for premises and rules that are derived from the Scriptural text. Then, the context and outcome of each case are carefully debated and assessed—is this the correct way to interpret the Law? Jewish law is thus a modified and interpreted law, capable of change when new facts are presented by new cases, brought to the rabbinic discourse. Consequences, once they are enacted because human communities follow the law, are then reexamined and debated: how did that work in that place and time? What about anomalies? Pragmatic encounters, knowledge of precedence, historicity, the tactile, all become a part of the rhetorical even fantastical narratives about the law, which in a sense, resist being a theory of law, unless one is speaking of the second-order scholarship of later philosophical authors. One of the premises here is that human beings have the capacity to be rational actors, in need of reasons for moral agency. Human reason is needed both to negotiate the system and to interpret intelligently the sensory world, but the logic of rabbinic discourse is a logic of language and word games, not abstract premises. Case by case, text by text, the system is explored and described. Talmudic methodology was a long historical argument, structured by text, history, and community experience, this latter called *minhag* or customs. These local practices had to be understood and considered, because the Jewish community has long been scattered among different nations. Both Islam and Christianity influence the law and the language; Hellenism and Persian thought influence the discourse as well. All these elements, and the use of reason to decipher them, modify the deontological method of Jewish ethics. It was *deontological*, because it assumed an imaginary in which Torah law was motivational, commanded, central, and binding; and *casuistic* because it was also inductive and modified and shaped by cases and their context.[16]

The rules, duties, and norms, however, are critical, especially when humans are not consistently rational. Bounded by the system of legal behavior that is called *halachah*, the individual Jew, once past the age of maturity (thirteen years old for boys and twelve years old for girls), is responsible for the performance of *mitzvot*, or divine commandments that direct moral behavior. There are said to be 613 such commandments in the traditional reckoning, a metaphorical number that stands for the completeness of obligation, for there are actually more than 613 commandments to be found in the halachah corpus. (Six hundred thirteen corresponds to the number of limbs of the body, in rabbinic reckoning, 248, which added to the number of days of the year, gives the number 613.) Many are concerned with the daily details of life that structure and lend gravitas to the smallest moments. Some authoritative rabbinic commentators do not see ordinal commands as "ethical commandments." They consider as "ethical commands" only those mitzvot that address the broadest set of social relationships—for example, the injunction against murder, commandments to "do justice" and to make peace, and the like. But others strongly disagree and argue that it is exactly these habits of the commanded life, even commandments impossible to understand rationally, that undergird moral behavior.[17]

Judaism is both a deontological and a casuistic system, rooted in rules, duties, and normative conduct and concerned with motive and process. But it is unlike a purely deontological system because the real world, and the context and outcome of each case, counts in their assessment. Judaism is a modified casuistic deontology. Consequences, once enacted, are reexamined and debated. The real-world matters: knowledge of precedence, historicity, the tactile and the theoretical. Human reason is needed both to negotiate the system and to interpret intelligently the sensory natural world. Talmudic methodology was argument structured by text, history, and community. All these three elements, and the use of reason to decipher them, modify the deontological method of Jewish ethics. It was *deontological* because it assumes Torah law as motivational, commanded, central, and binding; and *casuistic* because it was also inductive and case (context) modified. The terms of Greek analysis do not precisely fit the Jewish system.

The first procedural question that the system of Jewish ethics addresses is the problem of how to achieve good ends in a nonteleological system. How are the norms in a "modified deontological" system evaluated and enforced over time if neither classic consequentialist nor classic deontological ethics are part of the tradition? Judaism answers this in a way that is the unique hallmark of the method. The basic procedure for the evaluation of norms is the mode of argumentation, commentary, debate, and discussion. Essentially casuistic, the halachic system uses the encounter with the biblical text, and the encounter with the other's encounter with the text, to create a continuous discursive community. Cases are raised to illustrate points of law and then to illustrate alternate interpretations of the law. Narrative, in a variety of literary forms (metaphor, allegory, historical reference, intertextual mirroring) called *aggadah*, are embedded in the Talmudic text. Aggadah "narrates the Law," according to Barry Wimpfhiemer, and these narrative forms are found throughout the Talmud, as a form of reasoning, of biblical interpretation, as a part of the larger linguistic puzzle that allows the unfolding of the law.[18] This narrative form was used to grapple with and embellish the discussion of the details of the practices of the halachah, which is nearly always explained by way of a story, with examples and history, and commentary from rabbinic figures across the centuries between 200 BCE and 600 CE during which the Talmud took shape as a written literary document in close to its present form.[19]

The Process of Discourse as Citizenship: A Postmodern View

And more is gained from the textual turn: it is the methodology of the discursive community, a disparate collection of arguments and additions, redactors and disputers, that forms a reflective canon that is the critical aspect of halachah.[20] The central claim of Jewish ethics is that truth is found in the house of discursive study—the bet midrash.[21] Such a public discourse is created when we argue, face to face, about the meaning and relevance of the narrative, symbols, and referents.[22]

This is not merely a postmodernist insight about the fluidity and mutability of text (although it is in part that). It is an historical-literary observation that anyone can make upon opening a page of the Talmud, the literal record of the oral tradition of proof text, argument and counter text that circles and circles virtually any truth claim. Revelation is given to the imperfect world, to nomads, and recently freed slaves, to the rabbinic decisors of the Talmudic and post-Talmudic period, who were shoemakers, and tenant farmers alike, to Lithuanian wise men of my grandfather's town, and to me, and to you, any listening reader.

You might wonder why we need the disagreements of halachah at all. Why not just start with a general discussion of ethics and values? Perhaps principles, as is the case in American bioethics? But Jewish ethical reasoning cannot be fully separated from this religious legal system. It is this carefully preserved dispute, and the tradition of dispute itself, that is preserved. It is the nature of justice that it must be proven in the specifics of the actual.[23,24,25,26]

There is an assumption of reversibility in the text (if it happened this way then, it may happen that way again; if it happened to him, it may happen to you), a recollection of a concrete moment of human gesture, an internal textual logic based on the effort to identify the hearer of the story or aggadic midrash (something like a morality tale) with the players in the narrative. The story makes sense of the textual quote from Hebrew Scriptures, itself a sign of the argument about the original query. The text, the example, and the explanatory narrative serve to create a tension that places the hearer of the argument in the position of the subject, and thus the hearer is given the opportunity for reflexive analysis. The problem, the narrative, and the textual fragment exist at different historical moments, allowing the contemporary account the same privilege as earlier commentary. The text is reversible in a variety of circumstances, each slightly unlike the other, linked by an analogy that places index and subject against context, conversational.[27] The multivocity of the form itself insists on the questioning of the solidity of the text. For many of the proof texts there are strong countervailing premises and correspondent inimitable truths, and rabbinic authorities, or teachers, who defend differing positions; the proof texts, then, are not only a narrative, but a dialogic notation.

Why is all of this of importance? My understanding of the method displayed in the rabbinic literature is that it arrays the first task of Jewish ethics as creating the possibility of a discursive venue for wildly difficult and fiercely contentious ethical debate. Beginning in this way allows us to confront each other, and one another's promises, face to face, as Emmanuel Levinas noted, and to disagree in full public voice.[28] Argument is not the roadblock to, but the first premise of social citizenship. "The banal fact of conversation, in one sense, quits the order of violence. The banal fact is the miracle of miracles."[29] It is this attention to the argument that makes exilic journey possible, and provides continuity, what scholars such as Daniel Boyarin have called a textual traveling homeland, a journey in which both detail and the dispute matter terribly. We will return to this point. Finally, it is essential to remember that much of the case law turns on elaborate constructs that never happened or could never be expected to happen but are explored fictively as limit cases.

Much of the legal discussion is about work, for example work on the lost Second Temple, that can no longer be performed, or work on land in Israel that had been under Roman control for generations. Long prior to the modern environmental movement, the limits of agricultural and craft production were the subject of careful theological reflection and yet nearly entirely imagined. It is clear that human beings' ability to stop work—even imagined work—is critical to understanding God's sovereignty, for it was the one thing that slaves could not do.

The capacity to stop as an act of human will, to create limits on consumption, in particular, is found in many religious traditions. Samuel Raphael Hirsch, the nineteenth-century founder of modern Orthodoxy, saw the triumph of rationality and modernity in nearly every Jewish law and custom. He saw the structure of Shabbat as the organizing principle of Jewish practice: a practice that called for a constancy of attention to place, task, and limits for the marketplace.[30] It is this deep biblical structure of cessation, of voluntary retreat from the endless possibility of production and consumption that is found in every agricultural law. We are enjoined always to take less than we could, to wait longer to harvest the first fruits, to let the land rest every seven years, in an entire year of Shabbat, and finally to declare a year of Jubilee every fifty years, when not only the land rests, but the marketplace and social hierarchy itself are restored to their point of origin. This original position is also imagined: when the moment of origin itself, when The Land was only a theory, a promise, a consequence of the choice for goodness and of flight, and the tribes stood, in full and public view of one another, receiving their promised location within the Land, and their responsibility. I will return to the key concept of the sabbatical year in a later chapter. The laws of cessation always connected to the complex gift of a homeland carefully remembered for centuries after it was lost.

These moments of attention to and acceptance of the law are moments of moral identity and accountability; they are the moments that, for Emmanuel Levinas, using the metaphoric language of rabbinic thought, are redolent of "the scent of paradise"[31]—of the possible. It is a moment at once both intensely personal—you are the one commanded and you carry the responsibility for actions, your choice for good and evil itself, and your witness of the acceptance of responsibility of your community. In his essay, "The Pact," Emmanuel Levinas reminds us that this act, the first act of a people liberated from slavery, was into the service of mutual responsibility, a taking on of the other's responsibility.[32] It is not only the minutiae of consumption and production and social life that are both taken and witness, but also the commitment to witness itself, the interlocking network deeds and debt that will hold the exilic community together. It is the obligation toward the stranger that is at your side, and her to the one at her side, that will make the time in the desert bearable.

Levinas reminds us that the moral agent in Jewish thought is corporate, communal, and infinitely ceaseless, 'sleeplessly' responsible for the other.[33]

It is a truism in much of new theology, and communitarian philosophy, but it is an absolute organizing principle in Judaism that the community has a stronger appeal than the autonomous individual. The *golah* is a collective noun—an exilic population, and the Exile that so defines Jewish life is a shared fate of peoplehood. To act only for oneself, even to act only on behalf of one's family, is not only proscribed, but it would also be shortsighted to the point of folly. The community must act on behalf of the promises collectively made in order to expect a world in which the minimal promises of order are returned. To break the oaths of justice and fair dealing is to literally stop the rain. I will return to this.

Recounting general statements about religious and ethical systems sounds, in this instance, vaguely laudatory. This is not the case in the systems of Jewish ethics (or any ethics), for in fact, the rain stopped all the time: droughts drove desperate people around the Mediterranean. Commanded deontological systems work in many instances to hold societies together, but not always, and not always in the face of enormous external forces. I am claiming that Jewish ethics does not focus on elegiac return to a natural world, nor a critique of mastery to anchor ecological literature, but there are resources to explore ethical issues that arise when societies fail or when the powerful whose actions threaten the welfare of the entire fragile diasporic community emerge. What of the careless ones, the selfish ones? Evil, sinfulness, and idolatry are hardly new theological problems. Hubristic destruction of a local landscape, exploitation of the poor, and excessive and greedy use of the resources held in common were in fact quite possible in antiquity. Biblical accounts speak of the ability to utterly waste the land we travel in. The option to husband the wealth of the biblical world for the benefit of the most powerful, or to distribute the social goods of the whole unfairly, has long been an option. And of course, the Jewish narrative stands as testimony to what can happen when the evil is unchallenged. What is possible is extinction, the loss of the Temple, the exile from the land, the ultimate borders of the Shoah.[34]

But one does not need to go to the ruptures of Jewish history to see how evil is considered. Sinfulness is everyplace, failure ordinary, in the course of human interactions. Because the marketplace presented (and presents) such opportunities for deceit and deception, the rabbis had opportunities to adjudicate disputes and judge wrongdoing. In general, they saved their most severe judgments for the gentile nations that held them captive, whose idol worship and choice of the incorrect Messiah seemed to them to drive history in the opposite direction, away from Home. The rabbinic texts consider the many ways that human can "miss the mark"—in Hebrew, *chet* and in English, *sin*. To have Jewish membership was to be faced constantly with given law, which detailed nearly every embodied possibility: love, work, cooking, candle-making, business, and communal duties, for both men and women. Because of the intimacy of the law, every gesture was a moral gesture, a position we can clearly understand when we consider global warming, where every action is laden with the ubiquity of its cost. Of course, there were highly complex and thought-out methods of *tsuvah* or return and repair after sin, first, by expiation and animal sacrifice when the First and Second Temples were intact, and after, with prayer, the ritual reenactment of expiation at Yom Kippur, charity, and restitution to the wronged party. This is not to suggest an answer to the question of human evil, only that the ethical systems of judgment also included methods of, if not forgiveness, of restructure.

Methods of Jewish Ethics

As I noted above, there has been a long and essentially unbroken chain of methodology that is used when disputes or questions arise within the Jewish community, or when individuals or communities interact with the larger societies in which they live. An ethical question arises, and it cannot be easily settled. It is brought to a local rabbi and if he (in Orthodoxy, rabbinic ordination is restricted to men, although this may be changing) can respond to the question, he will do so, but if he cannot, or cannot find the correct source upon which to base his answer, he will formally ask the question of a nationally regarded expert or a circle of rabbinic authorities. This position of regard is based on a consensus that a particular scholar has a sound and convincing argument. In the larger sense, I am familiar with the process in bioethics, for variants of this method have been applied to a number of contemporary dilemmas, for example, stem cell research, organ donation, or in vitro fertilization.

In my own work, as well as the work of other contemporary academic scholars of Jewish ethics, this method is the beginning of the inquiry. For example, we will raise our question of how we ought to live in the face of global warming. And just as rabbinic authorities would classically do, we turn first to the traditional texts and commentary to seek the earlier solutions upon which to ground the argument.

Because of this, Jewish ethicists have searched for proof texts within the tradition to support a claim for a Jewish environmentalism, just like our Christian colleagues have found in their texts, and, to be sure, have found evidence that the rabbinic texts understand the value of the natural world—not as an absolute value, but as part of the Divine gift that is human existence. This "for-us" quality, the sense that the natural world is of worth relative to our lives, takes place in the rabbinic tradition. But this value is simply less important than other critical values, in part, because of the far more important worth of the Torah law and the act of study and interpretation and in part because nature is "for-us, " it has a purpose which is to sustain human persons. Let me demonstrate with an example that is important for our purposes in understanding a Jewish concept of nature. Clearly, there are texts like this one, which is the basis for the command of "bal tashchit" (do not vandalize or wantonly destroy). Here is the sort of text one might find valorized in the literature of ecology. Indeed, one does find it:

> When you besiege a city for many days to wage war against it to capture it, you shall not destroy its trees by wielding an ax against them, for you may eat from them, but you shall not cut them down. Is the tree of the field a man, to go into the siege before you? (Exodus 20:19–20)

But lest you think that there is a deep prohibition about cutting down trees, the very next verse (usually left out of the literature) makes it clear that there is no such prohibition. Whack away; just do not interfere with food production:

> However, a tree you know is not a food tree, you may destroy and cut down, and you shall build bulwarks against the city that makes war with you, until its submission.[35]

And while it is true that there is a blessing for the first annual sitting of a fruit tree in bloom *("Blessed are You, Lord our God, Ruler of the universe, Who has made a world with nothing lacking, and created in it good creatures and good trees to give humans pleasure.")* and this is often cited as a proof text about the goodness of nature, it is more complicated.

This is because blooming trees are to be seen instrumentally, part of the object world given to humans to use, and the verse praises God not for the tree, a priori, but the tree as a beautiful object giving humans pleasure, and perhaps, since fruit trees are the ones that bloom, as an anticipation of food in a hungry world. And lest one think that trees have value outside of their use, consider texts like this one from the Mishnah:

> Trees must be kept at a distance of twenty-five cubits from a town; carobs and sycamore trees fifty cubits. Abba Saul says that all wild fruit trees must

be kept at a distance of fifty cubits. If the town was there first, the tree is cut down and no compensation is given. If the tree was there first, it is cut down, but compensation must be given. If there is a doubt which was first, it is cut down and no compensation is given. (Baba Batra 24b)

And finally, we have this text, from *Pirke Avot* (The Ethics of the Fathers), a small tractate of the Talmud, which is traditionally read and studied on the long Shabbat afternoons, and taught to young children:

Rabbi Ya'akov says: One, who while walking along the way, reviewing his studies, breaks off from his study and says, "How beautiful is that tree! How beautiful is that plowed field!" Scripture regards him as if he has forfeited his soul (as if he should be killed). (Ethics of the Fathers 3:7)

This is the problem with rabbinic proof texts, the one that Bernstein noted, for they stubbornly insist on a very particular and, of course, very different view of the natural world than you usually find in the literature of the ecology movement, for the rabbis are concerned with the pagan aspects that may accompany too much love of those trees. Moreover, because any statement in this long tradition will have a counterargument and many explanatory claims, even ones I have made earlier, will have a perfectly available alternative counterclaim in the literature.[36] It is a complex tradition! It is for this reason that in this book and in my work in general, I also turn to the tradition of Jewish moral philosophy to consider contemporary dilemmas in bioethics, and in this instance as well, I will ask you to expand the architecture of halachah to include these thinkers. In Jewish thought it is particularly important to contextualize the arguments within traditional texts, take note of the texts themselves, and finally ask what they imply. It is, in Levinasian terms, exegesis on exegesis. I argue that the task of contemporary Jewish ethics is to consider all the competing moral appeals, as expressed in arguments, narratives, and law, and make a judgement. We will return to this "necessity for judgement" in a later chapter.

Part III: The Phenomena of Exile as Ethical Ontology

All of the claims in Part II of this chapter are made to introduce a general reader to the systems of Jewish thought, and the Jewish reader to how this system is undergirded by a particular method.

In this part of the chapter,[37] I want to attempt something different from an accounting of disparate proof texts which has correctly troubled Bernstein. I intend, rather, to create a description of my central theological argument that, while derived from the texts of Jewish Scripture and interpretation, is metaphorically applicable to the ontological situation of humanity.

It is the argument that not only do Jews live in an historical exile after the occupation of their land by the Roman Empire, and their expulsion, first from ancient Israel, then again and again from other lands, but that the human situation itself is an Exile in the largest and most profound sense. We all live in an overreaching, existential Exile, a *Galut*, forced into a world that is not Edenic, but is agonal, thorny, risky, and ultimately, of course, fatal ("from dust you shall return"). In this world, in which we are all in this difficult diasporic condition, and in which we are small, fragile creatures, there are constant demands and terrible obligations from each one of us toward each one of us. We live in a community of sojourners and strangers of which we are a part, because we are thrown into a world, if we take the Hebrew Scriptures seriously, that renders any claim of indigeneity useless, for none of us are quite at home, in this metaphorical sense. We fragile creatures try to build cities and states, but the ground under them shifts, and this is an agonistic account of the condition of human life, far from the assumption of harmony, or easy comradery. It assumes that the work of a human life and of a human community is serious, death-defying, and usually, a failure, and that the goal of a human life is not simple happiness, or even simplicity (certainly not simplicity) but uprightness and courage on the road. Exile, hunger, the way closed behind you, and the future stony, difficult, and as yet unredeemed: this is the starkness of the world that we are given, an Exile that is repeated over and over again in later Scriptural texts.

Consider the Beginning of the Story of Humanity

God has planted an abundant Eden, placed humans within it, and given one command: Do not eat this tree.[38] But it is eaten—already a breach in perfection—and then, the first estrangement. God calls to his creatures and they hide, suddenly aware of their naked, vulnerable, soft bellies, and failing arms. Here the narrative continues:

> 3:13 And the Lord God said unto the woman: "What is this thou hast done?" And the woman said: "The serpent beguiled me, and I did eat."

48 ETHICS FOR THE COMING STORM

> 3:14 And the Lord God said unto the serpent: "Because thou hast done this, cursed art thou from among all cattle, and from among all beasts of the field; upon thy belly shalt thou go, and dust shalt thou eat all the days of thy life.
>
> 3:15 And I will put enmity between thee and the woman, and between thy seed and her seed; they shall bruise thy head, and thou shalt bruise their heel."
>
> 3:16 Unto the woman He said: "I will greatly multiply thy pain and thy travail; in pain thou shalt bring forth children; and thy desire shall be to thy husband, and he shall rule over thee."
>
> 3:17 And unto Adam He said: "Because thou hast hearkened unto the voice of thy wife, and hast eaten of the tree, of which I commanded thee, saying: Thou shalt not eat of it; cursed is the ground for thy sake; in toil shalt thou eat of it all the days of thy life.
>
> 3:18 Thorns also and thistles shall it bring forth to thee; and thou shalt eat the herb of the field.
>
> 3:19 In the sweat of thy face shalt thou eat bread, till thou return unto the ground; for out of it was thou taken; for dust thou art, and unto dust shalt thou return."
>
> 3:20 And the man called his wife's name Eve; because she was the mother of all living.
>
> 3:21 And the Lord God made for Adam and for his wife garments of skins and clothed them.
>
> 3:22 And the Lord God said: "Behold, the man is become as one of us, to know good and evil; and now, lest he put forth his hand, and take also of the tree of life, and eat, and live forever."
>
> 3:23 Therefore the Lord God sent him forth from the garden of Eden, to till the ground from whence he was taken.
>
> 3:24 So He drove out the man; and He placed at the east of the garden of Eden the cherubim, and the flaming sword which turned every way, to keep the way to the tree of life.

I want to spend some time on this text, for it is the first exile. This is the disobedience that leads to the Fall, a central motif in the Christian narrative, one that animates so much of Western literature and theo-political tradition. While in some Jewish texts, the claim is made that it is not so much of a sinful fall as an entrance of sorts into a complex adulthood, a beginning of time after timelessness, a beginning of history, and this is also the case, the text clearly tells us that expulsion is the reason for the terrible puzzle of mortality. Humans are thrust into an economy of scarcity, of impossible loss, and of finitude. The natural world, in this text, is brutish; the land is covered in thorns, childbirth is tragic, and animals are dangerous. God both "sends forth" and "drove" humans out of Eden, a doubled exile, from a place where nearly every tree is pacific and where animals talk. Scholar Arnold Eisen emphasizes this important point:

> The earth is "cursed" in opposition to the blessing which it originally enjoyed, blessing in its primary connotation of fertility. Now the earth shall sprout only thorns and thistles, and only with the greatest human effort will it provide food for man. Earth and humanity still need each other, but they shall be locked in struggle until they are reunited, in death. Whether Adam and Eve had been meant to be immortal or only learn of their mortality once "their eyes are opened," is not important here. What matters is that images of death and estrangement now dominate a narrative previously given over to images of life abundant. Finally, and most crucially, Adam and Eve are forever banished east of Eden, "to till the soil from which (humankind) was taken"—"taken" in three senses: birth, alienation, and exile.[39]

But the Earth on which we live is not Eden (surely not America, surely not even Yosemite). It is fundamentally out of balance, not in order, or at least, not hospitable, but, like the serpent, terribly dangerous. Human life is still possible, but it will take a lot of work, and in the texts, there is a violence in the work of agriculture: the land needs to be subdued, for it always can return to chaos and thorns. But the humans, who, dressed like animals in little furry outfits, in the last tender act of God, cannot return, for the way is barred, on the one hand, by angels with flaming, Miltonian swords, and by the other, by death itself. We move forward into time, into failure, floods, war, a deeper exile, traveling along with Benjamin's Angel of History, who is blown backward by the storm from Paradise.[40]

Indeed, it is not much further in the story that the tragic possibilities inherent in this tilling of the earth are revealed. Cain, the first born, does indeed "eat the herb of the field" and offers it as a sacrifice. It is rejected in favor of his younger brother, Abel, who offers his dead lambs, the first blood that is shed. His is next, of course, after a murder by Cain that sends him into a deeper exile, and soaks the dust that created Adam with blood. Cain is "cast out from everywhere, a ceaseless wanderer (*na'va-nad*) who can settle only in the "land of Nod"—the land, that is, of "wandering."[41]

Arnold Eisen has pointed out that the original banishment of Adam and Eve was metaphysical and existential, and was redoubled by the political and social exile of Cain, banished from everywhere, and from all human society. Argues Eisen:

> Cain will suffer the fate of the alien denied the protection of his clan. "Anyone who meet me may kill me." God must therefore become Cain's sole protector—an eerie foreshadowing of the destiny of God's people Israel. They too will be made strangers, by God's will, in strange lands, and safeguarded only because God's blessing proves a shelter as well as a curse.[42]

Adamic exile is a nakedness beyond naming, a stripping of all but the scent of Paradise, carried on the animal skins of Adam and Eve, later in the animal skins of Esau that Jacob steals, later on the coat of Joseph, a divine "scent" which will reemerge again and again in the world of rabbinic midrash, and in the work of Emmanuel Levinas, as a hint of the infinite possibility of what Levinas calls "infinity." But Cain is also in political exile, outside of human contact; he is outside of human sovereignty, and he leaves with only the mark that is the stain of his terrible error. Cain, the farmer, cannot count on the world to offer up berries and rabbits to eat, for like his father, he must farm by the sweat of his brow. It is all he knows. We are his descendants:

> (T)he curse remains a curse, further estranging us from God, from the earth, and each other. Cities, farming, music, "tools of copper and iron," all follow from Cain's murder of his brother—human culture developing inextricably, so it seems, from homelessness. It is this tool making, copper and iron smelting, that will construct the bars of our present situation.

Eisen claims the exilic state as emblematic of the Jewish condition. I want to extend his insight to include that metaphor to a humanity that is profoundly not at home in our chaotic world of modernity, and of rapid climate change. We have never lived in Eden, and we never will, for this Exile will never be ended until the Messianic era. We are both lost and at fault, both at risk and accountable, both bearers of that faint scent of Paradise and lovers of the pleasure of the desert, easily seduced by idols, losing track of the dangerous column of fire in the night, but most of all, we are in transit, and we live as guests on this earth, thorns at our throat as we give birth and plant seeds.

The Fence around the Torah: A World of Limits

The Exile into time, labor, and grief, the deeper exile created by violence, is replicated by the tension between being lost and wandering and the profound uncertainty of the patriarchs and matriarchs of biblical history itself. Abraham and Sarah, bearing their homelessness, nomadic, the flights from hunger into Egypt, the wandering in the desert—in fact, little of the Torah narrative of their progeny actually takes place in the Land which is promised. In the wanderings of Jacob, famine is always at stake:

> There are famines—the most graphic reminder to those "at home" upon the earth that its bounty is not theirs to control. Famines highlight the link between the existential and political dimensions of exile, by collapsing the space in which the patriarchs and their neighbors had managed to live with minimal friction.[43]

Of course, as we will see in the next narrative of Hebrew Scripture, it is Joseph's fate to be exiled by his brothers, and then to construct the debt system that will eventually enslave his great grandchildren into a four-hundred-year exile in Egypt. The great liberation of Exodus is to a new exile, not to the Land, but to forty years in the desert to burn out the slave in the bone. The Torah that moves from this Exodus ends not with redemption, but on the shores of the Jordan—the home is in sight, but not entered. At this nearly there, but not, place, Moses delivers his tragic speech, the first prophecy of despair. Even in this Land, the promised homeland after centuries, the Israelites are doomed to fail, he tells his people, and to turn away and seek the pleasures of others, and the punishment will be to wander, enslaved yet again. This ends the five books of Moses, the Torah, and this is what occurs over and over in the narrative, throughout the next centuries until the Romans finally end the precarious Jewish state's existence.

The time which is spent on the Land is fraught with prophetic rebuke. It is clear in the midrashic understanding of the later rabbinic reflection about the last exile that God is also seen as a wanderer, "like a King without his retinue" in the desert.[44] In the depths of exile, with the Temple in ruins, the rabbis of the next six hundred years will carefully create a memory house, with the Center of lost Jewish life discussed in detail, a fantasy Temple, with fantasy sacrifices rebuilt in their thinking, arguing, and writing. The Talmudic argument and the responsa literature struggle with the realities held in tension, exile and the possibility of redemption. Even while discussing when it was acceptable to bathe in the Greco-Roman bathhouses, or where and when to sell in the Gentile market, they never forgot to rehearse the details of the sacrifice of doves, that the poor would bring to the Temple that had not existed for centuries. The exile seemed so final; the might of Rome so complete.

For these Jewish communities, it was the method of halachah that offered a way to talk about the relationship between small personal acts of daily life and the largest possible social order. For Arnold Eisen, this is an historical feature that emerges directly from the reconstruction of Jewish religious life after the Roman destruction of the Temple, the center of Jewish identity and statehood, and forced exile and dispersion on the Jewish community. Thus, the Talmud itself is a colonialized text, the quintessential text of exile, the portable homeland. Eisen notes:

> The world was hopelessly out of joint and history a jumble, or at best, a cipher the hidden meaning of which as yet escaped discernment. Those who should have been punished for their wickedness reigned triumphant over half the world.... Exile, indeed, had become co-extensive of the world itself, in crucial respects... embracing even the Land of Israel in its stranglehold. This was proof positive, if proof were needed, that sense could not be made out of such a predicament. The rabbis of course, had to try nevertheless, and even more important, to resist.[45]

In the Mishnah, they responded to their situation with attention to every detail, with a code that surrounded the community with a sacred imaginary, a "four cubits of the Law," a small, but determined space and a time that keeps the community, living surrounded by strangers and idolaters, soldiers on alert and temptations everywhere, intact, even as the Jews are forced to walk, bathe, eat, and trade with idolaters. The notion of a system of faith that depends on habits of order that surround and encompass a human life is how the ordinary world is rendered holy. At all times, the minutia of the moral gesture is important: exactly thirty-nine acts prohibited on the Sabbath, the animal killed in precisely this way and no other, articles counted, measured, weighed, compared precisely, with the exactitude of consumption and commerce all watchfully addressed in rabbinic literature. Of course, the rabbis of the Talmud were aware of Roman rule, of the vastness of the cosmos, and of the impossibility of control. But the covenantal relationship, the promises of exiles to God-in-exile were intact. One must live in a pragmatic world of exchange, but there are halachic limits to economic exchanges, to relationships between unequal parties, and to encounters with strangers, all intended to preserve a vivid communal life.

In the Gemorah, the questions about the injustice of colonialism and Roman imperialism are raised more directly. In many sections of the law, the rabbinic discussion veers off to raise question about contingency, just deserts, or the prospering of the wicked. How could the temple have been destroyed, they ask, over and over again.

> Israel stood alone as never before, even if God continued to dwell among them in their wonderings. They had been punished in the traditional manner—with destruction, dispersion, and exile—but without the traditional comforts of explanation. Sacred order would therefore have to be improvised, in both the homeland and diaspora, until such time as the situation at the Center was more propitious.[46]

It is not that individual acts of exiled Jews had the power to change the Roman world, any more than habits of recycling change how the Pepsi corporation uses world resources. It is that to live a fully human life, a moral life, one must act as though it does. The messiah will be brought, not to perfect the world, but the day after the world is perfected by the cumulative weight of such acts. At least, during the tragedy of exile, a human life could still continue. Eisen notes:

> Avodah Zorah is an exercise in facing the abyss so as to avoid falling in; in constructing a fragile and shifting guardrail, wherever possible, so that Jews could live at the precipice with some impunity. The rabbis could not turn the world right side up. They could not depose the Roman rulers, establish the jurisdiction of Jewish courts, or restore the Temple to its glory. All they could do was protect the purity of the Israelites who followed their lead by eating, drinking, and having sex and marrying in accord with the rabbis own comprehensive regulations. For the rest, they relied on imagination to

set right, through fantasy, what no amount of demarcation could salvage. Their time and their place—their exile at home and abroad—allowed no more.[47]

The intellectual problem of the Jewish leadership is to make meaning of the wandering into Babylon and then beyond, Spain, renewed expulsion, Western Europe, again expulsion, then the Pale of Settlement, and finally exile from the Enlightenment, science and rationality of modernity itself, into the horror of the Shoah.[48] In the splintered postmodern landscape, a landscape where, once again, the explanatory story is riven and must be retold, where the mark of chance and of escape from death is born, like a sign, on the forearm. Of course, the modern State of exile and Zionism itself represents the determination and the power of the physical return to the Land, if not the existential one.

The rabbis sustained the exile because they had faith it would end. The waiting was not passive, as Max Weber assumed,[49] as so many assumed about the Jews, but an active if ultimately insecure creation of a state of exile that lived in full awareness of contingency.

The rabbis imagined Abraham, in the beautiful and hopeful midrash, below, turning up at the site of the Temple's destruction, the foxes prowling the broken stone steps, the smell of salt and blood, all that he has dreamed of, sacrificed for, all that was promised, and now only this. His children, Israel, have gone into exile, the entire project of Jewish peoplehood seems undone. The writer of this narrative wants the reader to remember that this is the same Abraham who had argued with God about the injustice of destroying the cities of Sodom and Gomorrah in fire and flame, because of the evil that was done there, arguing for the possibility that innocents would be killed along with the guilty. "Shall not the judge of the world do justly?" he asks. In this text, too, he argues with God, who has seemingly found Abraham at the site of the ruined Temple, in despair:

> R. Isaac said, At the time of the destruction of the Temple the Holy One, blessed be He, found Abraham standing in the Temple. Said He, "What hath My beloved to do in My house?" Abraham replied, "I have come concerning the fate of my children" ... Said He, "Thy children sinned and have gone into exile." "Perhaps," said Abraham, "they only sinned in error?" And He answered, "She hath wrought lewdness." "Perhaps only a few sinned?" "With many," came the reply. "Still," he pleaded, "Thou should have remembered unto them the covenant of circumcision." And He replied,

"The hallowed flesh is passed from thee." "Perhaps if Thou waited for them, they would have repented," he pleaded. And He replied, "When you do evil, then you rejoice." Thereupon he put his hands on his head and wept bitterly, and cried, "Perhaps, Heaven forfend, there is no hope for them." Then came forth a Heavenly Voice and said, "The Lord called thy name a leafy olive-tree, fair with goodly fruit: as the olive-tree produces its best only at the very end, so Israel will flourish at the end of time." (Menachot 53b)

Abraham argues on behalf of the exiled Children, and God quotes Jeremiah back at him, flinging the prophets imbrications as proof text, until Abraham weeps bitterly, "there is no hope for them." But God relents, and a "Heavenly Voice" reminds Abraham of the Covenantal promise, that in the end, Israel will be restored.

Our Exilic Lives

"What occurred to our fathers is a sign for the children."
"I will tell you a rule; go understand it. In all of the following portions about Avraham, Yitzchak, and Yaakov, and this is a significant topic, our Rabbis mentioned briefly and they said, 'Whatever happened to the fathers is a siman (sign or signal) for the sons.'"[50]

For medieval Jewish commentator Nachmanides, quoted here, the Torah's exile prepares us for our own. We are heirs to the rabbinic tradition of practical prophecy as well as to their exile, wherever we live. The work of faith was to provide tools for the details of daily life in the Exilic present. It is to the specificity of response to the condition of *galut* as a synecdoche for all that is modernity under the threat of global warming that we now turn.

Unlike traditions of rights-based philosophy, Jewish ethical norms do not support a completely unbridled autonomy but focus more intensely on two other concerns: the nature of human duties toward the Other; and the exploration and boundary setting of the limits on human desire. Because of the near hegemony of the assumption and power of autonomy in both ethics and in the discourse of public policy, it is important for Jewish ethics to offer some reflection on the tenuousness of that claim. Jewish thought struggles not only with the nature of the self, relative to the Other, and the self, relative to the community, but whether the embodied self has what post-Enlightenment thinkers describe as rights at all. The notion of the good in this formulation rests not on the promise of voluntariness, but on the promise of obligation. Thus, since in Jewish thought, human creatures live in exile both in an existential and in a literal sense, it will be fruitful to consider the promises of exiles, the obligation of sojourners, the limits of our use of the natural world, and the nature of possession and accumulation. Our collective human exile, marked by our exit from an Edenic reality, is to a world of limits: of temporality and specificity. There is the terrible temporality of each human life, of the seasons of harvest and of growth, of lunar and seasonal cycles, and for our discussion, a new temporality must be considered: the amount of time that humanity has before the negative effects of atmospheric carbon can be halted—in the United Nations Intergovernmental Panel on Climate Change (UN IPCC) report (August 2019), that period is a decade. For each event ordered by the natural world, rabbinic law proscribes detailed additional human restraints. Acquisition, consumption, and sexuality are all seen as unequivocally good acts and are not unregulated acts. Limits are not tragedies, but social realities. Desire, seen as infinite, is not rebuked, but refined; expected, but contained by collective necessity creating a moral finitude.

Wilderness and Cultivation

In much of the literature of the ecological movement, the needs of the natural world, left as untouched as possible, are set at odds with the needs of human persons: we are urged toward "fewer people and more bears."[51] But in Exile, not Eden, people need to eat, and thus, nature must be cultivated. Hence the command to all humans, given early in Genesis, "*leshev et ha'aretz*" ("to settle the land"). When the Israelites are told of the Land they are to be given by God, it is Land to farm and to raise animals, but it must be done within limits or the Land itself will "vomit you out." But if you will be a moral people, then it is possible to live there.

> 'If you will listen." Thus begins the Sh'ma, the prayer Jews are liturgically commanded to call out two times a day, every morning and every evening. This is a daily prophecy, and it could not be clearer:
>
> ... if you will listen constantly and diligently to My commandments that I command you this day, to love HaShem your God and to serve God with all your heart and with all your soul, then I will give the rain of your land in its right season, the early rains and the late rains, so that you may gather in your grain, and your wine, and your oil. And I will give grass

in your fields for your cattle, and you shall eat and be satisfied. Watch yourselves, beware, because your heart can be deceived and seduced, and you will turn away astray, and serve other gods, and bow down them;

Then the anger of HaShem be blaze against you! And He will shut up the heavens, so that there shall be no rain, and the ground shall not yield her fruit; and you will quickly be banished, starving, from off the good land which HaShem gives you.

It could not be clearer or more forthright: justice, the Sabbath, the care of the stranger, the ordering law, and the narrative of exile; you must repeat this all, for it is your moral actions that keep the world a good world.

Thus a powerful argument within Jewish theological ethics is one that linked care for the order of the natural world to the issue of social justice. "The heaven will shut its skies and there will be no rain" is the punishment for injustice to the poor. Such a text argues that we are obligated by Hebrew Scripture to care for the poor, the marginal, the desperate, hungry one. When this is done, it is not because one is nice, or charitable, or that it is tax deductible. One does this because the members of the reception community have bound the words of Torah to the body, flat out right between the eyes—*tzedakah*, the word for charity, is the same word for justice, *tzedek*, and charity is given because it is a public act that means one understands that one lives in a theo-political economy, an imperative moral economy, that is far more important than the marketplace which deceives and seduces and tells the enormous lie that the earth can be destroyed, its energy sucked off and burned for profit. One doesn't say: Look at me, I am so kind; instead, one ought to say: Look at God's world, in which the poor are central actors in the working out of moral order, look how abundant are the corners of the field, which belong to the poor, look at the richness of the second harvest, which belongs to them. And in Jerusalem, Rome, and Medina, similar texts remind the faithful: Look at our awesome God who cares for the land so we can care for the poor, so we can steward the land so that it will be abundant, green, and golden to the corners. And if we do not, says Deuteronomy, the entire productive cycle will stop—because what is it all for, the abundance of it, the way it returns, really despite everything and all our petty sins, if not for the poor?

The *golah*, the exiled population, between Sinai and Babylon and America, must make for themselves an order. The text reminds us that what cultivates the earth is not war or submission, but justice. The rules of encampment in the desert, and the rules of agronomy, worked out carefully far from the facticity of the Land of Israel, by people who were living in crowded, dark medieval cities, suggest how we exiles are obligated to live in our world: by remembering the social fact of our own estrangement—this place, this forest, this mountain, this is not ours to own. Enjoined to know the heart of the stranger and to see that he can live by your side, the *golah* is thundered at by prophets and reasoned to by teachers: the wealth and resources into which you walk are not yours; they are transient gifts in a world which is not fully yours even if you, as Adam Smith and John Locke write, mix your labor power with the land. This uneasiness, homelessness, alienation, nakedness, then, is only mediated with careful attention to the most fundamental needs of the Other, the poor, the widows, the orphans, who have nothing if not for you, in their poverty.

What tediously transforms the curse of wakefulness and wariness, of danger and chanciness into a blessing is community, the ordinal structure of sociability, the recognition of vulnerability that mutual and universal estrangement brings. Embodiment is a condition of the creature, its first cause and structure. The labor of birth to which Eve's daughters are given is the work of loving the terribly weak, whose vulnerability requires human community. It is tempting, because it makes one feel safer, to think that the homeless guy, or the immigrant kid on the wrong side of the wall, is not like you, because here you are in your house that you bought, in the chair you bought, eating the food you possess. But really, you and the homeless guy, and the immigrant kid, are all in exile, in a world that is quite literally melting under our feet.[52]

The move of theological ethics toward a consideration of exile is an approach that is promising. It allows us to think about our duties as exiles, as opposed to our rights as landowners, and to fear their curtailing. Now we can begin to envision a world that is a cultivation with limits, between physical necessity and ethical task.[53] It is promising as well, in a world so full of lost chances, when one remembers that the world is fundamentally unredeemed, yet redeemable. To discuss the details of the renewed Temple, as the rabbinic commentators did, to describe the garments of the priests, and the order of songs, commits one to a homecoming that is absolute, no matter how dark the broken world or how remote the vision, or how impractical.

Personal Action in a Public World

Yet, it is fair to ask, how specifically does such an exilic ethics compel substantially different behavior from a world leadership that organizes consumption and commodity exchange? Such behavior is, for each of us, of course, personal as it is political. In this book, I will consider this question on several levels—personal, familial, communal, and at the state level—for all will be important. The rabbinic imagination engaged every aspect of human life, making every choice rich with meaning, and I would argue that there are two reasons to begin at the level of these personal choices as long as that is understood as insufficient. First, there is the reason that emerges from Maimonides's account of moral action, which he derives in part from his reading of Aristotle and Averroes, the Arab Islamic philosopher, and in part from his reflection on Scriptural texts.

> [E]very commandment from among these six hundred and thirteen commandments exists either with a view to communicating a correct opinion, or to putting an end to an unhealthy opinion, or to communicating a rule of justice, or to warding off an injustice, or to endowing men with a noble moral quality, or to warning them against an evil moral quality. Thus all [the commandments] are bound up with three things: opinions, moral qualities, and political civic actions. (Guide, III, 31, p. 524)[54]

Maimonides argued that one could shape one's character by intellectual achievement, and that the commandments could, in theory, be perfectly understood. Even without perfect knowledge, the enactment of the commandments helped one's moral qualities, a virtue theory about how to become a person with better qualities (with the main virtue being intellectual). Acting in concert with your rational sense is Maimonedes's standard. Thus, one should act on a personal level for the sake of developing personal integrity. Secondly, one should act personally because the sum of all such actions can shift things in the political world, particularly if the actions involve marketplace decision or voter choice. Consider: My own grandfather Nathan Cohen, who saw his village burned to the ground in the pogroms of 1905, never saw Yosemite, nor much of wilderness, and walked on the beach in laced-up black leather shoes. He made his small living, happily painting the hundreds of new houses of immigrant Los Angeles that filled up and destroyed the fragile California desert. He liked cities, studying Talmud inside rooms. He planted his backyard carefully, gloried in his grape vines—that was the natural world, something he could tend. He loved progress, the fact of cars, the curly neon signs of the 1950s, the endless fecundity of American grocery stores. He studied the same arguments as the rabbis studied in the year 150 CE, and in 1100 CE, and in the eighteenth century when Locke was writing about America as Eden, and when two world wars ripped apart the family he had left behind in a seacoast town in Russia, and this never altered his dedication to the commandments, or to the small minyan on the corner of Pico and Genesee that he founded. But he always believed that the world was going to change and that Israel would be redeemed, and so he bought shares in theoretical Palestine, hoping to go Home, long before it was a real State.

It is at once maddening and compelling to think that the catastrophe in the climate, the destruction of vast ecosystems, has anything to do with his, or my, paltry choices; after all, I can reason, vast forces far outside of my control actually govern the world economy, an economy at an absurdly far remove from my moral gestures. Consider the following, from David Korten:

> As powerful as the large corporations are, they function increasingly as instruments of a global financial system that has become the world's most powerful governance institution. The environmental, social and even economic consequences of financial decision involving more than a trillion dollars a day are invisible to those who make them... the basic point is that the globalizing economic system is reconstructing itself in a way that makes it almost impossible for even highly socially conscious and committed managers to operate a corporation responsibly in the public interest.[55]

This is almost impossible, in a world governed solely by economics or scientific theory. But not impossible in a world also moved by considerations of faith and human community, a force, despite falling on skeptical times in the late twentieth century, that has historically and contemporaneously reorganized the odds of the fixed and given order more than once. It was in large part the small stubborn acts like those of my grandfather, that supported the creation of the State of Israel. It was not the end of exile, but millions of small acts shifted something in the larger world of politics.

We live always in exile in a world that we cannot possess, for it is already spoken for (and spoken into being, in the language of the New Testament). It means that one walks in a continent not of one's making, on a land soaked first with the blood of Abel (Genesis 14:11) and then with the blood of so many other brothers and sisters. A possible stance would be to abandon the actions of the self entirely, to surrender to a sense that the problem is too large or too "wicked" or too complex. But this choice would be animal, not human.

To be human, and to have a profoundly human task, is to understand that the condition of exile can be, must be, altered by a myriad of human choices.

Jewish ethics does not offer a theology of return to Eden, nor a time when plants or animals are animated with equal moral worth. The very blessing of the human is the ability to work, and to rest, to tame, subdue, harvest, alter, and co-create nature. The environment, in Jewish texts, is not Paradise; it is the actual world, and it more than needs us—it would be a restless wilderness without our hands, a place for beasts, not children, not learning, not *avodah*, the word for both service and for prayer.

Hence, parking lots, neonatal ventilators, PCR machines, plastic Legos, spaceships, and electron microscopes are a necessary part of what it is that humans do, and their beauty and their compromises are the reverse side of a deep appreciation that both dolphins and roaches, and redwoods and kudzu are part of creation. It is foolish to waste or ruin the land, to poison or to strip it, but in Jewish thought, it is not morally incorrect to manipulate it. It is our work, as much as anything about us, that makes us holy.

More than conversations about ethics allow us to agree, they allow us to argue. The work of Jewish thought has always been to make ordinary meaning out of impossible events and to answer the question, "Now how are we to live?," as we stumble out of the last place we have left.

An ethics that speaks to our duties relative to climate change must do at least two difficult things. If it does not, it will be no more than sweet and peripheral, a sort of moral Muzak. The first task is for each person in the exilic community to act according to her promises of accountability—daily, habitually, and against the sense of futility that envelops such acts. I am not going to rehearse the list here, for there is an entire literature to tell one how to use a minimal amount of carbon, starting with the limits on what one eats, and avoiding meat entirely, so I will only comment here that these changes are difficult little sacrifices, but not impossible ones. The moral template is the system of discipline in all religions, but the moral boundaries, limits to total and individual personal action, can exist without reference to the specificity of any view of God. Each self will have to also pick up one's head and expand the gaze, understanding that the self is in full view of the Other. The notion of the good in this formulation rests not on the promise of voluntariness, but on the promise of obligation. The commitment of daily action simply because it is the right act and because it is demanded of you because of your moral location on the planet confronts directly the post-Enlightenment model of the unencumbered disconnected trader in the open and "free" marketplace. Such an approach would insist on the community of others that are dependent on, and dependable on as part of the process, and questions whether unconstrained accumulation is either possible or the ground for human freedom.

The second task for ethics is to seriously consider the problem of power. How difficult an act! It is tempting to only rail against the powerful other guy, or to yearn for a retreat to Eden, or Egypt, or the shtetl—from wherever was the last expulsion. But the rabbinic turn takes us from this. We are enjoined to go beyond complaint, far beyond nostalgia. We need to see the other, and the choices of the other, as our responsibility, and our business. We need to find clarity in the religious voice and claim its power, rather than acceding to its privatization. The prophets of the Hebrew Bible and the rabbis who took leadership of the Jewish communities consistently spoke to the necessity of justice, to the vulnerable, to the laborer, to the land. But of all of these prophetic rebukes, the most compelling is to the powerful, to leadership itself. My community and yours must reflect on their alliances: when the poor tell their stories, will they speak of the solidarity of our community, or of its compliance with evil? We must insist that all of us strangers in the exile have the courage to name evil. The stakes for such engagement are high. But if we do not call the ethical question, if we, too, are lulled into a somnambulant despair by the pursuit of commodities, and the coolness of the silk on our cheeks, the pleasure of the company we keep, and that company's proximity to power, then who will?

Calling the ethical question in the marketplace that orders so much of the largest environmental decision-making is of necessity very difficult. The one who brings moral imperatives, much less God, into the equation will be told, patiently, that the tangible, the tough, and the actual way the world works is by the fulfillment of desire, by the call of the marketplace. Yet the prophetic tradition can tell us much about the imperative of the outsider who can see an alternate vision. Challenging the "is" with the "ought" leads us to fruitful understandings about the role of the alternate claim, leads us to challenge the givenness of the relationships as presented, and leads to an ironic view of diagnostic certainty. Such language is neither safe nor endearing. That the historical place of the philosopher as well as the theologian was to remain the outsider can easily be forgotten.

The first responsibility of any ethics is to remember that it is the brokenness of the world itself that calls us to the work of repair. It is not a new call: Jeremiah (21:1–15) reminds us that long after the cedars were stripped from Lebanon, we still had a chance to reflect and reconsider what we mean by wealth. It is a task for each to insist on, a performative as well as a theoretical commitment.

> "Administer justice every morning;
> rescue from the hand of the oppressor
> the one who has been robbed,
> or my wrath will break out and burn like fire
> because of the evil you have done—
> burn with no one to quench it.
> [13] I am against you, Jerusalem,
> you who live above this valley
> on the rocky plateau, declares the LORD—
> you who say, 'Who can come against us?
> Who can enter our refuge?'
> [14] I will punish you as your deeds deserve,
> declares the LORD.
> I will kindle a fire in your forests
> that will consume everything around you."

Jeremiah, the prophet of exile, speaks here to the exiled people, and they remember and carry his words to read every year on Tisha b'Av, the day that mourns the drama of exile itself. The paradox in the holiday of midsummer comes one-half year after Tu b'Shevat, the midwinter holiday of trees, land, and promise of harvest. Rebuke in August abundance, assurance in January barrenness, the world a place that is capable of anything. It is, says Jewish sources, not a world in harmony and not a world in which we are "at home," but a world in which promises can be made to struggle toward some place where justice is possible. We are in exile on an earth that each year will be smaller: the coastline pushed inland, and the deserts larger, and the places where it is possible to grow food shifted north to poorer soils. While most of the world's population now lives in cities, the land that surrounds them is the only place where food is grown, a simple reality that is not obvious, but our relationship to this earth is one of utter dependence.

> Land provides the principal basis for human livelihoods and well-being including the supply of food, freshwater and multiple other ecosystem services, as well as biodiversity. Use directly affects more than 70% of

the global, ice-free land surface. Land also plays an important role in the climate system. People currently use one quarter to one third of land's potential net primary production for food, feed, fibre, timber and energy. Land provides the basis for many other ecosystem functions and services, including cultural and regulating services, that are essential for humanity.[56]

If Cain's industry, copper, guns, and steel, is something that emerges out of exile, cultivation is something that can be lost. Land is a complex, divine gift: first the perfect garden, then the exile of Adam and Eve, then the gift of the Promised Land, and then exile again. "Property is as much a gift from God as the rains which make it valuable. What God gives, he can take away,"[57] notes Eisen. The fragility of the gift is clear, for the way the earth is warming threatens food production, especially for the marginalized.

> Warming has resulted in an increased frequency, intensity and duration of heat related events, including heat waves, in most land regions. Frequency and intensity of droughts has increased in some regions (including the Mediterranean, West Asia, many parts of South America, much of Africa, and North-eastern Asia), and there has been an increase in the intensity of heavy precipitation events at a global scale.[58]

Jeremiah is thinking of one place, one set of forested hills. We are now living after the exile, deep into the exile, and the hills all around us are in flame. This is a new climate. The terrible heat and torrential rain are directly attributable to increases in atmospheric carbon. In the UN IPCC report on Land Use, from the summer of 2019, this is described clearly:

> Since the pre-industrial period, the land surface air temperature has risen nearly twice as much as the global average temperature. Climate change, including increases in frequency and intensity of extremes, has adversely impacted food security and terrestrial ecosystems as well as contributed to desertification and land degradation in many regions
> From 1850–1900 to 2006–2015 mean land surface air temperature has increased by 1.53°C while GMST increased by 0.87°C.

This will result in increased food prices, which has social effects. For example, food prices from 2007 to 2011 when up 240%, due to a drought in the Eastern Mediterranean, the worst in centuries. In Tunisia, Tarek el-Tayeb Mohamed Bouazizi set himself on fire, in part in frustration at rising prices, setting off the Arab Spring. I will return to the far-flung effects of the drought when I discuss the link with the Syria refugee crisis.

> Climate change can exacerbate land degradation processes including through increases in rainfall intensity, flooding, drought frequency and severity, heat stress, dry spells, wind, sea-level rise and wave action, and permafrost thaw. Ongoing coastal erosion is intensifying and impinging on more regions with sea level rise adding to land use pressure.

Keeping the land, and raising children, and cultivating a life is contingent; it could be otherwise if you forget how to treat the stranger. "Retention of property depends on how one uses it, even more than on business acumen."[59]

"Response options" say the UNIPCC, might be able to mitigate some of the worst effects, but they will be limited in the very countries where the degradation, desertification, and seawater incursion may be the worst. There is, in the careful language of scientists, uneven burdens, as is documented by the UNIPCC:

> (U)neven distribution of impacts among populations of both environmental change and intervention responses to this change. . . . Vulnerability reflects how assets are distributed within and among communities, shaped by factors that are not easily overcome with technical solutions, including inequality and marginalisation, poverty, and access to resources (Adger et al. 2004; Hallegate et al. 2016). Understanding why some people are vulnerable and what structural factors perpetuate this vulnerability requires attention to both micro and meso scales (Tschakert et al. 2013). These vulnerabilities create barriers to adoption of even low-cost high-return response options, such as soil 20 carbon management, that may seem obviously beneficial to implement (Mutoko et al. 2014; Cavanagh et al. 2017). Thus, assessment of the differentiated vulnerabilities that may prevent 22 response option adoption needs to be considered as part of any package of interventions.[60]

It is not only villages in Burkina Faso, rice paddies in Cambodia, or a third of all land in Pakistan that are affected. It is also parts of Locke's paradise. If "all the world was America," even America was not spared from violation. Consider this from the *Washington Post*:

> Today, more than 1 in 10 Americans—34 million people—are living in rapidly heating regions, including New York City and Los Angeles. Seventy-one counties have already hit the 2-degree Celsius mark. Alaska is the fastest-warming state in the country, but Rhode Island is the first state in the Lower 48 whose average temperature rise has eclipsed 2 degrees Celsius. Other parts of the Northeast—New Jersey, Connecticut, Maine and Massachusetts—trail close behind. While many people associate global warming with summer's melting glaciers, forest fires and disastrous flooding, it is higher winter temperatures that have made New Jersey and nearby Rhode Island the fastest warming of the Lower 48 states. The freezing point "is the most critical threshold among all temperatures," said David A. Robinson, New Jersey state climatologist and professor at Rutgers University's department of geography. Rhode Island is the first state in the Lower 48 whose average temperature rise has eclipsed 2 degrees Celsius. In the past century, the Earth has warmed 1 degree Celsius. But that's just an average. Some parts of the globe—including the mountains of Romania and the steppes of Mongolia—have registered increases twice as large. It has taken decades or in some cases a century. But for huge swaths of the planet, climate change is a present-tense reality, not one looming ominously in the distant future. Pests, no longer eradicated by cold winters, are attacking people, crops and landscapes alike. The ⅛-inch-long southern pine beetle had been largely confined to southern U.S. forests—hence its name. But the warmer temperatures have spurred the beetle's migration north, where it has damaged more than 20,000 acres of the state's Pine Barrens, a vast coastal forested plain that Congress has defined as a national reserve. "They are changing the Pinelands," says Matthew Ayres, a Dartmouth researcher who has studied the beetle. "It may not be too long before people are driving through the Pinelands saying, 'Why do they call it the Pinelands?'"[61]

No matter what we do now, the divine gift of the land cannot be completely secured. Exiles have had to leave before, and now the IPCC verifies it. No matter what we do now, there will be increased demands for water, and there will be water scarcity. By 2050, the report says, when the tropical zone can no longer support cultivation, and less and less soil is fertile, people will be on the move, our status as exiles confirmed, our nakedness but for the grace of God, fully exposed.

In this chapter, I have discussed how thinking through Jewish texts about exile and the loss of one's homeland is tied to our current situation of exile, and asked you, reader, to reflect on what might be the response, our response, if we want the good land and the good rains, and the harvest, to continue. It will take more than understanding our situation, of course, for it will take caring for the strangers, for that is the organizing principle of much of Jewish ethics: Land use is tied to the moral world we create, or the moral world that is a catastrophe.

I Will Kindle a Fire in Your Forests That Will Consume Everything around You

There were two pictures in the California newspaper after the fires of the late autumn of 2018 swept the state. One was of the long line of cars creeping slowing along the highway along the coast near Los Angeles, which was, it turns out, in front of my family's house, and in the background, looming, enormous, billowing, the black and red clouds of the fire that was roaring down from the coastal range all the way to the Pacific's beaches, just behind them as they fled, strangely beautiful in that eighteenth-century sense, sublime. They fled in their numbers, running from home, so many that the cars had stopped, the highway full. The second picture was also of cars, but it was not so beautiful, for it was a road of burned-out cars, all the people who did not get away from the terrible fire in the ironically and metaphorically named place called Paradise, in the golden brown foothills of the high Sierra. The cars were the subject of the image: in one case, the people tiny, trapped inside; in the other, the people dead inside, in cars that in a very real way had been a part of the world system that drove the temperature, that caused the weather, that meant that one spark is fatal. Now we have to run from a world on fire; on the road, it turned out to be better to leave the car behind and run. And I can think of no better way to describe our quickened exile this summer, each year the hottest year even known.

Again, and again, the forests burn: in Australia, in Greece, in the Western Rockies and the High Sierra. In the summer of 2022, it was the whole of the Northern Hemisphere that broke records for heat, the great lawns of the French and British imperial palaces crackled and flattened into dust, the olive groves planted in the medieval centuries, withering, and the hunger stones revealed in the lost rivers of Europe. "If you see me, weep," they read, and still the water drops, and ceases. It is not an easy exile. We are in the time of fire, and what are we to think? In the next chapter, I will turn to another way of thinking and tell the story of the great fire that marked the end of another imperial power, the earthquake and the fires that destroyed Portugal and opened up a new way of thinking to the world.

3
Making a Place
Lisbon and the Narrative of Disaster

This is a chapter in Four Acts, with a Prologue.

This is the Prologue.

The great West Antarctic ice sheet, larger than Mexico, is thought to be potentially vulnerable to disintegration from a relatively small amount of global warming, and capable of raising the sea level by 12 feet or more should it break up. But researchers long assumed the worst effects would take hundreds—if not thousands—of years to occur. Now, new research suggests the disaster scenario could play out much sooner. Continued high emissions of heat-trapping gases could launch a disintegration of the ice sheet within decades, according to a study published March 30th, heaving enough water into the ocean to raise the sea level as much as three feet by the end of this century. (*New York Times*, front page March 30, 2016)

Act 1: Making the Case

The world is an optimistic one, and we imagine ourselves as more powerful than ever before. After all, the world is flatter, and we have powerful new technology that has enabled us to travel to all parts of the globe, exchange products, peoples, and skills, making a world with more in common than ever before in human history. Our thoughts are shared with new communities of people who we will never see. We have a sophisticated new economic system, and the optimism has deep intellectual roots, for the many disparate fields of ethics, theology, sciences, and philosophy are considering new ways of thinking about the self. This creativity is expressed in art, architecture, and poetry as well as a new form of public/personal essays. We are a rich world, we in the West, with libraries and art galleries, gilded homes and painted elaborate halls in which we gather. Communities of faith have large and passionate followers, and the arguments for faith are clearly and forcefully heard in the public square.

Yet into this world has come a great interruptive tragedy—the very ground of our security is threatened, and thousands of lives are at stake, and it may well be that the tragedy we are suddenly faced with is in part caused or at least potentiated by the very way we live. Nature, the earth beneath our feet, some argue, rebels against our sinful ways, a moral reaction to our excess and our power. But others argue that Nature, the earth beneath our feet, is not moral, and turns with the logic of scientific necessity; it is a dangerous place, to be sure, but it is only made more violent by our cities, our crowds, our greed. It is hot, flat, and crowded, and humanity may be at an end. We face a catastrophe beyond telling. So, reader, what year is it? The world I am describing is the capital of Empire, the third largest city in the known world; it is Lisbon, it is Portugal, and it is All Saints Day, November 1, 1755.

And I am describing this because I am interested in methods of Jewish ethics. In the last chapter, we considered classic methodology in Jewish discourse, that of the presentation of a question, or *shilah* to a rabbinic authority, and the discourse that surrounds the response which is based in textual interpretation and narrative meaning. The method is derived from the model of the rabbinic period, and it is still in use today. However, as in many religious traditions that are not primarily or as heavily textually based as Judaism, the ethical norms are also derived from oral traditions or histories. Jewish thought can operate in this way as well. So when I was asked to think about "Nature and Its Power," for a climate change and religion conference, I decided that rather than consider the usual texts, described in the last chapter, I would turn to another source. I was curious about disasters, and curious about what sort of debates had emerged in Jewish responsa literature after disasters. I wanted to look historically, but that meant that I would not find, I thought, disasters that involved our problem of global warming and climate change. I, ever the Californian, began to think about earthquakes. And I quickly found the vast literature about the single most important natural disaster of the eighteenth century, one that many historians called the first modern disaster.

In 1755, just as new machines, imperial power, conquest, and enlightenment all contended for attention, one of history's largest earthquakes–thought to be a 9 on the Richter scale–struck off the coast of Portugal, destroying most of Lisbon, followed by a tsunami and then followed by an enormous, city-wide fire that killed a full quarter of the inhabitants. The earthquake shock waves were felt as far as Finland and Africa. "Such a Spectacle of Terror and Amazement, as Well as the Desolation to Beholders, as Perhaps Had Not Been Equaled from the Foundation of the World" read the headlines in the newspapers of the cities of the world. On November 20, 1755, a shaken English merchant, driven from his breakfast tea into a street he no longer recognized, wrote of watching the entire shipping industry and Imperial Navy of Portugal that was anchored in the port be swept under a tidal wave, and flatten into emptiness in one moment. The "Late dreadful Earthquake which laid the Capital of Portugal waste," he wrote, and it seemed perhaps the end of the world itself, a portent of the end of human life as he knew it.

> No Words can express the Horror of my Situation at that Instant, involved in almost total Darkness, surrounded with a City falling into Ruins, and Crowds of People screaming, and calling out for Mercy, while from the violent and convulsive Motions of the Earth, we expected every Moment to be swallowed up. Such a Situation I apprehend is not easily to be imagined by those who have not felt it, nor to be described by those who have. God grant you may never have a just Idea of it, which is to be had only by Experience. (Letter #4, BL, Add. 69847)

An English nun, living in Lisbon, wrote home about the many who burned to death, or starved to death, screaming in pain, begging for help, trapped under mountains of debris, and of aftershocks that sent her out to the streets in terror, for months afterward.

In the months and years that followed, theologians and philosophers struggled to make meaning of the deaths of utterly innocent people, killed randomly, indeed, killed in church on All Saints Day, the clergy, moaning, scarlet blood on scarlet robes. The king and his family were only spared because a young princess had cried because she wanted a picnic on the holiday and could not bear to spend the fine day in church. Her parents had indulged her. The king and queen, arguably two of the most powerful people in the world, sat huddled in a carriage for hours, homeless and alone, a fact which fascinated all of Europe. They never again lived indoors, instead, setting up the court in a series of white, billowing tents, outside the broken palace until they died.

Thus began a debate that has ranged for centuries. There was the idea that the tragedy of Lisbon was due to the error of living in cities, or that the earthquake was due to a divine intervention, a punishment for the deep sins of Portuguese and Jesuit imperialism abroad, or that the world was just a capricious and contingent place, or that the living in this particular, terrible nature was primarily a difficult moral task, with a universe that was entirely indifferent to our creaturely choices. For Pierre Bayle, for Rousseau, for Emmanuel Kant, for Voltaire, nature's force was indicative of the reasons that science and reason would need to be the ground for ethics, for the literal instability of natural order could not hold societies together and the explanations about a God capable of such chaos could not either.

For the eighteenth-century philosophers, the concept of beauty in nature was split away from the concept of "the sublime," a word which was used to describe how nature's power, including catastrophic power, is displayed. It is a turning point. For Rousseau, the earthquake was made into a tragedy by our human actions. It would be far better for all of us to live outside the city, in the tent of nature, he argued, happy, safe, and free amid trees, and not markets and cathedrals. For Kant, who avidly and somewhat obsessively clipped newspapers and exchanged letters with other scholars about the earthquake and then published an early work on the tragedy, the problem was that the city needed to learn from what we would now call the "indigenous wisdom" of the Chilean Indians, with small huts and thatched roofs. Like Montaigne before him, Kant turned to admire anthropological inquiry. Why was it that the Portuguese built such tall hubristic structures, unlike the Tupinamba? In the Republic of Letters, it was a constant topic for the learned men writing across the Atlantic—What is freedom? What is fate? Voltaire, mocking Alexander Pope's *Essay on Man* "whatever right is right"), writes:

> This is indeed a cruel piece of natural philosophy! We shall find it difficult to discover how the laws of movement operate in such fearful disasters *in the best of all possible worlds*—where a hundred thousand ants, our neighbours, are crushed in a second on our ant-heaps, half, dying undoubtedly in inexpressible agonies, beneath débris from which it was impossible to extricate them, families all over Europe reduced to beggary, and the fortunes of a hundred merchants—Swiss, like yourself—swallowed up in the ruins of Lisbon. What a game of chance human life is! What will the preachers say—especially if the Palace of the Inquisition is left standing! I flatter myself that those reverend fathers, the Inquisitors, will have been crushed just like other people. That ought to teach men not to persecute men: for, while a few sanctimonious humbugs are burning a few fanatics, the earth opens

and swallows up all alike. I believe it is our mountains which save us from earthquakes.[1]

Four years later, Voltaire will publish "Candide," mocking the concept of metaphysical optimism, his ironic critique of Leibniz's causality, using the earthquake to prove his point. But others, clearly torn between the new Enlightenment ideas about human freedom and the traditional representation of God as "first cause," were sober. Consider this from the *Maryland Gazette*:

> However the natural Causes of earthquakes may be accounted for by the Learned in the Theory of Nature, no sober Man will suppose that those causes ever act in any remarkable, Manner, without the immediate Direction of the FIRST GREAT CAUSE, the Creation of all things, the Governor of the World.[2]

Lisbon represents, then, the first great modern debate about fate, freedom, the responsibility of the state and the citizen, and the goal of creating a sustainable society. Unlike earlier disasters, in which it was theorized that the natural world acted in direct accord with divine manipulation, the theologians and philosophers understood the complex and nuanced set of choices, had a view of a moral agency that can make nature more or less unjust. Rather, they argued, we live in a natural world, in which we can speak of a distinction between the moral evil inherent in a world made thus and the tragedy, unfairness, and harm that befall the world and its breakable creatures, and a moral evil that exists when we make cruel, unjust, and self-interested choices to harm our neighbor.

The Jews of Lisbon

In Paris, Amsterdam, and Northern Africa, Portuguese Jews in exile waited anxiously for news. In Germany, Rabbi Jacob Baden declared a fast day and assembled a new book of prayer for the Lisbon community destroyed in the earthquake. Jews worldwide heard the news—and stopped to pray and, in this way, reorder the world. It was an event so resonant that nearly two hundred years later, Jewish philosopher Walter Benjamin will discuss it, naming it as the moment when philosophy is liberated and can use science for predictions. Adorno will liken its significance to the Shoah. We locate the fault lines of the medieval world as breaking and falling as surely as the great cathedral that became a tomb, crushing the thousands at mass.

Back to Global Warming

But the way I caught your attention, of course, was for a different reason—it sounds so very familiar. We live in a wealthy West, grown chubby with the goods we bring from the developing world, grown so prosperous we could afford to hire the poor of the world to come from everywhere to serve us. I will argue that we face the sort of tragedy that the Lisbon princes faced—a devastating crisis of unheard proportions, a world we have worked over so carelessly that, because it is made thus and so, threatens to trap us under a great canopy of greenhouse gases, swept by hurricanes and tidal waves. This is a grim textual reality: to remember 1755 and see in it our own time is far closer, I would argue, to the actual news we are hearing about climate change. We live in a world shaken by the collapse of the foundation of capital, to be sure, but we know that our capital markets are linked to the way we built our cities as surely as the King of Portugal knew that the teetering seven-story homes of Lisbon, built in haste, were unsubstantial. We know that the precipice awaits. Only we have the chance of surviving, for we have a warning. It is the contention of this chapter that we can learn from the reactions to 1755, and to the ongoing reception of the story of that day as we look for thoughtful and meaningful responses to the catastrophes of our time, a time in which the fragility and paradoxical power of the natural world challenges our faith traditions, and when I contend we will also need to turn to our text and traditions to draw a different language for our response.

Act 2: Making Theological Ethics

Like earlier scholars, nature's force is the subject of our moral problem—in this case, in the way that global warming threatens human life, the way that the rising seas, three, six, twelve feet, threaten the lives of all creatures who live near the shore. Global warming is not like an earthquake, we know, but consider this: once we have initiated the process of global warming, the way that the natural world responds is very like an earthquake, with out-of-control force. Once the Atlantic is warmer, the hurricanes out of our control; once the ice caps are melted, the floods are out of control. Suddenly, the analogy seems ever more apt, especially because the way that human action was deeply believed, by the eighteenth-century world, to affect such events.

Let us then turn to the problem of how nature's force can be understood in a fragile moral universe in a Jewish theological sense. First, let me also begin with a warning about certainty in theology. As I noted in the last chapter, many of the categories within religious studies do not quite fit the categories of Jewish thought. A systematics for theology is one such category. What I cannot do is give one answer from the Jewish tradition to our Lisbon problem. In fact, the arguments about our proper stance in the world are long-standing. Jewish perspectives on the place of the human person in the natural world, or the relationship between the forces of nature itself, and divine will and human action are complex, competing, and in many cases, utterly contradictory, as I pointed out in the last chapter. There are many competing texts—some that profess an affection for the innocence and beauty of the world and yet a sense that the world is only the background for human action; others that see the world itself as created only after Torah, and in some way, "with Torah," hence, see the world as a legal creation; and still others that human wickedness is the cause of nature catastrophe. All of these ideas are in tension. It is this tension that is at the heart of the remarkable frankness of Genesis, in which two completely different theologies of creation are carefully retold. The first, in which humans and animals were brought into being on the same day, seems to place us within nature, as creatures, with our actions determined by the sense of *tov*, of goodness. But the second story of creation, the one in which it is clear that Adamic human persons have a specific and legal authority even before the tree of knowledge has been tasted, is one in which our power and our judgment are constantly at stake—we are *shomerim*, guardians of a world, set free but with a duty toward mastery. We are given, notes Natan Levy, "two stories of creation at once, the world begins with two possible narratives." For Levy, we are both moral actors in the narrative in which we are created as separate from animals, with the command to *kivshuha*, to subjugate, and populate the earth. We are *baal taschit*, a power that can easily get out of hand when we are to make a human place, not of the created world, using the animals as an extension of our power. And we are moral actors in the narrative in which we are creaturely in the *tov* sense, in the same narrative breath as the animals of the natural world.

And it is against this both/and possibilities that we are held, if we are to be honest about our text and tradition. I have made this point before, and I will repeat it throughout this book: the Jewish theological tradition is multivocal. One cannot explore the history of aversion to paganism, which is so dominant in the tradition, without mentioning the way that mystical, pantheistic themes reoccur in the work of Rav Kook, A. D. Gordon, and in contemporary terms, with Waskow and Green. I know and respect a large and emerging literature from my contemporaries that recovers each text that describes our need for care of the planet, or the prayers for the moon's cycles, or the centrality of the texts of caution in planting and harvesting. Yet we cannot be jejune. Monotheism and patriarchy, if we are to understand them, are built in large part on an argument against the pagan, and the idolatrous, and the temptation to worship the world as a divine thing apart, with its separate moral authority. Here, I will introduce an argument that I will expand in Chapter 8, an argument for a theology of interruption which enables a call to attend to the present moment, but to allow for radical breaks into one's theological certainty. In this chapter, I am going to first briefly suggest two theological concepts. First, a theology of interruption and, second, an ethics of hospitality which I will explore in Chapter 4. You will see how these two ideas work together as we return to the events in Lisbon and then consider how they allow us to think, in Jewish terms, about our situation.

There can be no more interruption as startling as an earthquake. Thus, for Jews, earthquakes were always understood as nature's force both connected and unconnected to humans, a feature of the Mediterranean world so pervasive that there is a separate and discreet prayer in the Yom Kippur liturgy, a prayer for the protection of Jews who live in unstable earthquake zones, against the tragedy that they will create. Like many prayers, this one praises a world of such terrible power, and then moves toward a prayer for protection. Earthquakes are both seen as an example of the pure, disinterested power of nature and of the possibility that God has a hand in the retributive terror they evoke. Both ideas surely exist in the text, and this tension is a critical part of all textual, traditional, and contemporary reactions to crisis in the natural world.

For example, this first text, a rabbinic midrash on a line of biblical text in the Book of Samuel, suggests earthquakes come to "awaken" sinners:

And it came to pass, in the days that the judges judged: Slothfulness casteth into a deep sleep (Prov. XIX, 15). [Israel was cast into a deep sleep] in that they were negligent in paying the appropriate honours to

Joshua after his death. That is the meaning of the verse "And they buried him in the border of his inheritance . . . on the north of the mountain of Gaash" (Josh. XXIV, 30). R. Berekiah said: We have examined the whole of Scripture and we have not found mention of a place called Gaash. What then is the meaning of 'the mountain of Gaash'? That Israel were too much preoccupied (*nith-gaashu*)[7] to pay proper honor to Joshua after his death. The land of Israel was divided up at that time, and they became unduly absorbed in the division. Israel were all occupied with their tasks. One was occupied with his field, the other with his vineyard, yet another with his olive trees, and a fourth with quarrying stones, thus exemplifying the words, And the idle soul shall suffer hunger (Prov. XIX).[1] They therefore neglected to show honor to Joshua after his death, and the Holy One, blessed be He, sought to bring an earthquake upon the inhabitants of the world, as it is said, Then the earth did shake (*wa-tig'ash*) and quake (Ps. XVIII, 8). "And the idle soul shall suffer hunger." In that there were among them those who deceived God by idolatry; he therefore starved them of the Holy Spirit, as it is written, And the word of the Lord was precious in those days (I Sam. III, 1).[3]

What are the rabbis suggesting in this narrative? There has been an earthquake (*wa-tig-ash*) but why? What causes earthquake. They debate. The text suggests it is overattentiveness, or a preoccupation with production, preoccupation being a similar word in Hebrew (*nithgaashu*), to the word for earthquakes, a preoccupation especially about the commodities of the marketplace, and that attention to all this making and having creates a lack of community cohesion—a busyness that paradoxically creates a spiritual "sloth" that is akin to unconsciousness—a moral "sleep." The people are so busy with the business of commodities, says the midrash, that they bury their leader, Joshua, who has led them since Moses, carelessly, on some random mountain (Gaash) that nobody has ever heard of, but which is somehow connected to all this preoccupation, for they were too busy to pay proper attention to their grief or to do honor to their spectacular, dead, leader. Everyone is personally occupied, as it were, inhabited by the spirit of industry, but not by any connection between the self and the Other; thus, each one is guilty of sloth—a paradox that the texts plays with by speaking of fullness and starvation, in which "things" and "Torah" are placed in tension as necessary for human sustenance. Here, earthquakes are clearly a punishment for misdirected thinking: thinking of the self, not the Other. Earthquakes are meant to get the community's attention.

Yet in this other text, a Mishnah that articulates the special blessing that is said over earthquakes, it is clear that they are one of the moments in which God's power is indeed noted, and seen, in contrast to the previous text, as a wonder, as sublime.

> [On witnessing] shooting stars, thunderclaps, storms and lightnings one should say, Blessed be he whose strength and might fill the world. On seeing mountains, hills, seas, rivers and deserts he should say, Blessed be who wrought creation. R. Judah says: If one sees the great sea one should say, Blessed be he who made the great sea [that is] if he sees it at [considerable] intervals. For rain and for good tidings one says, Blesses be he that is good and bestows good. For evil tidings one says, Blessed be the true judge.

I will return to this idea.

Act 3: Making a Place

Yet the catastrophe of Lisbon cannot be understood without the problem it raised theologically, which was the death of so many who seemed completely innocent. It was the beginning of a modern theodicy (think of Adorno), yet the contemporary philosophers were not completely aware of another story, another narrative unfolding at the same time. It marked the end of the Inquisition, which had been a terrifying and brutal feature of Portuguese theo-political life for three centuries. For the Jews of Portugal, the earthquake was an extraordinary moment of liberation. For when it destroyed the court of Lisbon, it also destroyed the prisons of Lisbon, into which the Jews from all over the empire had been sent to be tortured and killed in the Inquisition. The Jews fled into from the ruins, free to live as Jews, into a deeper exile, leaving the Spanish and Portuguese world where the Golden Age of toleration for Jews and Muslims had at least existed, occasionally, prior to the fifteenth century. In flight from the prison houses of Portugal, they were able to become citizens of the Enlightenment world.

Let me return to our Mishnaic text about prayer, as promised, which the Gemora discusses in more detail:

And over earthquakes [Zewa'oth]. What are Zewa'oth? R. Kattina said: A rumbling of the earth. R. Kattina was once going along the road, and when he came to the door of the house of a certain necromancer, there was a rumbling of the earth. He said: Does the necromancer (even) know what this rumbling is? He called after him, Kattina, Kattina, why should I not know? When the Holy One, blessed be He, calls to mind His children, who are plunged in suffering among the nations of the world, He lets fall two tears into the ocean, and the sound is heard from one end of the world to the other, and that is the rumbling. Said R. Kattina: The necromancer is a liar and his words are false. If it was as he says, there should be one rumbling after another!

He did not really mean this, however. There really *was* one rumbling after another, and the reason why he did not admit it was so that people should not go astray after the necromancer.[45]

Here is a rabbinic fight! The theology of this passage is again complex. There is a blessing to be said over an earthquake, which we know from the earlier Mishnehic text, and a series of words to mediate the news it brings. Yet then the odd little story, in which the magician seems to have a better sense of God's grief at the exile of the Jews than Rabbi Kattina. Rabbi Kattina knows that the suffering in the human world is boundless; it is what shakes the world constantly. But one cannot live like that, waiting for the next catastrophe, and the next, and the next. So Kattina is the liar, not the magician, as you the reader can plainly see. But the rabbi needs to keep the social world intact, which will point toward another theological task. While earthquakes are important because they provide an interruption of human business that allows for a recognition of more meaningful obligations, it is also important to be able to exist in a world where humans can live despite the constancy of human suffering without resorting to despair or magic.

In 1755, exilic Jews in Western Europe were just turning toward science and technology, and seeking practical and technical knowledge as an emerging means to control fate and contain suffering. How should earthquakes be understood? Is this causal question imperative? Yes, of course, for understanding causality would begin to affect the moral activity of instrumental and effective new civic policies to avoid human suffering.

In Portugal, the dispute over causality was exemplified on one side by the Italian-born Jesuit Gabriel Malagrida, a famous missionary to Brazil and a favorite of the Portuguese court, and on the other by António Nunes Ribeiro Sanches, a Paris-based Portuguese natural philosopher, who had been forced by the Inquisition to renounce his Jewish faith, but who reasserted it in exile. For Malagrida, who bore witness to the horrors of the Portuguese colonial massacres, a God of justice and memory had taken his revenge. Lisbon is destroyed, he writes, and the causes

> are not comets, are not stars, are not vapors or exhalations, are not phenomena, they are not natural contingencies or causes; but they are solely our intolerable sins. . . . : I do not know how a Catholic subject dares to attribute the present calamity of this tragic earthquake to causes and natural contingencies. Do not these Catholics understand this world is not a house without an owner?"[6]

Ironically, this house metaphor has been used in the rabbinic discourse as well. Yet it was the Jew Riberio Sanches who was the author of the pamphlet that so outraged the priest. In it, he described both the physical observations that led to his conclusion that the earthquake had natural cases, linked to the way the earth was formed, and having an essentially stochastic, not a retributive pattern. In fact, his chapter "The Force of Vapor and the Exhalations of the Interior of the Earth" had been written prior to the Lisbon quake. These observations were appended to his widely read text about the need for public health and the role of the state in building cities, and in restoring a compassionate and just system of social goods after disaster.

The Portuguese king, still terrorized, had handed over the task of rebuilding to his first minister of state, Sebastião José de Carvalho e Mello (1699–1782), better known to history as the Marquês de Pombal, who had first published Ribeiro Sanches's book on public health and, in the aftermath of the Lisbon catastrophe, ordered it to be distributed to all public and religious officials. Father Malagrida began a public campaign to oppose the book as Jewish heresy. He was promptly condemned by Pombal. As Kenneth Maxwell notes, Father Malagrida was outraged. He wrote to his friend, the German-based retired Father Ritter, the former confessor to the Queen:

> Do you wish to know my crime? Read the booklet you will receive with this letter and you will know all. They criminalize me for daring to oppose this booklet and the pernicious doctrine that is propagated in this Court and City, that one should not attribute the earthquake to our sins and the anger of a God, punisher of our crimes; but instead to purely physical and natural causes. It is for this that I am accused, sentenced and condemned without being heard.[7]

Pombal was not one to let such an overt challenge to his authority go unanswered. He was already engaged in an increasingly bitter dispute with the Jesuits, which would eventually lead to their suppression and expulsion from Portugal and its empire in 1759. Pombal personally denounced Malagrida to the Inquisition. Pombal was intent on crafting the public health and welfare response that marked the modern governmental response to catastrophes from then on, making recovery public, not based in private charity or acts of faith. This, of course, was a part not only of his drive to secularize the instruments of the Church for his own ends but was also a rebuff to Malagrida. He also sought help in rewriting the laws of the Inquisition to punish illiberal Jesuits, including ones who might be outraged by state policy in the colonies. Malagrida, now seventy years old, bound and gagged, was burned, the last person burned by the Inquisition. Soon thereafter, Pombal abolished the designation of 'New Christian,' a designation that had been used to identify Portuguese Jews forcibly converted to Christianity. He forbade slavery in the colonies and ended the Jesuit colonial enterprise altogether, seizing most of their holdings for the state. He instituted broad health and safety measure, and planned the rebuilding of Lisbon, the beautiful mosaics that lace and loop, down the long hill to the harbor. In drafting these new laws, Pombal had called on the advice of none other than Ribeiro Sanches. It was a formidable historical irony, notes Maxwell: the Jew reforming the Inquisition, the Jesuit its last victim.

But, still in exile, Ribeiro Sanches, writing in his diary, repeats the private aside of the Talmud, echoing the words of Rabbi Kettina: "But can this law extinguish from the minds of a people ideas and thoughts they have acquired from their earlier years?" The rumblings of injustice are actually constant, thus the human task of response; especially for the sort of response that reorders the violent natural world for habitation, hospitality is the constant task.

Act 4: Making a Place Again

Thus for the Jew, the exile becomes the way the world is apprehended, and survived, always the narrative of exile and expulsion, always, like the trembling of the earth itself, the constancy of the danger. One knows that evil will interrupt, like an earthquake in a terribly planned ghetto or a tidal wave on an eroded shoreline, or moral sinfulness will interrupt. The Inquisition, the pogrom, the poor getting the worst of the tragic possibilities of the earth, the poorest always the worst affected by whatever tragic fate is propelled into being. This is how I want to end, by tying together these themes of disaster, exile, and place. In this chapter, I described the great interruption of the Lisbon earthquake and noted that the suffering of the world is constant and familiar. In 2023, we have come to understand this, for now the disasters that follow global warming come faster and faster, happening all over the globe, unprecedented, like the constant low rumblings of the earth that Rabbi Kattina and his buddy the magician both could feel. What does one do in the face of this? Once we are interrupted, and our attention is focused, then what? What sort of lesson do the earthquake and the reconstruction of the city teach us?

Here is the theological claim, and because it is a Jewish ethical claim, it is phrased in the linguistics of moral action: we must build a hospitable world; we must practice hospitality. This is a theo-political task, imperative even if we fail to stop global warming at this or that conference or in this or that new treaty. I will write more, in a later chapter, about the sort of work that would be required to create the possibility of averting disaster, and the sort of treaties humans would need to turn away from the use of fossil fuels, and many others have written about ways to mitigate disaster, too. But here, I want to consider more about why acts of hospitality always involve a reconstruction of the world, making a place for the displaced.

First, I must note the problem with the term "sustainable" as a descriptor for this action. Here is why we need to move, in caring for our world in which we are travelers ourselves, exiles always, from the idea of sustainability, a good place to start, to hospitality. Creating a sustainable place does not allow us to go beyond the deep injustice in our place. Sustainability is a sensible goal, of course, and it only asks us to retreat a bit, buying, say, a Prius instead of a big gas SUV, or eat tofu instead of turkey. But reader, the world is not defensible as "sustainable" if it is so poor, so broken. It really is good to have windmills in the harbors, and solar panels for the wealthy that can afford them, but if it is called sustainable to do so in a world of our neighbor's hunger, if the solar energy fuels the mansions of the wealthy ecologist or the private university, while the farmers in the central valley of California must let their farms lie fallow, or our neighbors in our town need a park, then we surely we need another word for what I am suggesting. Let me argue for something larger, a goal that is far more difficult, that asks much more of us, that reminds us that the world is held in balance by attention not only to our freedom, our economic and productive exchange, but by the way we are bound, obligated, interrupted, by the needs of the neighbor, both the neighbor we can know and the neighbor we can only know of, whose distant, urgent need is yet intimately connected to our front porch. I am proposing that we aim not for "sustainability" but for "hospitality," for a hospitable world. This will return us to the centrality of hospitality as an aspect of ethical and theological response.

Why is this more ethically and theologically coherent? First, because the world we would want to "sustain" is an unjust one. Let me be more specific. Worldwide, in the year I wrote this eight billionaires in America possessed as much wealth as the entire bottom half of humanity (3.6 billion people).[8] We are completely dependent on a system of capital exchange that still leaves too many in abject poverty.[9] And while standards of living are improving for many if not most people on earth, two things are extremely problematic: the concentration of wealth and power in fewer and fewer hands, and the steady rise in global temperatures. Additionally, because we have made serious progress in essential civil liberties, and tolerance, we cannot go backward, for either if things remain just as they are, or if they pulled backward into 1940, in a Wendell Berry sort of way, when small farms were lovely and sustainable but African Americans were excluded from voting and lived in segregated towns near the lovely farms, it will not be just.

Second, the acts of hospitality are open to anyone, and they are particularly important among exiles. And, unlike so many of the sacrifices that will be needed if we are to contain our carbon use, it is a practice of abundance. It requires an outgoing of the self, instead of a reduction. It can be done—it is done—by the poor and by the wealthy, and in fact, in this, the poor are our teachers. It represents the antithesis of the gated community, the tinted windows, the private jet; it is making public, open to the directions, living in a tent—the model is Abraham, with his tent flapping in the wind.

Third, making a place requires we make a place for the stranger, too. In the discourse of the self and the other, there is a third, and it is this third that allows for justice to be in the discourse, notes Emmanuel Levinas. The encounter needs a home for a stranger without one. It is not about me and Nature as other, for making a place requires judgment, for it allows this third to enter between Nature and the self.

Fourth, this ethical act requires we make a place, which means that our making is an act that centers on the most vulnerable. A world that is completely safe for humans is not available to us, for the natural world is not made thus, as we all now know after COVID-19. We live in a world of limits, of signs and wonders and loss. But the act of hospitality creates doors that open after the limits of the world are set. One can say, welcome.

Exile, as I have written in the last chapter, is our state of being. Climate change is not a disaster, a fallen, failed star, or an earthquake. It is an error, an ontological error, followed by a technical mistake. The initial error is the belief about having; it is to think we "have" the earth, that it is ours, that our habitation and our cultivation are possession. And if it is ours in that entrepreneurial sense, then we own it and can utilize its products to make us rich. But to have it is to misunderstand our position. We are not masters; we are only here to work; we are, as it were, tenant farmers, and contingency and precarity mark the phenomena of our existence. Lisbon is our metaphor, our midrash, on this fact.

Earthquakes interrupt our social fiction. Are you too busy to honor the dead leader? Then, perhaps, think the rabbis, there is a divine interruption. Are you too cruel to the natives of Brazil, so you extract the gold beneath them, enslave and murder them? Then, perhaps, thought the witnesses to Lisbon, you need to be interrupted. Do you think that your beautiful built cities and tall, ornate buildings will protect you from the tidal wave? You are in error.

But after earthquakes, we rebuild. Pombal took the opportunity to plan a city that was a reflection of Enlightenment values, rationality and open squares, the light literally filling the Baixa, the old medieval area of the city.

> If anything, the planning ethos that governed the plan for Lisbon, as an abstraction, focused upon the conquering of nature. Though the earthquake had, in effect, revealed its power over reason; Christianity had taught man to conquer nature. It was the duty of the State, as the people's secular interpreter of reason and protector of the nation's welfare, to show that it was making an effort to reinstate human power over the elements. This is reflected, for example, in the grid-iron layout of streets. This design was not common to any of the Portuguese cities during the eighteenth century, did not fit into the natural contour of the Lisbon landscape, and did not, in any way, lend itself to resolving questions of property realignment. In essence, the grid-iron pattern was a foreign concept that was brought to Lisbon as an expression of the will of the state. There was nothing natural about it. To impose such a design on a city that was so organically patterned before the earthquake was to announce that a new order was at work.[10]

This is interesting. For I have just argued that the error of possession and the fiction of control needs to be interrupted. But I have also argued that humans must rebuild after interruptive destruction, and that this rebuilding has the potential for liberation. The earthquake destroyed the prisons and the Jews were free. The new city valorized the secular over the Catholic Church, the people over the royalty, the new philosophy over the Inquisition. The open debate about what sort of sin had made the destruction is complex and unsettled. This is not a chapter in which I do more than invite you as reader to the story. Ribiero Sanchez was correct, after all. The new order which replaced the old one would contain some of the same tragic fault lines, for even the beautiful Enlightenment cities were not enough to contain what still rumbled beneath them.

We must understand that we are witnesses to everything, every moral action, every good act and every failed one, for all the moral gestures we see, we partake in. If we allow moral evil to exist without our judgment and our outrage, the good society we yearn for will be only a vision. And the converse is equally the case: everything we do here, in our little American neighborhoods, is done in full view of the witnessing world.

I began writing this chapter because I was seeking other ways of thinking about global warming, or rather, to find other arguments that might make this point more vivid and persuasive for my students, to shake them from the complacency about this topic. Clearly, we needed new ways of thinking, for our cheerful ecology language was not enough, and that, while good, it has done little, really, to avert the danger and disaster that we see. And that is why I turned instead to how Jews reacted after natural catastrophe, and I found this one complex response: rebuild, recover, make a new city, make a Lisbon that has wide open streets with beautiful black-and-white patterns and well-thought-out places to live high above the tide lines. It was, I thought, a complicated enough story for our time as well.

That is why I argued, then, we need to look beyond the Genesis narrative, for we are so long out of the Garden. There are no easy or simple answers to the problem of causality. In the book of Job, which is the book in the Hebrew Scripture that asks the darkest questions about how to live with grace, freedom, and justice in the darkest of times, there is a discussion about emptiness and its possibilities. Job's neighbors come over and tell him to curse his fate, yet "Do not curse," says the text; "bless" instead. But the book does not end with words, actually, but with action, and the action is that Job ends up praying for his stupid neighbors' lives, saying blessings after all, but for the other, for his cursing, bitter, neighbors. And his first act of abundance, after catastrophe and loss, is to make a sacrifice. It is this act that allows the world to return from chaos and loss to renewed fullness. For it is hospitality he understands is necessary now; nothing is sustained without interruption, and even a life that is good enough can be unfairly undone. It is tragic until we make it right.[11]

Let us return to the earthquake then. I have told you a story: a beginning, a crisis, a resolution, and an end. A text condenses, makes dense the details that carry the ethics yet make it more elemental. In this chapter, I have brought a narrative to consider and used the event of destruction to serve as one data point, one midrash for our time.[12]

Ethical analysis asks us to judge the right act, and what makes it so, and it asks us: To what to attend? To what to be wary of? To whom do we have duties? Interruption offers a way of thinking about thinking, a willingness to think about unknowability, corporality, contingency, a location for meeting for moral action, with questions from different disciplines, for questions about why, not only how or how big. It offers an actual account of human life and a disjuncture of the quotidian.

In thinking about how philosophers in 1755 turned away from a totalizing theology of causation to the modern sense of action, repair, and human response, we also can count the cost of this strategy, because of the stochastic nature of knowledge. Urban planning, as Levinas, reminds us, also has a cost.

> This adding up of the sum total is the economic life . . .(here) the face plays no role, human beings are terms, they come into an ensemble, adding themselves up. The adding up of totality is, concretely, economic life and the state; economic life is concrete in the State."[13]

An earthquake is a metatexual event or, as Timothy Morton suggests, a "hyperobject." However, human beings did, in fact, find a way to grasp its significance, of which they were aware almost immediately, and to understand some of what it took to address its power. It had an impact on philosophy as well, with the idea of the sublime, the nature of fear and awe. But why it is important now is that as we consider the hyperobject that is climate change, that will derange the world, it is critical that we learn as many narratives as we can. In reflecting on this earthquake, we see it disrupts the former truce between religion and science, and allowed victory in that debate for science, reason, and the eighteenth-century ideas of liberation to extend even to the

Jews. But of course, what was lost was the older notion of a God that would punish for the sin of exploitation, and that surely smoothed the way toward the empires that Ghosh reminds us were the first to be managed by industrial power. How we live in the natural world is the major ethical problem of our generation. It will take all our resources, from all our disciplines, to seek the answers, and it will take, I would argue, the interruption of the moral question to make sense of our story. But after the interruption, how to respond? Here, I have begun to suggest that an ethics of hospitality is one way. Build a new city, open the door.

In the next chapter, I will explore another way of thinking about climate change, by thinking more about the primacy of hospitality as we are faced with destruction not just in one city, but globally, and deepen the discussion that I began by considering the event of the Lisbon earthquake. To live in a good society is to live by welcoming the stranger into our midst; of course we know this, because it is one of the primary tropes of the Hebrew Scripture, the Gospels, the Quran, and the stories of the Buddha. The complex trick is to do this when we feel most vulnerable ourselves. We feel like we have less and less: less money in our savings and for our retirement fund, our stuff is worth less, there is a climate of scarcity—and it is just at this moment that we must understand, say the texts of ethics, that we must be most generous, which will mean a sacrifice far more inconvenient than we have yet understood. Moving from a sustainable to a hospitable world[14] is a critical first step, if we are to constantly do more to make the city rebuilt, to make our place good.

4

Risky Hospitality

Ordinal Ethics and the Duties of Abundance

Imagine that you are a loyal government official, a scientist charged with studying your country's climate. It takes you five years to write your report: you are a careful person. But as you tour the country's north, you find something strange. Whole villages are abandoned; fields of peppers seem to have vanished; the rice croplands have shifted and sunk under the yellow winds. You prepare a report for your president, a beautiful 164-page document with a picture of the country's most ancient and beautiful city on the front (a city that, in three years' time, will be destroyed entirely). In it, you explain that thousands and thousands of families have left the dying farms, which once provided 30% of the entire gross domestic product, and are streaming into cities. They need water, sanitation, health care, schools, and jobs. You tell him that the region is staggering under a drought that has lasted for four years, the worse drought ever recorded in the history of the country, one of the world's most fertile areas, the cradle of human civilization. Here is the news interview about that conversation:

> "Where villages once thrived growing wheat and cotton, often what he found were empty houses and despair due to the lack of water. Between 2007 and 2008 we found 300,000 people had left the countryside to come to Damascus and Aleppo. We felt this was a big problem for us. Maybe it's a reason for the war now. . . . There were poor people. This area suffered from a lack of rain and precipitation . . . it was very affected," he says. During his field visits to villages in the North he remembers asking where all the people had gone. "I saw at that time only buildings, houses and nobody was there. People said we didn't have rain for 3–4 years . . . they left their houses and went to the big cities."[1]

You tell the president that not only is the situation bad today, it will be worse in the years to come:

> A major shift in long-term annual rainfall patterns and a rise in temperatures are projected over most areas of Syria by the year 2100. This will predominantly have negative impacts on the agricultural sector, which currently employs 25–30% of the total workforce and contributes the same percentage of the country's total GDP. Economic sectors are highly affected by climate change, leading to a decrease in the ability to achieve balanced socio-economic development.[2]

But the president in question is not responsive, and the country is question is Syria. And this is no theoretical construct. This drama took place in 2009. And as 1.5 million internal refugees crowded outside of Aleppo and Damascus, the protests grew, as the displaced demanded water. Two years later, thousands of frustrated, landless farmers—a full quarter of the country's population—staged protests in the Arab Spring of 2011. But unlike other states of the region, Libya, Egypt, or Tunisia, President Assad killed the protestors and bombed their makeshift neighborhoods. And thus began the long civil war. It started over famine, water, heat, the loss of land, the desperation of homelessness. It is these same families that now walk, in the thousands and thousands, into the cities of Europe.

> Beginning in 2011, about 1 million Syrian refugees were unleased on Europe by a civil war inflamed by climate change and drought—and in a very real sense, much of the "populist movement" the entire West is passing through now is the result of panic produced by the shock of these migrants. The likely flooding of Bangladesh threatens to create ten times as many or more, received by a world that will be even further destabilized by climate chaos, and, one suspects, less receptive the browner those in need. And then there will be the refugees from Sub-Saharan Africa, Latin America and the rest of Southeast Asia—140 million by 2050, the World Bank estimates, meaning more than a hundred times Europe's Syrian "crisis." The UN projections are bleaker: 200 million climate refugees by 2050 . . . the high end is "a billion or more vulnerable poor people with little choice but to fight or flee."[3]

The dedicated scientist, Dr. Yousef Meslmani, was project director on the study. It was one of his last acts as a government official before he left the country with his family in 2013 to escape spiraling levels of violence. It was the last report that Syria sent as a part of the United Nations Intergovernmental Panel on Climate Change (UN IPCC), and it is why, in the fifth report, the prediction that the Eastern Mediterranean will face increasing heat and drought is so very sound. He saw it firsthand: the empty villages, the dry wells.

In an earlier chapter of this book, I argued that our essential condition as humans in this period is the exilic condition. Here, I will consider the implications of that claim, which is, I believe the necessity for hospitality. Hospitality is the first and the last moral gesture of our time, hospitality that is both urgent and difficult, and hospitality is the final possibility for the world as we face a common condition of exile. I am an academic, just like Dr. Meslmani. All I have is words. This chapter is about talk about global warming, and it will have four parts: a justification for the imperative to talk about a specific critical issue; an analysis of our duty as people who call themselves believers, toward this public speech; a brief journey into a theory of theological citizenship; and finally, a way to talk about climate change that I hope allows both a repair of ethical method and an argument for what we need to do when even our best efforts toward mitigation will still not be enough to undo the damage we have already caused. For as I will repeat in the book, even if we stopped releasing the vast quantities of carbon into the air right now, we would still inevitability live in a world changed by global warming. This changed climate is already, without doubt creating human migration on a vast scale. Here, I suggest that one of the critical tasks of theological ethics is to address this reality, using scriptural reasoning to develop a moral gesture of hospitality as one preliminary response to the crisis to which we speak.

The Polis and the Duty to Speak: Come to the Public Square

Consider this thesis: *Americans, as citizens of our country, have duties to the world.* Why?

First, because the capacity to live in our society is a privilege that is directly contingent on the duties carried by each of us within our society, and as Americans who live in worlds that are relatively protected, socially and physically, we hold more profound obligations. Our university campuses, even if they are community colleges in the inner cities, are still protected by special police, still well-lit and paved, lined with trees, with libraries with open access to millions of texts, with safe and healthy food brought to campus, with watered lawns like parks, and tidy places to put our used Volvos and new Prius cars. It is a world beyond imagining for the vast majority of the world's poor. Our place, our location, our relative status as members, in this sense, of Pharaoh's court, implies a duty, for we are as Joseph, the interpreters and analysts of the dreams of the past and the projects of the future, complicit in the organization of economies, the order of statecraft and institutions.[4] Linked to this fact is the new fact that we are the place where climate refugees want to go. This paragraph is also true of British, French, and German democracies, but as I write, it is our American walls and our American policies that are keeping desperate, hungry families from entering our country.

> Guatemalan migration to the U.S., which had been steady since the late nineteen-seventies, has spiked in recent years. In 2018, fifty thousand families were apprehended at the border—twice as many as the year before. Within the first five months of the current fiscal year, sixty-six thousand families were arrested. The number of unaccompanied children has also increased: American authorities recorded twenty-two thousand children from Guatemala last year, more than those from El Salvador and Honduras combined. Much of this migration has come from the western highlands, which receives not only some of the highest rates of remittances per capita but also the greatest number of deportees. Of the ninety-four thousand immigrants deported to Guatemala from the U.S. and Mexico last year, about half came from this region.[5]

And why, you might ask, were so very many Guatemalans making the terrible trip north? Because a drought there has destroyed the agrarian economy. Even the cleverest farmers were not able to adapt successfully. It was better to be a refugee than to watch your children starve.

> The population in the highlands is mostly indigenous, and people's livelihoods are almost exclusively agrarian. The malnutrition rate, which hovers around sixty-five per cent, is among the highest in the Western Hemisphere. In most of the western highlands, the question is no longer whether someone will emigrate but when. "Extreme poverty may be the primary reason people leave," Edwin Castellanos, a climate scientist at the Universidad del Valle, told me. "But climate change is intensifying all the existing factors." Extended periods of heat and dryness, known as *canículas*, have increased in four of the last seven years, across the country. Farming, Castellanos has said, is "a trial-and-error exercise for the modification of the conditions of sowing and harvesting times in the face of a variable

environment." Climate change is outpacing the ability of growers to adapt. Based on models of shifting weather patterns in the region, Castellanos told me, "what was supposed to be happening fifty years from now is our present reality."[6]

Second, we have obligations that arise from the brokenness of the world, a contingent, fragile, and unfinished project that, on its own, at the moment of rupture, interrupts the constancy of our being and pulls us to attention. The world comes to us, is experienced by us, if we are at all alert, if we listen at all to the cries of the other, as broken. This is a Scriptural truism, of course, but it is also a matter of data. Consider the number of people who are hungry (805 million)[7] or without clean water (one in every nine people in the world). The other side, in the moral sense of the fact of the world's brokenness, is the fact that we have the ability to repair, and this "can" implies "ought."[8]

Third, the needs of the poor create another justification for the duty. What I do, how I live, is a moral act, every single gesture. And while the gestures seem innocent, they are cumulative, and they set in motion a chain of action that, given the structures of exchange, is part of the systemic order of the world. And the world is so shaped, the production and exchange and consumption of the goods and services, so that the wealthiest have garnered the vast majority of wealth, at the expense of the lives and the health of the poor. As readers of scripture, who of course know this and who are deeply aware of the specially regarded place that poverty claims in Scripture, we have a duty to speak to this regard. In Hebrew Scripture, the New Testament, and the Quran, the relationships between production and the laws for structural charity are made clear. Moreover, we have an obligation to teach the language of prophecy and of the justice such language implies. We have an obligation to teach our texts and their real-world implications for social justice and structural, political repair, with the same seriousness that, say, a molecular biologists will teach that Darwin's text implies certain realities about the spread of adapting bacterial diseases, or an engineer will order structure on the basis of the facticity understood by Roman bridge builders.

Let me expand on this point. We now live in a world in which nearly every system of justice has been stripped of legitimacy. Socialism, much less communism, a courtly system of obligations, or the *noblisse oblige* expressed by local barons, or the rules of decency and polite conduct, are all thrown over in the face of the "justice" of markets, which, despite having nearly collapsed in 2008, have recovered just enough so that the economists can, with straight faces, argue that climate remediation plans are too costly. Even the truth discourse heretofore found in science is funded by private capital, and the languages of the market shape notions of what it is "worth."

Fourth, we are the sort of creatures, as any Kantian will note, that are possessed of a "plight" and the plight into which we are each born is that we cannot *not* act. Thus, there is no "doing nothing," for the doing of nothing is a something, is a moral act, one in which you support the existing constructs of carbon use and the policies of the energy companies, and it looks for all the world like you are then acting as if you have a duty to them, one that you enact every time you get into the car.

And finally, our abundance as Westerners creates special duties. We would, of course, have obligations toward protection even if climate change was act of random chaos, as we do as neighbors, for example, when an earthquake occurs. But in this case, now that we know that when climate change is related closely with the way that we—me, you—live every day, with our abundance and our ease, then we in that sense, are the perpetrators. It is the "now that we know" aspect of our lives, the way in which the ordinary, careless, causal acts lead to the devastating yet unseen events: that is the moral failure. We are, as Jewish philosopher Emmanuel Levinas noted, all dwellers in the Cities of Refuge, people who have committed manslaughter, sort of by mistake, like the man in the Talmud who, when tearing down a wall, tosses the stones onto a refuge heap, where the poor huddle and are killed.

Let us examine this idea of our culpability in some detail. We return to the rabbinic discussion once again as they consider the problem of inadvertent murder. Here is the Talmudic text, a conversation about the blame for the death of the poor, from Babba Kama 32b:

> If a man throws a stone into a public thoroughfare and kills [thereby a human being], he is liable to take refuge. Now, does not [the offence] here committed inadvertently approach willful carelessness? For surely he had to bear in mind that on a public thoroughfare many people were to be found, yet it states, 'he is liable to take refuge' (in the city of refuge, and not be tried for murder)?
> —R. Samuel b. Isaac said: The offender [threw the stone while he] was pulling down his wall. But should he not have kept his eyes open?
> —He was pulling it down at night. But even at night time, should he not have kept his eyes open?

—He was [in fact] pulling his wall down in the day time, [but was throwing it] towards a dunghill. [But] how are we to picture this dunghill? If many people were to be found there, is it not a case of willful carelessness? If [on the other hand] many were not to be found there, is it not sheer accident?

—R. Papa [thereupon] said: It could [indeed] have no application unless in the case of a dunghill where it was customary for people to resort at night time, but not customary to resort during the day, though it occasionally occurred that some might come to sit there [even in the day time].

—[It is therefore] not a case of willful carelessness since it was not customary for people to resort there during the day. Nor is it sheer accident since it occasionally occurred that some people did come to sit there [even in the day time].[9]

A man is pulling down an old brick wall, perhaps to build a big new building, a significant one, perhaps a home for the wealthy. The text does not say. But nearby are the garbage heaps of the city, and there is so much waste that it has become a little hill, place for the poor to sleep; they sleep without any home at all, on the heaps of garbage, and even in the daytime, there are people there, for perhaps there is nowhere else to rest, or perhaps it is as it is in our time, that the glittering cities are surrounded by mountains of garbage and the children of the poorest and the most desperate live there, and just like the man in the Gemorah text, we do not even know. In Berkeley and Los Angeles, tent cities line up under the concrete, bridges beneath the hum of the freeway overpasses, and the poor lie in the parks and in the grass that divides the hustling streets.

It is so easy to kill in this way, not to even see the poor or know their lives. It is ordinary, even, to live in such a way, produce in such a way, consume in such a way that our actions, our life choices, and our hungers are the cause of their deaths. Our cheap t-shirts are made in distant, oppressive sweatshops; our yummy chocolate picked by twelve year olds who have never tasted it, whose bodies are crippled by the need to pick cocoa beans. Perhaps this is why, notes the Talmud, the roads to the Cities of Refuge where the people who kill by mistake are exiled, are exponentially wider than any other roads except the King's Highway, for so many, if justice were really enacted, would be crowded into the route.

Let me turn to the ethics of our abundance and the reason that our scholarly duties are also political acts as well as speech acts.

What Duty Does

We are urged—and we should teach—that ordinal acts really do matter. They do in the sense I spoke of earlier, in that my existence is contingent on millions of others bearing my burden and they do as ethical acts that emerge as obligations, necessitated by the place I am situated and the person it allows me to become, necessitated by the identities that are created by speech, act, and the invisible but coherent moral argument every single act implies, and by which my character as well as my world is shaped. We teach in the broad daylight of the public discussion of religion, and we live as if surrounded and witnessed by this public of which we are a part.

I depend on thousands of invisible others to make the world stable and safe. I am served by people who wake before dawn, by people who clean up the places I go, and harvest the food and bring it to my city, which has been built by thousands, over a hundred years, working on streets and sewers. Even in our academic or professional conferences, we are tended and served by people whose lives are invisible. It is not inevitable that this is the case. For by acting "as if" I can see the face of the Other, I might even create a world in which everyone's work is seen and the actions of all matter. And the next step in this logic, the logic of democratic citizenship, is to recognize the brute fact that our ordinal acts are moral arguments either *for* or *against* a certain kind of world, *for* or *against* the reality of the faces of the others who surround us. Thus, the first step in creating a democratic moral life is to look around. It is to understand how the polis is created, where "it" and "we" are. If we see the relationships, intersubjective, always present, we know we are not alone. The private act, our act making ideas into words spoken, can be taken out of its isolation and flown as an identity and as a public appearance, and by this way, creates the public. How does speech create a public? What can the political act be, as opposed to the merely social act? It is a core question of political philosophy, and I would argue, in political theology as well.[10]

Consider Hannah Arendt. Arendt, writing philosophy in a one-room apartment, in exile, in New York, her entire world, its spaces and squares blown to pieces, like smoke, vanished in the winds of the Third Reich. She had, she wrote, "lost the world," a term for the erasure of the public sphere of public truth telling, parrhesia, and the actions that public speech implies and its replacement by the deep interiority of private lives, lived in silence, or of economic exchanges between strangers, or of social administration over public democracy.

What will it take to create moral and democratic action once again? How does the public world exist? She argues for an argument, activity that is an enabling agency, valued for its dissonance and disagreement on the nature of "worth" or "good" as opposed to the celebration of a universal norm of goodness. The power of the pluralistic discourse is that it needs citizens who are willing to discern, judge, and advocate for positions, and willing, moreover, to when convinced, organize others toward "concerted action," a praxis of action that arises out of speech acts allowing political changes even when all the power of the givenness of history is arrayed against them.

This public space is rare and endangered by the trivialities of the market, the loneliness of the individual, the pervasive idea that history is organic, and not created by the acts of citizens. In the place of the political, another sort of public emerges, of the anonymous polls, or of the beautiful shops, or the easy charm of markets. This rise of the social is opposed to the solemnity of the political. In the social, discernment is lost to accumulations, capital, objects, and social wealth. And the values of the social—the novel, the mutable, the quick, the abundant, the expedient, the sense of fashion—are in direct conflict with the values of the political: endurance, freedom, solidarity, responsibility. For Arendt, the actions of citizens in public are the actions that define them as individuals with particular, irreplaceable identity, for in the social what matters is not their being, but their social role, and as consumers or producers, they are, like their products, completely replaceable, expendable. Agency in public allows for the defining acts of freedom and equality that are critical to our humanity.

Arendt understands the need for private life, called "labor," in which people are sustained as creatures, and the need for "work" in which the structure and objects of materiality are made. But what is critical for the "natality" of the citizen, the full and flourishing person, she recovers from Aristotle, is the second miracle of being, is action, the capacity for a speaking, arguing adult to begin again to act in public and to convince others of the need for action. This can happen anywhere there is a community of speakers:

> The *polis*, properly speaking, is not the city-state in its physical location; it is the organization of the people as it arises out of acting and speaking together, and its true space lies between people living together for this purpose, no matter where they happen to be.[11]

As philosopher D'Entreves comments, in a review of Arendt:

> For Arendt, therefore, the *polis* stands for the *space of appearance*, for that space "where I appear to others as others appear to me, where men exist not merely like other living or inanimate things, but to make their appearance explicitly." Such public space of appearance can be always recreated anew wherever individuals gather together politically, that is, "wherever men are together in the manner of speech and action" (HC, 198–9). However, since it is a creation of action, this space of appearance is highly fragile and exists only when actualized through the performance of deeds or the utterance of words. Its peculiarity, as Arendt says, is that "unlike the spaces which are the work of our hands, it does not survive the actuality of the movement which brought it into being, but disappears not only with the dispersal of men—as in the case of great catastrophes when the body politic of a people is destroyed—but with the disappearance or arrest of the activities themselves. Wherever people gather together, it is potentially there, but only potentially, not necessarily and not forever"[12,13]

If there is not appearance, no self-to-Other speech, no texts debated nor talk exchanged, then the capacity for democracy is unwound. The public square can be filled only by social noise or the exchanges of stuff, but the premise of a state is the first act of gathering, of occupation, as it were, of the community. Says Arendt:

> Power needs no justification, being inherent in the very existence of political communities; what it does need is legitimacy.... Power springs up whenever people get together and act in concert, but it derives its legitimacy from the initial getting together rather than from any action that then may follow.[14]

But the first act is the courage to appear to one another, face to face, so the differences can be seen, and the commonalities seen, and of course, to see that there are many in the square, and that one is not alone. My talk, my thinking and my idea for action, I see reflected on your face, but only if we are standing as citizens, together. And there is no escaping the fact that one stands, counted by one's actions, in a community to which one is responsible. Arendt argues:

> We can escape this political and strictly collective responsibility only by leaving the community, and since no man can live without belonging to

> some community, this would simply mean to exchange one community for another and hence one kind of responsibility for another.... The question is never whether an individual is good but whether his conduct is good for the world he lives in. In the center of interest is the world and not the self... no moral, individual and personal stands of conduct will ever be able to excuse us from collective responsibility. This vicarious responsibility for things we have not done, this taking upon ourselves the consequences for things we are entirely innocent of, is the price we pay for the fact that we live our lives not by ourselves but among our fellow men, and that the faculty of action which, after all, is the political faculty par excellence, can be actualized only in one of the many and manifold forms of human community.[15]

The inescapable community is one that is threatened by a danger that is hard to manifest, one that we as scholars can know and teach so that the human community to which we have a duty to teach, a collective responsibility to be among the people seeking ways to respond, to change the practices that have led us to the intense consumption, the accumulation, the business, the peripatetic seeking that define our world.

Thus, we are always travelers, not just in the literal, Walter Benjamin sense, the Jewish philosopher finally fleeing from the most hideous of rumblings of the twentieth century, the Shoah, with his work and what was left of his beloved library, packed in his one suitcase, but in the sense that we know we need hospitality, too. But we also know that whoever you are, there are neighbors in worst straits, and one's door must be open to them, the solidarity of exiles.

Communities are difficult to construct, and they are necessary for human order. It is the loss of community, one thing, that is deadly about being a climate refugee, but it is the loss of the self that is ontologically destabilizing. Notes Hannah Arendt:

> The calamity of the rightless is not that they are deprived of life, liberty, and the pursuit of happiness, or of equality before the law and freedom of opinion—formulas which were designed to solve problems within given communities—but that they no longer belong to any community whatsoever. Their plight is not that they are not equal before the law, but that no law exists for them; not that they are oppressed but that nobody wants even to oppress them.[16]

What about the children at the border, the families waiting at the wall? They are the first wave of what will be a torrent, but no one even wants to see them, much less offer them a home. They are the "surplus people" Arendt has told us are of no use to the State and without rights, they, quite literally have no place in the world.

Arendt, of course, spends nine years of her life as a stateless person, hiding in France for there was no place for a Jew to go, lucky to be even a refugee, and she knows it. She writes:

> The story of our struggle has finally become known. We lost our home, which means the familiarity of daily life. We lost our occupation, which means the confidence that we are of some use in this world. We lost our language, which means the naturalness of reactions, the simplicity of gestures, the unaffected expression of feelings. We left our relatives in the Polish ghettos and our best friends have been killed in concentration camps, and that means the rupture of our private lives.[17]

Even with her brilliant ideas about community, she stood outside, stateless. To be a Jew in 1942 was to be a refugee no matter where one was. Human beings, she wrote, "have ceased to exist for quite a while," for actual hospitality is remarkably hard to assemble:

> If it is true that men seldom learn from history, it is also true that they may learn from personal experiences which, as in our case, are repeated time and again. But before you cast the first stone at us, remember that being a Jew does not give any legal status in the world. If we should start telling the truth that we are nothing but Jews, it would mean that we expose ourselves to the fate of human beings who, unprotected by any specific law or political convention, are nothing but human beings. I can hardly imagine an attitude more dangerous, since we actually live in a world in which human beings as such have ceased to exist for quite a while, since society has discovered discrimination as the great social weapon by which one may kill men without any bloodshed; since passports or birth certificates, and sometimes even income tax receipts, are no longer formal papers but matters of social distinction.[18]

Jewish ethics is also grounded in this history, and in particular the recent history of forced exile in which the plight of the Jews was merely, for Arendt, a prefiguring of the fate of all peoples.

> Refugees driven from country to country represent the vanguard of their peoples—if they keep their identity. For the first time Jewish history is not separate but tied up with that of all other nations.[19]

The climate refugees of Syria, of Guatemala, and of California are the vanguard of the many who will be forced out by global warming. The UN IPCC warns of more extreme weather and loss of land.

> Climate change has already affected food security due to warming, changing precipitation patterns, and greater frequency of some extreme events. In many lower-latitude regions, yields of some crops (e.g., maize and wheat) have declined, while in many higher-latitude regions, yields of some crops (e.g., maize, wheat and sugar beets) have increased over recent decades. Climate change has resulted in lower animal growth rates and productivity in pastoral systems in Africa. There is robust evidence that agricultural pests and diseases have already responded to climate change resulting in both increases and decreases of infestations. Based on indigenous and local knowledge, climate change is affecting food security in drylands, particularly those in Africa, and high mountain regions of Asia and South America. The likelihood, intensity and duration of many extreme events can be significantly modified by changes in land conditions, including heat related events such as heat waves and heavy precipitation events. Changes in land conditions can affect temperature and rainfall in regions as far as hundreds of kilometres away.[20]

Bring Your Book

Arendt tells us that in situations where injustice arises, we must speak. But speak of what? It is here that we can lift up an argument that Scriptures hold a critical place, and more: these are the voiced moral appeals that we as scholars and as citizens have held dear, and whose voices we in this sense carry into the world and speak: theology.

There are many rich resources in theological traditions that argue for the need to limit desire so as to be a just steward of the world and in many, there are stories of refugees who come to your door when famine drives the world into disorder. In the Scriptural traditions of Judaism, Christianity, and Islam, the story of hospitality to the poor stranger is a central motif, reoccurring to remind us of the precarity of our position and of the place of the poor in our theo-political economy.

In the last chapter, I have looked at how the Jewish tradition sets norms in place by commandments and exemplary behaviors in reaction to catastrophes.[21] Here, I consider a text not necessarily thought of as a text about ecology. I am interested in ordinal acts of ethics and in the Torah's ideals about hospitality. But how can the gesture of hospitality work? If the projections about the way that climate change will affect food production, especially in the global South are taken seriously, we surely have strangers who knock on our door. Already, when crops fail, the poor move to the cities— they are already standing at the door. Massive climate change however, has already begun to shut down whole regions as we have seen in the case of Syria, or Central America.[22] What will we need so that we can respond? Let us turn to how the actual event—ecological disaster, the collapse of the land, and the poor who show up at your door—has been considered scripturally. Will you invite the stranger in, as you are commanded to do? This coming to the door is familiar to readers of Scripture. Consider the narrative of Joseph and his brothers which is told in an entire chapter of the Quran, in addition to the long narrative in Genesis 42 of the Hebrew Bible.

> The seven years of abundance in Egypt came to an end,[54] and the seven years of famine began, just as Joseph had said. There was famine in all the other lands, but in the whole land of Egypt there was food.[55] When all Egypt began to feel the famine, the people cried to Pharaoh for food. Then Pharaoh told all the Egyptians, "Go to Joseph and do what he tells you."
>
> When the famine had spread over the whole country, Joseph opened all the storehouses and sold grain to the Egyptians, for the famine was severe throughout Egypt.[57] And all the world came to Egypt to buy grain from Joseph, because the famine was severe everywhere.
>
> When Jacob learned that there was grain in Egypt, he said to his sons, "Why do you just keep looking at each other?" [2] He continued, "I have heard that there is grain in Egypt. Go down there and buy some for us, so that we may live and not die." And he said, "Behold, I have heard that there is corn in Egypt; get you down thither and buy for us from there and we may live and not die." And Joseph's ten brothers went down to buy grain in Egypt. And the sons of Israel come to by grain among those that came; for the famine was in the land of Canaan. And Joseph was the governor over the land and it was he that sold to all the people of the land and Joseph's brethren came and bowed down themselves before him with their faces to the earth.[23]

Here is the same story, continued, but in the Quran, in the chapter Yosef:

> When they entered (Joseph's) quarters, they said, "O you noble one, we have suffered a lot of hardship, along with our family, and we have brought inferior goods. But we hope that you will give us full measure and be charitable to us. Allah rewards the charitable."
>> [12:89] He said, "Do you recall what you did to Joseph and his brother when you were ignorant?"
>> [12:90] They said, "You must be Joseph." He said, "I am Joseph, and here is my brother. Allah has blessed us. That is because if one leads a righteous life, and steadfastly perseveres, Allah never fails to reward the righteous."
>> [12:91] They said, "By Allah, Allah has truly preferred you over us. We were definitely wrong."
>> [12:92] He said, "There is no blame upon you today. May Allah forgive you. Of all the merciful ones, He is the Most Merciful."[24]

The story of Joseph, opening the door to his failed and broken brothers, men who themselves are oddly unclear on family obligations or moral realities—this is not the hospitality of Abraham, all busy, happy, rushing about to serve the beautiful, beatific angels. It is the risky hospitality, the grudging uneasy welcome to strangers. They look familiar but also just like your enemies. They do not deserve your welcome, and they cannot bless you. The relationship is asymmetrical, as in all encounters with the Other, says Levinas. You have so much, storehouses of stuff, and they are so hungry.

You have so much. This problem of abundance (and while scholars of religion are no doubt underpaid, there is not one of us who could not find a place for another to sleep in our house, no one who could not share a meal, or a week of meals for another) is twofold. First, abundance is a problem, because it is insatiable, circular in its action; and second, it is a problem because counting up one's stuff is expressive of a fundamental confusion, the confusion between humans and things, between knowing and owning. With so much at stake, as one adds up the stuff that defines one, it is easy to slip into counting "things"—even relationships have a weight and quantity. It is easy to forget the theo-political economy, in which the possessive capacity, the ability to dream up plans, the land itself, the capacity to work, all of this, is on loan to you to use to create more than enough for yourself and for the strangers who are a part of the plan, who come after the harvest. As Emmanuel Levinas, in "Outside the Subject," argues:

> Face to face with the other man that a man can indeed approach as presence, and that he does approach as such in the sciences of man, had not the thinking one, (*le pensant*) already been exposed—beyond the presence of the other, plainly visible in the light—to the defenseless nakedness of the face, the lot or misery of the human? Had he not already been exposed to the misery of nakedness, but also to the loneliness of the face and hence to the categorical imperative of assuming responsibility for that misery? The Word of God in that misery committing him to a responsibility impossible to gainsay. A uniqueness of the irreplaceable and chosen. From unique to unique, beyond any kinship and any prior commonality of kind—a closeness and a transcendence outside all subject, outside all synthesis of a mediator ... Justice means we are responsible beyond our commitments ... You are not free, you are also bound to others beyond your freedom, you are responsible for all. Your liberty is also fraternity.[25]

A risky hospitality transforms the stranger into brother, your abundant possessions, your stuff into gifts, liberty into fraternity.

Here is another text: the rabbinic midrash on the moment just prior to the moment of hospitality, which gives us more details about the desperation that drives Joseph's brothers to Egypt. Here Jacob sends his sons into the world of famine:

> Now Jacob saw that there was *seber* (hope).
> That there was *sheber* (disaster), viz. famine; that there was *seber* (hope), viz. plenty. That {Gen. 832} there was *sheber* (disaster)—And Joseph was brought down to Egypt (Gen. XXXIX, 1); That there was *seber* (hope)—And Joseph was the governor (ib. XLII, 6). That there was *sheber* (disaster)—And shall serve them, and they [the Egyptians] shall afflict them—the Israelites (ib. XV, 13); that there was *seber* (hope)—And afterward shall they come out with great substance (ib. 14).
> Another interpretation of, Now Jacob saw that there was corn in Egypt. Was then Jacob in Egypt that Scripture says, Now Jacob saw that there was corn in Egypt? Did he not say to his sons, Behold, I have heard that there is corn in Egypt (Gen. XLII, 2)? Since the day that Joseph was stolen, however, the Holy Spirit departed from him [Jacob], so that he saw yet did not see,

heard yet did not hear. Now, why does it not say, "Jacob saw that there was *bar*," or, "There was *okel*," but, there was *shebber* (Corn)? Read not *sheber* (corn) but *seber* (hope): he saw in the glass of vision that his hope was in Egypt, viz. Joseph.[26]

In the midrashic account, the rabbis are making a point using the similarities between the words "disaster," "corn," and "hope," which sound closely similar in Hebrew. Hope and disaster are always paired, something that the broken Jacob, could understand despite his physical blindness. The act of giving used the term *shebber* and not the usual word for grain, *bar* or *okel*, so that it become the sign of hope in the middle of disaster. Again, the transformative alchemy of disaster into hope, because of hospitality, done with the moral language game of rabbinic theology.

Of course, Westerners, moderns, you, reader of this book, we are very much like Joseph the bureaucrat, who is management for the storehouses and the distribution: culpable, able to see the coming famine, to convince the king, to be in technological charge, and able to organize a response. And because we have this power it is possible, that my argument, or the argument of the text, is true, is obtainable, is possible. If we can learn to risk hospitality, we make the hope within even disaster—if we can bear to share that grain. Look how the rabbinic imagination plays with what Jacob/Israel sees: that hope in the name of welcome can be found even in the middle of hopelessness, the obliteration of the natural world of grain, the violence of a broken nature, can be redeemed by a single human act: you are welcome inside.

Come to the public square: bring your Book, and tell this story, because nowhere else will the risk of hospitality and the grace of forgiveness be lifted up as possible. In fact, to risk in this way in the context of our current public squares, the real ones, with the desperate beggars, the neon, the broken sidewalks, and the old men who sleep in the doorways, would be considered absurd. But consider why we are "surd," or silenced, unable to speak: it is because we largely speak without text, and it is soundless indeed.

"Whenever there is disaster, whenever there is drought, people move, and whenever that happens, there are walls," says Ronni Ellenblum, a geographer and political scientist. It is the case in 2023 that the discourse is about walls and we have not offered much in the way of hospitality. It will be a virtue that we have to learn, because the habitable spaces and the existing populations are not stable, but will constantly be part of a larger struggle for survival.[27]

There is much more to say about this, both this Joseph text and about other ones and about the larger problem. In the next chapter, I will explore how the issue affects women disproportionally, as one possible extension of my argument. But our texts illuminate the speech between us: they remind us that despite the impossibility of the task, the terrible crisis we face. It is, a crisis that needs our careful reflection, our best ideas, and the arguments written, spoken, rewritten, and restated across the centuries: here is what you need to do when all might be lost, when the crisis engulfs the world, how to be able to open the door to the need, and see the face of your family: they look so like you.

Into Praxis

There was a terrible rainstorm, and the dark waves pounded against the shore all night, and we woke in the morning, and walked to a beach covered with trash, the large and the small detritus of the world. Or rather, of Los Angeles, not quite the world. There were beer cans, and bottles of salsa, many condoms, and bright, broken toys, and shiny paper that both attracted and then sickened the gulls, and the bodies of gulls lay about. It looked broken as if after an assault, and it was partially the nature of Pacific, of course, but partially the citizens, our trash. There was, oddly, amid the trash, a 1940s radio tube, covered with barnacles, and a plastic, fold-out Navy flight map of the Afghan-Pakistan border, with directions about how to move "only at night" if captured, and the berries that one could eat. All of the stuff, all the abundance of our careless world, things tossed over the side of the big boats and the big cars washed down to the sea. The storm was the very worst in many years, and it narrowed the beach to a rocky sliver. But the city turns its back on the sea, and like all the hundred-year storms, on the evidence of disaster. The public square is far from the edges of the city, the sea, river, or the mountains, so it is possible to speak there about the marketplaces which fill it, or the power that animates it, and never to look up, to understand what is happening. It was the only rain that season, and California lay brown under the daily sun, deep in drought, while the rest of America staggered under the deepest, coldest, longest winter in decades. It is coming, this climate chaos, every small place beginning to alter. We need to live here, and we will need the public arguments only theology can know, for the hundred-year storms, and the hundred-year heat waves, and the hundred-year floods are coming every year, and we will need the thousand year texts.

All theology, then, this speech between us, the saying of the Word, is political, separating light and darkness, creating a world. But the world not only needs to be said into being every morning, it needs our praxis, repetitive, ordinal. This will mean not only speaking and teaching as if we intended to save the world from this crisis; it will mean me and you acting in public this way. It is very hard, more than inconvenient, but not harder than, say, raising children or any other forward into the future work, in which one acts with certainty that things said and done this day will leap beyond me into a time in which I will not live. Act now as if your actions could be seen and judged by the people in the square in 2050. Most of all, this will mean limiting desires, reconsidering the meaning of having and not having, and finding a different way to decide worth. Thousands of small acts: One big one—consider the weight of your acts, consider pausing them, turning, seeing the world, yes, saving it. Consider speaking, consider parrhesia.

Exile within exile. Hannah Arendt considered the tragedy of statelessness, in which her friend, Walter Benjamin, was trapped, and in which he died. Benjamin left France just a little bit too late, and unluckily, hiked up to the mountain crossing over the Pyrenees to escape Occupied Europe on a day when it seemed that the border was closed, a decision that was reversed by the next morning. But sometime in the night, Benjamin, terrified that he would be sent back to France and again questioned by the Gestapo, and taken to the death camps, decided to swallow the arsenic he carried while he had the chance, and killed himself in a mountain hut. Arendt, his friend, was devastated by the loss. She wrote for him a eulogy poem:

> Mournfulness is like a flame lit in the heart,
> Darkness is like a glow that leads us through the night.
> We only need to ignite this small light of grief,
> To find home, like shadows, across the long vast night.
> The forest is illuminated, the city, the street, and the tree.
> Blessed is he who has no home; he sees it still in his dreams.

5
At the Last Well on Earth
Climate Change as a Feminist Issue

Part I: Finitude and Feminist Thought

There will be a time, in most of the world, when the last well goes dry. And this is because so much of the world lives already on the brink of a dreadful thirst, a life only made tolerable because women travel great distances to find the wells of water, or the rivers, or the ditches, and scoop it up and bring it home. They carry it on their backs, or their heads, or on their hips, as one carries a child. In Africa alone, women walk 40 billion hours to bring this water home.[1]

This is because in sub-Saharan Africa, women are responsible for 72% of all the water collected. This means that women and girls spend a significant proportion of their lives simply carrying water. And as the climate steadily gets warmer, droughts will become more frequent, water more salinized, and harder to find, further away from habitation. As it now stands, clean water is already unavailable to over 633 million people—one in ten of the people of the earth. Diseases from unclean water kill on the aggregate more people than any form of violence, including wars and acts of terror. Forty-three percent of these people are children under the age of five.[2] I have been thinking about how global warming affects women in particular, as the bearers of water. In this chapter, I am going to consider the question of gender, and how the differential structure of power in a world shaped by gender, race, and class is also a part of how one thinks ethically. A word of warning: this is not a comprehensive review of the feminist literature about climate change, which is quite rich, complex, and diverse. In this chapter, I will make the argument that a book about Jewish ethics and global warming needs to draw on some of these resources for making the claim that Scriptural texts allow a new language for thinking about our ethical problem. Persons live in communities; people live in families; and families are where the drama of global warming comes home. Women have historically, and textually, been the carriers of the crisis when it comes to your own kitchen table, when your own well is dry.

For babies born in the developing world, it is diarrheal illness that is most deadly. The struggle to get safe water is a large part of the embodied life of women who bear these infants. Without abundant water, it is hard to carry a pregnancy safely to term, to give birth to children, or to nurse them, or to wash them, to launder their clothes and clean their diapers, all the ordinal details to which women, and women alone, are largely responsible to attend. There are the daily deaths from ordinary waterborne illnesses, and in the last several years, there is cholera, carried in the water, deadly within hours, killing 4 million people a year.[3] In 2020, one of the worst cholera epidemic struck Yemen. It is still ongoing.[4] Speaking of the cholera epidemic in Haiti, the United Nations noted:

> Women and girls have a heightened risk of coming into contact with a high infectious dose of cholera through their domestic roles taking care of sick family members, cleaning latrines, fetching and handling untreated water, and preparing contaminated raw food. As a result, there appears to be an excess disease burden among women and school aged girls. . . . Women and girls shoulder a disproportionate division of the behaviors that cholera health education campaigns target. For example, a key cholera prevention message is to treat or boil water to kill v. cholerae bacteria, but the reality is that most of the responsibility for water purification falls on women and girls and that water purification requires extra effort as well as time and other resources that women and girls may not have available to them.[5]

It is not only a problem with waterborne diseases, but a more general issue about women and their precarity. Consider the United Nations report, "Gender and Development":

> Gender-related inequalities are pervasive in the developing world. Although women account for almost 80 per cent of the agricultural sector in Africa, they remain vulnerable and poor. Seventy per cent of the 1.3 billion people in the developing world living below the threshold of poverty are women.[6]

Consider the scenario in the Eastern Mediterranean in 2009 that I discussed in the previous chapter. At stake was the water table. The levels had fallen so drastically that the wells were all dry. It had become a region staggering under the worse drought ever recorded in the history of the country, one of the world's most fertile areas, the cradle of human civilization. And thus began the long civil war, a war that began when families needed water, when they abandoned drought-stricken farms in search of it. In 2020, a severe drought worsened in Latin American, and by the spring of 2021, immigrants crowded in desperation against the borders of the United States, abandoning villages and dying farms. From the highlands of Guatemala, to and along the length of South America, the drought was visible by NASA satellites:

> Large parts of South America are in the grip of a serious drought. Signs of the drought began to appear in satellite gravimetry observations of southeastern Brazil in mid-2018, and had spread into parts of Paraguay, Bolivia, and northern Argentina by 2020. "This is the second most intense drought in South America since 2002," said Matthew Rodell, a hydrologist based at NASA's Goddard Space Flight Center. "The calculation is based on the extent, duration, and volume of water lost during the drought as measured by the GRACE and GRACE-FO satellites." A drought in eastern Brazil and Venezuela in 2015–16 is the only more intense drought on the record.[7]

Consider the situation in the Tengger of China, where the Gobi Desert has overtaken the historic territories of the farmers and traders, forcing the relocation of tens of thousands, by the Chinese government, or the desertification of the Maghreb, where combined forces of overgrazing, lack of crop rotation, and increasing heat, and drought, have rendered large land areas infertile.[8]

It is when the land becomes inhospitable, when growing crops or watering the flocks, the oldest of human activities, becomes impossible, that entire families must take to the road. And here we have a paradox of modernity: the return to mass migration, in 2023, more families on the road than at any time since the end of World War II.

In all of these shifting populations, women are there, still with the responsibility to care for the work of the home, even the home on the road. All of this is why I will argue in this chapter that climate change is also an issue that feminist scholars should consider carefully. I will argue if that attention to the lives and fate of women, concern about women's bodies, or women's reproductive rights, or women's equal opportunities is a central tenant of feminist ethics, then feminist scholars like me must attend to the crisis that is climate change, which will throw these rights, bodies, and fates into chaos. In the environmental crisis, it is likely that women and children will be the first to be harmed. And for all the freedoms we have rightly obtained for women in the West, all the fine capacities for voice and leadership, it will mean little if we stand by and watch the world warm, the seas rise, the climate change, the refugees struggle, and the world we share disappear. Unless we turn our scholarly attention (which is, after all, the only sort of public voice we have) toward this crisis, there will be a time when the last well is dry. And then it will be too late.

Even as the quality of available water is constantly diminishing, in some places there is a growing tendency, despite its scarcity, to privatize this resource, turning it into a commodity subject to the laws of the market. Yet access to safe drinkable water is, in the words of Pope Francis's Papel Encyclical on Climate Change:

> "A basic and universal human right, since it is essential to human survival and, as such, is a condition for the exercise of other human rights. Our world has a grave social debt toward the poor who lack access to drinking water, because *they are denied the right to a life consistent with their inalienable dignity*."

This debt can be paid partly by an increase in funding to provide clean water and sanitary services among the poor. But water continues to be wasted, not only in the developed world but also in developing countries. This is largely because the way that water is used for the production of crops, especially grain for animals, does not prioritize the needs of the poor, a problem to which the Encyclical returns.

As the Pope reminds us,[9] the relationship between the water scarcity and the life of the West is bound up with issues of justice and relative privilege. In a world of finitude, every relationship is not only fraught with issues of power and inevitably, gender, but it represents a moral choice against a limited terrain. Human life is limited, both in its every gesture, and in its particular spanning narrative, something about which feminist thought needs to reflect, given that women are so often responsible for tending the bodies of the vulnerable at both ends of that span. But it is also played out within the particular plight of modernity, which is that every single entity, living, embodied, creaturely, or fixity, is also now revealed as limited, in short supply. Every animal, every source of water, every mineral, every forest, every wetland, all are mutable, fragile, diminishing, used up, all are commodified, and going fast. Unlike the conditions under which most of Western philosophy was historically performed, in which a sense of an infinite horizon—the Americas, or the Ocean, for example—was newly discovered, every place is vulnerable within its instrumentality, its capacity to come "to hand" as it is said in phenomenology.

Feminist scholars have historically drawn attention not only to the specifics of the embodied plight of women at the margins, and also drawn attention to systemic issues of allegiance, histories of distributive justice and injustice, and power that create structural and organizational relationships of oppression. The reasons climate change affects women more dramatically are not only actuarial (numbers of buckets carried and numbers of miles walked) but ontological, a matter of emplacement in a political economy that values the lives and work of women so substantially differently that solutions to climate change would require rethinking value systems themselves. It is the contention of my argument that one of the tasks of feminist ethics, especially when thinking about this issue in theological terms, as I argue is the task of this book—and I speak here in part as a feminist ethicist—is to also draw attention to the aspect of modernity that is its finitude. It is only with this realization that an accurate understanding of justice, discernment, distribution, all that we know as "political," can be held. And while the ethical is infinite, endless, and constant, politics is limited, finite, and temporally located.

It is my further contention that responding to climate change will require not only the acts we can understand as ethical: moral behaviors about individual consumption; but acts that are political: acts as citizens within democratic states.

Of course, the problem of drought in a changing climate is only one of many things that will affect the daily lives of women differently. A changed climate will occur in a world where the seas on which so many depend will be more acidic,[10] which will threaten fish supplies which offer food to millions. A warming world is also a world in which diseases expand their ranges—dengue fever, chikungunya, yellow fever, and the newly emerged Zika. Zika, because it targets pregnant women and their unborn children, has a particularly gendered aspect of the tragedy, sickening fetuses when they are inside their mothers' bodies. Thus the lifelong responsibility for care of children with untreatable and severe brain damage falls nearly entirely on the families of these children, usually, the women of the family, given the social structure of labor and caregiving, which is similarly gendered.

A warming world is also a world of food shortages, as crops fail and distribution networks falter. And finally, as we have seen in Syria, when the worst drought in instrumented history was recorded in the Eastern Mediterranean happened, it precipitated a catastrophe that sent millions to the road. When

112   ETHICS FOR THE COMING STORM

the rains stop, and the fields dry up, women and their families can only travel deeper into exile. When the well goes dry, what will we do?

Part II: The Turn to the Texts

If for we in the urban West, the idea that water from our taps could suddenly cease is unthinkable, it was surely an anxiety in the scriptural texts. For scholars of religion, such a crisis is familiar, and there is a rich array of languages to think about the issue. In the Middle East and Northern Africa, the setting of the texts of Abrahamic Scriptures, the loss of wells and the subsequent turn to the road of migration has been particularly intense. Are caravans traveling across the land to seek food and water? It is an astonishing replication of core scenes within Hebrew Scripture, the Quran, and the New Testament, these families we now see huddled against the wind, women desperate at closed shelters, women without water, yet all in an age of cell phones and chain stores, their desperation visible to all on our instant media.

The well is central because water is central—one can live only days without it, and it always the site of contention. I am interested in the problem of the "dry well" metaphorically, for of course, as a reader of Scripture, the description of the women walking hours for water in the Sahel is textually familiar. In the Hebrew Bible, the New Testament, and the Quran, the drama of scarcity and hospitality is played out by women standing at wells in the desert. The well is the sign, the fulcrum, the turning center of a crisis of scarcity turning toward abundance. Let me consider three texts about women at wells.

Let me turn to the first text, in Hebrew Scripture. Here, Abraham has sent his servant Eliezer from the mountains, to the East, to find a wife for his son Isaac, and he must go to the tribe of cousins that had settled in the valley and somehow find the right cousin for Isaac to marry. Eliezer sets off, and after a time, sits bewildered and exhausted, by a well of water, and prays aloud for:

13 "A girl to whom I say. 'Please, let down your jar so that I may have a drink'. May she be the one whom You have selected for your servant Isaac..."
And Eliezer waits and watches.

15 And it came to pass, before he had done praying, that, behold, Rebekah came out, who was born to Bethuel the son of Milcah, the wife of Nahor, Abraham's brother, with her pitcher upon her shoulder.

16 And the damsel was very fair to look upon, a virgin, neither had any man known her; and she went down to the fountain, and filled her pitcher, and came up.

17 And the servant ran to meet her, and said: "Give me to drink, I pray thee, a little water of thy pitcher."

18 And she said: "Drink, my lord"; and she hastened, and let down her pitcher upon her hand, and gave him drink.

19 And when she had done giving him drink, she said: "I will draw for thy camels also, until they have done drinking."

20 And she hastened, and emptied her pitcher into the trough, and ran again unto the well to draw, and drew for all his camels. (Genesis 24:15)

What is happening here? The instructions about how to find the correct person given by Abraham are a bit underdetermined, so the servant prays, asking God to send a woman "with a pitcher," her water a sign, so that he knows when the right women approaches. He is interrupted in his "speaking" to God, and sees Rebekah, just the proper cousin, "come out" and she is carrying a pitcher, literally the answer to the prayer. He runs toward her, as she runs back and forth to the well. The water is abundant, even in the desert, but it needs a moral agent to move it from the dark earth to the mouth of the thirsty. They are all running; it is urgent.

And the young woman is the central moral agent, chosen because of her capacity to draw water and organize repair. And while this may seem surprising, one teenager, to have an entire caravan of men and camels as subjects of her concern, it is not, for in the biblical world, as now, women were the ones who carried the water. Note that the radical hospitality is only possible because of the agency of the women. In this first text, the role of the man is merely evocative, not physical, in that it looks like the speech act (of prayer) moves the story forward. But it is the woman who drives the moral action.

A few chapters later in Genesis, and we read of another generation. Jacob, son of Isaac and Rebekah, is again going East, fleeing on his mother's advice, to the same cousins. He finds himself once again by a well. This time, the well is capped firmly, and the men gather around, waiting, once again, for agency and hospitality, which in this account, needs to be initiated. Jacob will act and then be textually handed off from his mother to his wife.

And he said, Lo, it is yet high day, neither is it time that the cattle should be gathered together: water ye the sheep, and go and feed them. And they said,

114   ETHICS FOR THE COMING STORM

> We cannot, until all the flocks be gathered together, and till they roll the stone from the well's mouth; then we water the sheep.
>
> And while he yet spoke with them, Rachel came with her father's sheep: for she kept them. And it came to pass, when Jacob saw Rachel the daughter of Laban his mother's brother, and the sheep of Laban his mother's brother, that Jacob went near, and rolled the stone from the well's mouth, and watered the flock of Laban his mother's brother. And Jacob kissed Rachel, and lifted up his voice, and wept. (Genesis 29:8)

In this textual excerpt, the well's use awaits a "they" that roll the stone off, and Jacob takes it on himself to do that act. Once the water is available, the woman Rachel, named by her matriarchal lineages ("his mother's brother") and her sheep, which she controls, also so named, are watered. Jacob then embraces and, vulnerable, weeps, reversing the roles swiftly, and here, as well, the act of water's exchange begins the deeper social exchange that culminates in marriage. Jacob and Rachel return to the community, and begin to live amid a world of others, with demands of work, obligations of family, and the competing pulls of tradition and debt.

The third and final rehearsal of the scene of The Man at the Well Meets the Women at the Well, from Hebrew Scripture that we will consider, is Moses's flight to the East, in this case, Midian, east of Egypt. Moses is the adopted son of the Pharaoh, although he has been born to a Jewish family and is thus a descendent of one of the sons, Levi, of Jacob, and he has killed a man, an overseer, in an attempt to right a cruelty to a slave.

> Now when Pharaoh heard this thing, he sought to slay Moses. But Moses fled from the face of Pharaoh, and dwelt in the land of Midian: and he sat down by a well.
>
> Now the priest of Midian had seven daughters: and they came and drew *water*, and filled the troughs to water their father's flock. And the shepherds came and drove them away: but Moses stood up and helped them, and watered their flock. And when they came to Reuel their father, he said, How *is it that* ye are come so soon to day? And they said, An Egyptian delivered us out of the hand of the shepherds, and also drew *water* enough for us, and watered the flock. (Genesis 29:8)

In the third telling, the infrastructure—the well—is more profoundly in the control of the men of the society; they guard it, they are hostile, and they drive the women away, who, presumably, perhaps, usually have to wait until the men leave. But Moses intervenes, actively aiding them, and in addition, helping, unlike in the previous two scenes, with the actual work of watering the flocks in their control. As in the other scenes, he marries one of the sisters, and by this act, sets in place a life and family.

This same story of a fleeing Moses, women, and wells appears in this version in the Quran:

> And when he came to the well of Madyan, he found there a crowd of people watering [their flocks], and he found aside from them two women driving back [their flocks]. He said, "What is your circumstance?" They said, "We do not water until the shepherds dispatch [their flocks]; and our father is an old man."
>
> So he watered [their flocks] for them; then he went back to the shade and said, "My Lord, indeed I am, for whatever good You would send down to me, in need." Then one of the two women came to him walking with shyness. She said, "Indeed, my father invites you that he may reward you for having watered for us." (Quran 28:22–24)

In the Quran, the characters are similar: the stranger who is thirsty, the women with flocks to care for, a well. We see the fugitive Moses, fleeing from Pharaoh into the desert, appearing as moral agent. In these two last texts, moral agency is active—not just acting on the well, but acting against other men who control it, a part of a strategic holding, a move in a water war, and the implication is that in some degree, the use or threat of force must be at play. Here we are now describing the move from ethical to political, an exchange of justice against a situation of scarcity.

Let me continue this textual exploration in the New Testament. We see this in a reading of a similar scene in the Gospel of John. Again, we have a women, and a well.

> 4 Now Jesus learned that the Pharisees had heard that he was gaining and baptizing more disciples than John—[2] although in fact it was not Jesus who baptized, but his disciples. [3] So he left Judea and went back once more to Galilee.[4] Now he had to go through Samaria. [5] So he came to a town in Samaria called Sychar, near the plot of ground Jacob had given to his son Joseph. [6] Jacob's well was there, and Jesus, tired as he was from the journey, sat down by the well. It was about noon.[7] When a Samaritan woman

came to draw water, Jesus said to her, "Will you give me a drink?" [8][9] The Samaritan woman said to him, "You are a Jew and I am a Samaritan woman. How can you ask me for a drink?" [10] Jesus answered her, "If you knew the gift of God and who it is that asks you for a drink, you would have asked him and he would have given you living water."[11] "Sir," the woman said, "you have nothing to draw with and the well is deep. Where can you get this living water? [12] Are you greater than our father Jacob, who gave us the well and drank from it himself, as did also his sons and his livestock?"[13] Jesus answered, "Everyone who drinks this water will be thirsty again, [14] but whoever drinks the water I give them will never thirst. Indeed, the water I give them will become in them a spring of water welling up to eternal life." (John 4:1-42)

In this text, the scene is repeated, but overthrown in the telling: stripped of men, of flocks of sheep, and finally, of actual water, the pitcher that appears in the first text as sign (of generosity and hospitality) is abandoned at the end of our final text, for the exchange is not about actual but metaphorical "water." And the thirst, the physical care, and move toward marriage and social order are all spiritualized and unhooked from the facticity of the tangible ("whoever drinks from me will never be thirsty again.") The women is specifically not married, an outsider, and the exchange this text is interested in is not reciprocity but undeserved and abundant, grace.

Part III: The Phenomenology of the Well

The Argument

I have made the case that it is sensible to turn to these texts simply because of the actual repetition of the act of thirst at dry wells in our twenty-first-century world order, and that to the extent that feminist ethics needs to dwell in the actual world of scarcity and finitude and address it, that these texts provide language and important language to respond. Here, exchange is possible between powerful men and relatively powerless women. But now let me turn to the reasons of philosophy and of phenomenology to deepen this account, seeking to answer the question under the narratives, which is—but how do we act justly now, in our present situation? My argument, stated in the last chapters, is this: we live in a world in crisis, and there is no place to flee that will be safe from its reach—there is no "East" to which to flee. Much of the crisis of climate change will be experienced as scarcity, and one of the most precious resources will be fresh water, just as it was in the world of Scripture and just as it is in the marginal areas now.

We all live four days from dying of thirst. In this reality, we all wait at the well with all that we love and for all whom we must care. If you live in a big city, as I do in Chicago, this seems remote, for you, like most readers of this chapter, will own, if not control, in a corporate sense, the water systems that are the endless wells of modernity. (And, even more absurdly, you in all likelihood carry a little red-topped bottle of special water around with you as if on a safari in a country with no running water.) Thus, the contingency of the well—Will the stone be on top? Will men drive us off? Is the water abundant?—is nowhere present, for we feel secure in our possession, our shiny quotidian faucets.

But the textual confrontations, including the New Testament reversal of the scene, are thematized in schematic terms. Consider the narratives. There is a powerful man forced toward the East, out of his land, unsecure, yet, even in his powerlessness, he is still structurally possessive of the core resource, water, the first instrumentality drilled out of the ground, the first human energy taken from there to here. Water wells foreshadow oil wells, of course, and in that, they mirror the productive relationships of ownership and power.

The men of these societies control the water. They have dug the wells. They are the only ones who can cover it with stone and take the heavy stones off. They control the space around the well; their proximity means priority. And this is true even in societies where women are not without their own power. After all, it is women in each of our cases who are in charge of the large, lowing, baaing, herds of goats, the essential economic capital, the main objects of worth in the herding societies of the biblical and Quranic Near East, but yet, without access to water, they would be lost. In other texts, Jacob or Moses or David will assume control of the flocks, and Jesus is metaphorically the Shepherd who guards the gate, but not in the well stories. Here, interestingly enough, it is women who bring the flocks and organize their care.

Yet the women come to a limit. They can begin the act of hospitality so central to all human exchanges in Scripture—the hospitality toward the stranger—but only after the systemic power around infrastructure shifts. In this sense, the *ethical act*—the recognition that the stranger is thirsty, lost, needing home, in exile—the recognition at the heart of the moral universe—is only made possible when the *political act*, the opening and defense of the well, the sharing of public resources, it possible. In the three retellings in the Hebrew Scripture, the Quran, and the New Testament, more and more moral agency is needed to make the phenomena of exchange possible. In the Hebrew Scripture, the stranger who has come to the well first is only required to show up, then to move a huge stone, then to fight off men who will not share the water. For all the individual acts of ethics, the recognition of the other, of his need, the hospitality, there is a need for adjudication. There are others at the well, the water needs to be shared, and societies need to be organized.

Finding the Language of Response

It is to this problem, the relationship between the ethical and the political, that Jewish philosopher Emmanuel Levinas often turns. We face a problem when we face the issue of climate change, and it is this: how ought one live at a time when the world is burning with our own desires, when our desires for stuff, for possession, for meat, and for water, cannot be fulfilled without pouring greenhouse gases into the air, making the climate steadily warmer? Even if individuals act well, how do individual acts, private acts, address problems of the magnitude on the scale of regional drought and millions of refugees in flight?

The language of Levinas clarifies the nature of the problem of climate change as a problem of justice, and justice, he claims is "the way in which I respond to the fact that I am not alone in the world with the other."[11] For Levinas, the face-to-face encounter (think, Jacob with Rachel) is the beginning of ethics. But the world surrounds each well, and the encounter takes place within a world that must be structured to respond to many needs. To respond to climate change in a world of scarcity will require some significant degree of sacrifice, which I have argued can be understood as the just payment of a debt owed to the poor because we in the West have already borrowed so heavily from the future. To respond to climate change will take individual acts, to be sure, but it will take political and social philosophy as well. Michael Morgan, in thinking about how Levinas understands justice, defines politics as a series of "principles for designing a system of norms, institutions, and practices that ought to organize the lives of individual persons living together in groups. There are various values that such principles should express and that the system itself should exemplify. Among such values are the security of the individual citizens, stability, fair treatment of all, some measure of equality... an effort to promote and protect general and group interests as well as the needs and interests of individuals."[12]

In short, what Morgan is interested in is how Levinas moves from his insistence on the interruption of the self by the face of the Other, to the creation of just societies. This happens, in Levinasian terms, with "entrance of the third." In everyday life:

> The act of consciousness is motivated by the presence of a third party alongside of the neighbor approached. A third party is also approached and the relationship between the neighbor and the third party cannot be indifferent to me. There must be justice among incomparable ones."[13]

The issue of climate change needs to be understood as a problem of justice which will require the sharing of resources among a plurality of people, some near, others unseen, others as yet unborn. It will require acting complexly, not only because of what is happening right now, in front of us (which for many in the West will not be apparently troubling or desperate) but for what will happen to future people. Because it takes decades for the climate system to respond to increased levels of carbon in most cases (although there may come a time in which a sudden tipping point is reached that creates a dramatic cascade of effects), we live in the climate system created by choices made by our grand or great grandparents. In 1905, when my grandmother was a young woman, she made her choices against a horizon without cars, or planes, internets, or 9 billion people, and her activities generated far less carbon than do mine. Yet even her choices were the ones that have created climatic changes that helped to create drought in Syria. Think of all the neighbors since, the pluralities of choices, needs, and desires since, and you will get a sense of the urgent need for a politics that is able to balance competing needs and to create stable structures for distribution of social goods under conditions of scarcity.

Thus, we must create social structures for response on a global scale. The role of the scholar is to create the linguistic justification for these responses; it is to create persuasive arguments that will change behaviors and move polities to call for changes on preventive regulations, profits, and repair for harms. All of these larger tasks need state action, state action that is predicated on an underlying ethics and is compelled by public action of people in mass movements.

For Levinas, it matters greatly whether politics assumes an ethics of encounter and infinite responsibility or competition and violence, whether it emerges from a Scripture or a "Greek" set of assumptions. Our texts imply that the first act of such exchanges is one of hospitality, but they are not naïve

120   ETHICS FOR THE COMING STORM

about the world in which the ethical act of one to another takes place. To have a coherent response to climate change means one must understand this, but having an analysis is only the beginning of our response.

Part IV: A Critique from Jewish Ethics

Until now in this chapter I have focused on what the insights of feminist thought could offer to Jewish scholars as we thought about global warming. I want to turn now to the ways in which a focus on feminist thought needs to be structured carefully, and is where the two theories diverge, remembering the distinctive voice of Jewish philosophy that attends to issues of justice so insistently. Here I raise a critique over a concept that might otherwise go unquestioned (and, of course, one needs to question everything). Let me turn then to a different set of texts, for I want to review some premises, ones that are often made within feminist sources, that nature is somehow both normative but also female in some way, and that the degradation of nature by human activity is somehow akin to sexualized violence. I wish to return to the question of our place in the natural world and look closely at how the standard feminist ecology literature has addressed the issue. I have noted some of these issues in the first chapter, and I will return to this problem now. But first, here is a text about nature as feminine from the Jewish medieval tradition.

Consider this text:

> Know! the philosophers call nature *Em Kol Chay* (Mother Nature). We, with our prayers, nullify nature. For nature necessitates such-and-such, and through prayer [the course of] nature is changed. This is the aspect of the Eighteen Blessings of prayer, not counting the blessing for [overcoming] atheists. For with the *ChaY* (18) blessings we nullify nature, *Em Kol ChaY*, subjugating and nullifying the atheists and heretics.[14]

For a long time, I have been curious about this passage, from a medieval Jewish commentary on prayer. It is one of a few times where nature is gendered as female and called Mother Nature in classic Jewish sources. What is it that the commentator is saying? He is talking about the central prayer of Jewish ritual, the Amidah, or standing prayer, said three times a day, four times on the Sabbath. For this author, prayer represents a necessary order, prayer makes nature habitable. There are prayers to do exactly what this passage says, to make the world more just, to allow the end of exile, to heal the sick, and free the bound, and create justice, and allow rain to come, and allow us to see the "many daily miracles," which we might otherwise forget. Nature, which in the classic Jewish tradition is usually understood as morally neutral, and because of nature's capacity to yield to desperation and to might, because famine is as old as humanity itself, needs our prayers to be good, and to be just. Jews do not worship trees, and to do so is a mortal sin, says the section of the Talmud called "*Pirke Avot,*" as I noted in a previous chapter. Instead, one is reminded to go back to study, to go inside and read. If one must plow the field, one must "take the Torah with you."[15] The natural world is the context for human use, in that passage as I have noted before. But attend to the way the commentator in this passage separates Jewish thought from the thought of "the philosophers."

Emmanuel Levinas reminds us in this quote, of something very similar:

The eternal Feminine, which the entire amorous experience carries from the Middle Ages through to Dante, up to Goethe, is lacking in Judaism. The feminine will never take on the aspect of the Divine, neither the Virgin Mary, nor even Beatrice.

This is a long way from how Mother Nature is portrayed in the literature about climate change, our subject here. And it is that characterization that I want to interrogate. Much of the literature in ecology is based on a concept from the Greek, as Levinas knows, not the Jewish tradition, the pagan, not the monotheist tradition: Gaia. Gaia as female, Gaia as both infinitely vulnerable and infinitely wise animates a trope of natural law, nature as providing, in its stasis, a model for moral worth. (I discussed the legacy of natural law for environmentalism in a previous chapter.) By using these terms, 'Greek' and "Jew" a reader of an earlier version of this chapter worried that I was making a simple argument based on a simple reduction or distinction between "Athens" and "Jerusalem," and pointed out that modern scholars of late antiquity have thoroughly critiqued this view. Here, I want to take care to avoid this, as I think Levinas does as well, while also pointing out the resonance of these mythic tropes, first encountered in Greek mythological narratives, because they really are used as proof texts in so much of the literature about climate change. What is happening to our argument if we rely on such an essentialist trope?

Part of the project of this book is to question both the nature of our situation and the nature of our response to it. In this way, I have come to see some aspects of this literature as problematic. In research on how genetic technologies intended to help the poor are being discussed, for example, I have found not only a recourse to this essentialist view of nature, but also a yearning for a lost past, and an odd glorification of the work of peasant women as a nostalgic symbol of that past. One famous nongovernmental organization has as its logo a young woman in peasant clothing, bent nearly double, hand-sowing seeds, a task, that if actually done by an actual woman, for hours on end, would be exceptionally oppressive and not at all romantic. Several of the debates in the literature that urge a resumption of earlier practices reveal confusion on the definition and borders of "nature." Nature, however, is not precisely defined. Was it temporally fixed? If so, at what time period? Are farmed fields "nature?" Or only wilderness, and really, where can that be found? We are asked to stop the use of new technology in the name of nature, and sometimes, in the name of sustainability or the cruel idea that we could return to a time when each family or little community could have an organic farm that would sustain it.

Reader, this is a fantasy, and a troubling one, a kind of denial that should have no place in a progressive movement, much less a feminist one. We live in a world with billions of others, and it is a collective action problem as we consider how to feed everyone, and some of our answers will be to use the tools we have to transform the natural world still more, the new tools of molecular biology, just as we have, miraculously, with vaccines for COVID-19, and not the deeply exploited labor of women. When a famous feminist ecofeminist calls for a return to an earlier time, or gestures to "ancient wisdom," we need to worry. Sustenance farmers lived a world in which women's lives were difficult, dangerous, and degraded, for all the valorization of the feminine deity, actual human women lived in terrible, deadly poverty unable to keep their infants from dying, largely unable to bear infants safely. Many of these societies believed, for example, that women were incapable of literacy, leadership, or voice. Our problem is not modernity—that is merely our moral luck, the train we are on, as I will explain in the next chapter. Our problem is the people who are reaping vast fortunes extracting oil and gas from the ground and burning it at enormous profit, and that is a problem as old as the world of capital exchange.

We are faced, globally with a deep yearning for the past—for the present can be a terribly uncertain place. There is a sense that medieval tropes are true or essential ones—that we live in a spirit-haunted world, with an affection for clarity in good and evil, for aliens, and witches, and pure natural beings that are linked to nature, as in the Lord of the Rings or Harry Potter.

But be aware, and we are aware, after fur-clad fascists stormed the U.S. Capital, that all of this yearning for the past, and all of this mythic symbolism of natural religion can be used by the powerful as well, if it suits them. The guy with the horns and squirrel skins demands organic food in jail, the anti-vaxxers describe their intuitive spirituality, they practice yoga, which, lest we forget, is in its present form completely inauthentic, a creation of Swedish army officers stationed in India, calisthenics used to civilize and attenuate a powerful premodern meditative practice.[16] Old prejudices reemerge, and fundamentalism is a powerful force politically and religiously. In such a period, there is a struggle with phenomenological knowledge—science, observation, empirical wisdom, and received knowledge from religious leaders. In the West, such fears are often the subject of intellectual discourse, but merely discourse, but in the developing world such theories had dramatic consequences. In Nigeria, polio vaccine was refused in fear that it would cause female sterility, and in Zimbabwe, grain was refused in a famine in fear of genetic engineering. In America, fundamentalists from all sides have taken up the questions about mastery and power based on a notion that an instinctual moral repugnance is more important, and of course, more natural. But what are we to think of moral repugnance when it means that babies are not given polio vaccinations, or women are not allowed to read, or five-year-olds go to bed malnourished, and now, oddly enough, masks are burned? In bioethics, the basic Heideggerian ideas—that truth can be recovered from a preliteral past, that authenticity is formulated by one strong "I," and that suffering and death are the fulcrum points of essential humanity have made a strong argument. And it is a brutal one, even when it is made in the name of nature, or Gaia.

But rationality, science, and what came to be understood as modernity have always been in collision with such ideas. Modernity is uneasy with received knowledge and seeks to learn from a process of trial and error, of open knowledge and phenomenology—in which the observation of the world, its description, its failure to comply with theory—was long noted by Galileo, by Vesalius. To be a citizen, that hard-won right for women, is to be an equal before a positive law. Science performs with an idea of progressive optimism, with its intervention to change fate, with an affection for machines, and with an attention to units of time. And in our evaluation, we need to separate modernity or science from oppression. This is why we need to see that scientific research always was radically violative of both the natural order, of the naturalness, and givenness of suffering and of death. In our time, think of how fiercely science has fought against the givenness of climate change. One should regard anti-science rhetoric with wariness, even if it is put forward in terms a feminist thinker might find persuasive.

It is the capacity to interrupt this narrative that allows for a far better analysis. When I raise the problems with some of the claims made in the literature of feminist thought about sustainability, it is because I have something larger in mind, something more audacious than sustaining the world as it is, or worse, as it was. Where to seek the justification for this sort of interruptive critique? A clear voice can be found in the texts of Jewish thought.

Jewish thought, however, does not usually understand nature as normative. In fact, Jewish thought problematizes the natural world as unjust, ridden with plague and coronavirus, and potentially a place of violence, the violence where the powerful win, where eating the weaker is the ordinary event, or chasing the weaker one for sport is a part of the natural order, and the worship of nature is the worship of this violence that refuses containment and refuses Law. How to change the natural world—I have argued that the rabbinic strategy is language, more precisely, argument—is the interesting problem, not how to revere it.

The rabbinic voice insists on the law, understood as Torah, on public action as opposed to a private experience of the Spirit, for it is only in the details within the conversation that allow a resistance to what seems as given, impenetrable, fixed without the possibly of parole, a resistance that allows for human progress. The rabbinic antipathy to spirituality arises because is the sort of concern with the potential to turn us from the work to feed the actual Other, it turns one inward, to one's harmony and peace, away from the screaming outside, the broken crossing outside, the unredeemed world that needs us every single day. As philosopher Franz Rosenszweig reminds us about the nature of law:

> That the world, this world is created and nonetheless in need of future redemption, the unrest of this double thought, is calmed in the unity of the law. The law—for viewed as world, it is law and not what it is, as the content of the revelation and demand to the individual: command—the law, therefore, in its comprehended multiplicity and power, ordering everything—the whole "exterior" namely everything of this life, that only a worldly law might somehow comprehend—makes this world and the future one indistinguishable. In the law everything of this world that is affected within it, every created existence, is already immediately enlivened and ensouled as

the content of the future world . . . for even in the case (of Jewish Law) it takes only this world as incomplete, but the law that it is prepared to impose upon the world, that it might proceed from this unto the future one, it takes as complete.[17]

Fundamental to this formulation is both the prophetic call for attention to the vulnerable and the overlooked within the natural order of things and the rabbinic insistence on human-scaled systems of organization and fairness against the disorder of the natural. This is why I argue that current calls for sustainability accept a view of the given hierarchies in the world, systems that need disruption. Let me return very briefly to the problem that this language of nature creates, the problem of sustainability which I discussed in my last chapter. Calling for sustaining practices maintains a view of history that privileges continuity over interruption, and resists creative technologies that historically have been liberatory for women. Yet it is only in interruption that the possibility of redemption is visible, an idea that we must make legible in the narrative of global justice in a warming world.

This is a sketch of what we will need to do to move beyond the goal sustainability and the concept of nature as good, female, and kind. First, a we will need a recognition of how very unkind and unjust is the nature world, next we will need a sophisticated analysis of how evil really operates and how it flourishes, not in some vague way, but as deliberate and decisive, and finally, a readiness for radical sacrifice and a willingness to change things to which we have grown accustomed and that we like very much. I will address this directly in the coming chapters.

I know that there is a class of the powerful, in the language of Marx, which can actually be named as flush with dangerous evil, I know that they have and will fight to the end to oppose the interruption of a very, very lucrative practice, the extraction, monetization and selling of fossil fuels something I will address in greater detail in Chapter 7. However, this does not mean that we are off the hook. Of course, Pope Francis is correct when he also names our own practices as part of the reason the wells have run so dry. We can get it wrong, for we can be so easily tempted. How? As feminists, we can be tempted by the easy tropes that allow us to focus on less scary advisaries—an abstract patriarchy for example, with no identifiable actors or on performative action that is only symbolic, or allow us to think that the answer is a problem of representation. That would be partially true, but ultimately wrong. Women have always been well represented in fascist movements; the mob that stormed

126   ETHICS FOR THE COMING STORM

the U.S. Capitol had a fair number of women, even leading the charge. There needs to be a task beyond the sort of self-righteous sustainability that it is too easy to propose. That is why I want us to think, first, about the ontological question, about who we are and what sort of evil we promote with our words, our acceptance, our situation.

To live as a Jewish woman is to enter a world in which the pieces are already in place. To live in this world is to live always in a world where you come late, where you were not here first, where the tracks are already laid. You wake up, your baggage already packed and with you, as Levinas says, aware of the previous ones, dead and living to whom you are responsible. They are outside the window, they are running for their lives, and they are a risk because of our choices, which so far, have been to go along for the ride.

Part V: The Tasks of Ethics

First, it is the task of ethics to understand, illuminate, and analyze relationships within political systems of exchange, especially ones that are hidden. The first of these tasks, as I have just noted, is to understand our precise place and thus our responsibility. For feminist philosophy, it is important to pay particular attention to the situation of women, if only because women's lives have been so long overlooked as subject of philosophy. In the West, women, all women, are Well Owners relative to the developing world. Our practices, our consumption, our gardens, even for the poorest American, surely for the reader of this chapter, mean that we have participated in the creation and control of the world's water. This is not an evil act on its face, for one is born into this world, thirsty already, and into the arms of a society of relative abundance, but there is no doubt that it carries the mark of sin, the trace of failure, and the deep, persistent throb of violence once you know that this is the case. Why violence? Because we would defend our resources from the traveler in need, because the systems of distribution have been set up as a sort of taking from the beginning.

> The warming caused by huge consumption on the part of some rich countries has repercussions on the poorest areas of the world, especially Africa, where a rise in temperature, together with drought, has proved devastating for farming.[18]

From this understanding of our taking comes the reality of our debt. If the relationship among humans, the interruption of the face-to-face encounter, is to be fully seen, then we must see the enormity, what Levinas reminds is the infinity, of what we owe the Other. I would add, it is not only that we are born into this ethical relationship, in our time, unlike his, where we know perfectly well that our consumption has caused much of their need. We live in the tightening noose of climate change, so we participate much more: we have not only *not* given to the Other what she needs to live, we have taken from her, and we owe her repayment. This is the ethical world under the political one, as Morgan reminds us.

Second, because we are aware of the ethical duties, we understand the way that politics and its pragmatic justice, its impartiality, and its distance, can seem outside of our capacity to control or act within it. But an awareness of the centrality and constancy of ethical exchanges means that they cannot simply be ignored or outsourced to "politics" in a sort of despair. What does this mean?

In the next chapters, I will argue that one must act as if every act was subject to the judgment of the poor, that acts like using bottled water, eating meat, wasting water and power, flying and driving, and excessive possession were important because they shaped you as a moral being. Such acts marked you publicly as an ally of the big oil companies or an ally of the poor, and such was their worth and value. But this argument adds to that assessment. Here, I argue that individual acts to affect the climate also remind us of something important philosophically. They remind us, or rather, they insist on speaking to us, of a world that is based on ethics and not Hobbesian competition.

At an historical moment in which the levers of politics seem particularly remote, when democracy itself seems at stake, in which even democratic forums such as the United Nations Global Climate Summits proved insufficient to protect the environment, ethical action is even more important, for it now serves the function of serving as collective memory, a terrain of human action in the "as if" of morality and the "what if" of lost power. We act "as if" when we act ethically, and we understand politics as an approximation, a compromise. But we act "what if" when we see politics as failed, and then, feminism, with its great tenderness for the private act as political, carries a redemptive power.

Pope Francis worries about the future: "What kind of world do we want to leave to those who come after us, to children who are now growing up?"[19] he writes. And indeed.

The encounters at the wells take place in a liminal space, a space just before the exchange that will allow the women and the strangers to be welcomed into a new social order, one in which there will be a plurality of needs, conversation, and structures. New families will emerge, and the future will open, if the contingent, fragile encounter goes well.

We, too, have come to a liminal space, a place in time that may be brief, when there is still a choice for hospitable behaviors, but only if we understand where we are in the time and the geography of the crisis of climate change. This clarity really is the aim of feminist ethics.

Third, we must develop a practice of feminist ethics that foregrounds the urgency of climate change on both a personal and political level. I argue that it is no longer acceptable to live in an unthinking manner, and that in particular, beloved individual habits such as eating meat, drinking bottled water, and so on must be reexamined. While it is must unusual to be this specific in an academic scholarly work, I do so here because I am convinced that our words must have some meaning if we are to be read seriously, and this meaning will come with a sacrifice. We must sacrifice some of our attention and our time to teach about this issue, to educate first ourselves (by reading and understanding and defending the science) and then our students and our neighbors and our families, all the others who surround us, about why this issue has a claim on us.

This issue has a long arc, for the environment has a long memory. The wells we have dug will need to go deeper and deeper, but the encounters that surround the drawing of the water are extraordinarily durable, and the texts of Scripture are received three thousand years later as signs for us, and as judgments on our acts. I return to these narratives, in addition, for languages and for authority. It is the intention of ethics to create a set of practices that will ensure that there will not be a last well on earth, but that solutions for social practices can emerge from the ethical norms that we have a duty to create.

This chapter has drawn on some concepts that allow us to consider how to think about the particularities of women's lives in a warming world, and how to think using a central and clarifying Scriptural encounter. In the next chapter, I will consider another problem, the complexities of moral accountability when the lines of responsibility are not so clear.

6

Strangers on a Train

Climate Change and the Problem of Responsibility

Part 1: The First Story

I was on the train from Los Angeles to Oakland, on the beautiful Coast Starlight (Americans name their trains), because I am the sort of person who has thought about climate change, and so did not want to fly or drive. It was a beautiful trip, away from the back end of the metropolis of Los Angeles, behind the low, browning coastal hills, opening to the glittering silver of the Pacific Ocean, and skimming along rickety, impossibly tall, wood trestles that hug the palisades to the sea.

On the cracked russet leather seat behind me sat a Polish philosopher, who told me that he taught at Copernicus University. We chatted about our students, and about life in Poland and Chicago, and why we were on the train; we were both pleased to avoid the long drive north (and self-righteous about our low carbon footprint), and we spoke about what we hoped for when we arrived. The train is a liminal space, neither in the past we had just left, the farewells, nor yet in the future, the greetings, but in the anticipation of the next step. We passed the coastal hills, which look, in winter, like worn children's stuffies, caramel grasses rubbed bare in spots, trails of cattle like the trace of fingers down their sides. At lunchtime, we sat, four strangers, the Polish guy, a tiny, old man who loved trains and knew the names of every cross-country route, a smiling, round-cheeked, woman, in a new matching top and sneaker shoes, from Fresno, who had just retired from the post office, bought the shoes, and was off to see the world. There was a white tablecloth and a little menu. Nobody is rich, because nobody who is rich takes the train in America, but the white tablecloth made us feel fancy. Later, the train ran along the Salinas River, scant because of the droughts which always stalk California now, and then we passed for hours along the long green ridges of lettuce and artichokes, water spaying above them in sparkly arcs, then past the outskirts of the tough farming town, Salinas, the flat Valley. Tomatoes under shimmering white

Ethics for the Coming Storm. Laurie Zoloth, Oxford University Press. © Oxford University Press 2023.
DOI: 10.1093/oso/9780197661345.003.0007

plastic, flapping silently as the wind died down and the late winter darkness descended. We were traveling now toward Gilroy, Garlic Capital of the World, and we left our seats by the window and rose to go again to the dining car. But then, the train skidded, shuddering, to a stop. It took a very long time to stop. It takes three miles to stop a train.

It was not scheduled, and after a few minutes, during which the porters on the train rushed past us, we realized that something was very wrong. It turned out, we were told very reluctantly, by the nice lady in charge of the coffee in the downstairs café, that the train has struck and killed four people, "probably the homeless people, maybe the illegals" who camp near the train tracks. It turned out, we were told, in a low voice, that "this was not the first time for the Starlight." We told her how sorry we were.

We had to wait a long time on the silent, shuddering train, because it was a Sunday and the county was poor, farmlands and pickers, and the coroner only on call, and miles away, and the area was in the fields between the jurisdiction of two cities, Salinas and Gilroy, and the bodies in terrible pieces, so the philosopher and I talked about moral luck, and about how we felt grief and guilt and powerlessness, and about what it was to feel these things. Moral luck is an idea from Bernard Williams, who was curious about the problem that so much of our lives, even the lives of rational and good persons, making rational and good choices, was still subject to random moments of luck or unluckiness. Writes Williams:

> There has been a strain of philosophic thought which identifies the end of life as happiness, happiness as reflective tranquility, and tranquility as the product of self-sufficiency—what is not in the domain of the self is not in its control, and so is subject to luck and the contingent enemies of tranquility. . . . Both the disposition to correct moral judgement and the objects of such judgement are on this view free from external contingency for both are, in their related ways, the product of the unconditioned will. . . . Yet the aim of making morality immune to luck is bound to be disappointed."[1]

He took as his example the truck driver whose brakes fail, just at the moment a child runs into the street and is killed. We had both read this article, for it is famous, and here we were suddenly the man in the truck. But he protested, we are not driving, so it is in no way our fault. And yet.

And yet we felt ourselves to be participants, implicated, implicants, more than standers-by, because we are the ones with the tickets. The name of this sort of guilt might be "being Westerners."

When I got home, I checked to see if the story had, as we say, "made the papers." I googled "4 killed by Amtrak train." What I saw was surprising, because there were over a million hits, thousands of stories, and this is because it happens over and over at that particular crossing outside of Salinas, and over and over a thousand times a year in this country at other crossings at the margins of cities and in the green and silent fields along the tracks in the dark. So what looked at first like bad luck, or chance, was not. It was policy; it was, as with so many things, indicative of deep structural injustice, and deep disregard for the poor, the homeless, the stranger. This happens because Amtrak is underfunded, and the guardrails are inadequate, the signals imperfect, the systems not fully figured out, the stations understaffed, the crossing not regulated, with no provision for humans who need to move around the land that is crossed by the rails. It happens because there are now large camps of the homeless in our cities, and a good place to camp turns out to be, quite literally, on the wrong side of the tracks, where is it dark and flat and abandoned at night; it happens because the signs are all in English, even in the Salinas Valley where the people that pick your grapes and your lettuce live, people who do not speak or read English. All of these facts are things that we could change.

But this is not a chapter about railway policy; it is a chapter about global warming, and about the task of faith, in particular, Jewish faith in thinking about it, and I am thinking here about the idea of collective and individual responsibility. Because we are Westerners, and thus have the tickets, we are on the train, so to speak, speeding along, living lucky lives in which we think we are making moral choices, but in which we are having dinner with white tablecloths as the land speeds by, on tracks across the fields, on the tracks made for speed and not for safety, not for the stranger. To be a Westerner is to be on a train that kills as it goes, in the ordinary way, on every ordinary day; it is to be participant and implicant in global warming. It is the argument of this chapter that to understand this is to take seriously the implications of being a citizen, living an ordinary, faithful life in a treacherous time, and perhaps to ask a question about Jewish ethics, which is in what way do the commitments of Jewish ethics matter to the rest of the polity? What I want to explore in this chapter is not entirely what to do about climate change, for, as I have said before, there are many other books that have such lists, but to think with you, reader, about who we are, and the sort of moral situation into which we find ourselves, the phenomenology of this moment. What have we done, and what are we doing here, selves that have been shaped not only by luck but by text, tradition, and the gaze of others, answered, and unheard, and turned toward and turned away from?

Part II: A Textual Story (a Second Story)

There was a text from the Talmud Bavli that I had long been interested in, or rather, I had been interested in one aspect of the text, the most abstract ethical bits, because, like so many Talmudic discourses, it seemed to trail off in a confusing and, frankly, grotesque set of details. But let me present the text as a whole, and you will understand why it is all important here, even the disturbing parts. It is a text about the dismembered body, a body dismembered by murderous violence.

It begins as a comment about an abandoned corpse, and it appears first in Deuteronomy, directly it turns out, after the oft-quoted section about not cutting down fruit trees during war, which I discussed in an earlier chapter. Here is the section:

> If, in the land that the Lord your God is assigning to you to possess, someone slain is found lying in the open, the identity of the slayer not being known, your elders and your magistrates shall go out and measure the distances from the corpse to the nearby towns. The elders of the town nearest to the corpse shall then take a heifer which has never been worked, which has never pulled in a yoke, and the elders of that town shall bring the heifer down to an harsh wadi which is not tilled or sown. There in the wadi, they shall break the heifer's neck. The priests, sons of Levi, shall come forward; for the Lord your God has chosen them to minister to Him and to pronounce blessing in the name of the Lord, and every lawsuit and case of assault is subject to their ruling. Then all the elders of the town nearest to the corpse shall wash their hands over the heifer whose neck was broken in the wadi. And they shall make this declaration: "Our hands did not shed this blood, nor did our eyes see it done. Absolve, O Lord, Your people Israel whom You redeemed and do not let guilt for the blood of the innocent remain among Your people Israel. And they will be absolved of blood guilt.[2]

Then, the biblical text returns to the subject of war: "when you take the field against your enemies . . ." Our section is a long interruption of the text about the commandments of a just war, and it is odd that it emerges here because it is not about war at all. The rabbinic discourse in the Mishnah will expand on some of the points, for example the innocence of the young calf, the innocence of the corpse, the transfer of this innocence to the priests, then "all the elders," then all of the people Israel. But then the discussion will add trouble and detail, raising issues of collective responsibility, unassigned guilt, ritual moral action, and finally, the problem of absolution itself when it might be luck or not that leads to catastrophe, or choice. Here is the conversation in the Mishnah:

> The declaration over the heifer whose neck is to be broken must be in the holy tongue; as it is said, "If a corpse is found slain on the land . . . then your elders and judges shall go out" (Deuteronomy 21:1–2)—three used to go out from the high court in Jerusalem. Rabbi Judah says: five, as it is said, "Your elders" two, "and your judges" two, and there cannot be a court of an even number, they add one more. If [the corpse] was found buried underneath a heap of stones, or hanging on a tree, or floating on the surface of the water, they would not break [the heifer's neck], as it says: "In the earth" and not buried underneath a heap of stones, nor hanging on a tree; "In a field" and not floating on the surface of the water. If it was found near the border, or a city whose majority of inhabitants were Gentiles, or a city in which there is no court, they would not break [the heifer's neck]. They only measure the distance from a city in which there is a court. If [the corpse] was found exactly between two cities, both of them bring two heifers [between them], the words of Rabbi Eliezer; Jerusalem does not bring a heifer whose neck is to be broken. If the head was found in one place and the body in another place, they bring the head to the body, the words of Rabbi Eliezer. Rabbi Akiva says: [they bring] the body to the head. From what part [of the body] do they measure? Rabbi Eliezer says: from the navel. Rabbi Akiva says: from the nose. Rabbi Eliezer ben Jacob says: from the place where he was made a slain person, from the neck. The elders of Jerusalem departed and went away. The elders of that city bring "a heifer which has never been worked" (Deuteronomy 21:3). And a blemish does not disqualify it. They bring it down to a hard (etan) wadi "etan" is understood in its literal sense of "hard." Even if it is not "hard," it is valid [for the ceremony]. They break its neck with a hatchet from behind. The site may never be sown or tilled, but it is permitted to comb flax and chisel rocks.
>
> The elders of that city then wash their hands with water in the place where the heifer's neck was broken and they say, "Our hands have not shed

this blood, neither have our eyes seen it" (Deuteronomy 21:7). But did we really think that the elders of a court of justice are shedders of blood! Rather, [the intention of their statement is that the man found dead] did not come to us [for help] and we dismissed him without supplying him with food and we did not see him and let him go without escort. Then the priests exclaim, "Absolve, O Lord, Your people Israel, whom You redeemed, and do not let guilt for the blood of the innocent remain among your people Israel" (vs. They did not need to say, "And they will be absolved of bloodguilt" (ibid), rather the Holy Spirit announces to them, "When you act in this way, the blood is forgiven you." (Mishnah Sotah 9.2–3)

Somebody is dead. Someone has killed him and fled, for the word is "found slain." There must be blood, and a sense of violence, someone has raised the alarm. It is, after all, in the textual middle of a discussion of war, that complete collapse of all human order. The place is desolate, a liminal space, far from habitation and the usual course of human affairs. What is this guy doing out here? The elders and the judges shall go out to see. We are to imagine the old men, the ones in nice suits, they go themselves, not the cops or the servants, but the most important fellows in the society, for it is a matter of great importance; they come even from the high court in Jerusalem, and they come prepared to judge, which is why there cannot be an even number, because a decision will have to be made: it is a matter of justice and courts.

The text then stipulates that the corpse has to be lying on the ground. It cannot be buried or hidden, or floating, or hanging, for, we will learn later, these might indicate that the death is an accident—a landslide, a flood, a fall.

> If it was found near the border, or a city whose majority of inhabitants were Gentiles, or a city in which there is no court, they would not break [the heifer's neck].[3]

There are places in the world of the Mishnah where the rule of law seemingly does not hold. We will circle back to this, but here the categories are described—we are not talking about the lawless border, and we are not talking about gentile cities, because violence, and social chaos is imagined to be common there. Here, the body lies in the field near a more ordered sort of world, the path is between two Jewish cities where justice is the norm, where good elders in good suits and nice people live far from the edgy border towns. There are courts of law, a Sandhedrin. But something has gone terribly wrong. So much so that the elders and priests of both cities bring sacrifices, pulling the mooing baby calves behind the well-dressed burghers of the cities all the way out to the muddy and desolate place between them, between, say, Jerusalem and Bethleham, or Salinas and Gilroy. A sacrifice for each city, for it is everybody's fault. We will return to this as well. The Mishnah then turns to the ghastly business of the coroner.

> If the head was found in one place and the body in another place, they bring the head to the body, the words of Rabbi Eliezer. Rabbi Akiva says: [they bring] the body to the head.[4]

The violence is so profound that the parts of the body are scattered, the head severed at the neck and the part of the person scattered, so much meat and limbs. And Rabbi Akiba and Rabbi Eliezar have an odd and seemingly petty discussion about whether to bring the head to the body, or the body to the head. What possible difference can it make now?

For Rabbi Akiba, the head, the face, is the part of the body that matters, that was a person and not an anonymous corpse, since the head is to be buried where it lies, it is the last honor, the last shred of dignity, to move the body back to it. Of course, when one writes about "the face" as a Jewish ethicist, one thinks of Emmanuel Levinas, for whom the face, as the mark of the vulnerable Other, was the synecdoche for the call of the Other in whom one was fully realized. Here is the passage from Levinas:

> I think that access to the face is straightaway ethical. You turn yourself toward the Other.... There is first the very uprightness of the face, its upright exposure without defense. The skin of the face is that which stays most naked, though with a decent nudity. It is the most destitute also; there is an essential poverty in the face, the proof of this is that one tries to mask this poverty by putting on poses. By taking on a countenance. The face is exposed, menaced, as if inviting an act of violence. At the same time, the face is what forbids us to kill... The face is meaning all by itself.[5]

Akiba and Eliezar repeat their positions in that matter of measuring. Measuring, the exact distance from the body to the city, is critical—it is the last bit of law left after the lawless act—because the guilt will rest on the city closest to the victim, and if it is perfectly equidistant, that must be known as well. But measured from where? Eliezar is back at the very center of the body again, all physicality and natality, the navel, one can measure and one can look away from the face to do so; it is like the headless, anonymous statuary in museums, it could be anybody, any body.

But Akiba measures from the very center of the face. One must get very close to the face to measure in such a way, one must look directly at the particular face, and it could be only that face, that one. The corpse's killer is unknown, but for Rabbi Akiba, the dead person still is a particular person, as much as one can be, alone, nameless, killed by a nameless killer, on a field by a road between two cities. Then Rabbi Ben Jacob, coming later, makes another claim—what matters here is the violence, so we must take our measure from the place of slaying, the slit throat. We are back to the violent act itself, facing the reality, no metaphysics for Ben Jacob.

> They bring it down to a hard (etan) wadi. "Etan" is understood in its literal sense of "hard." Even if it is not "hard," it is valid [for the ceremony]. They break its neck with a hatchet from behind. The site may never be sown or tilled, but it is permitted to comb flax and chisel rocks.[6]

The Mishnah tells us that the elders of Jerusalem then leave, presumably because the body is that much closer to "that city," the city in question, and the young calf is brought out, a baby cow, one who has never been used by a person for work, an innocent. And it is then suddenly, "from behind," "struck at the neck with a hatchet" and killed. In the rabbinic imaginary, it works as sympathetic ritual magic—an innocent person has been killed, maybe struck from behind unawares, and so we will reenact this with an innocent baby animal, sneaking up on it from behind, the men in suits and the judges, who wield a hatchet. One is reminded of Rene Girard here:

> How can one cleanse the infected members of all trace of pollution? ... Only blood itself, blood whose purity has been guaranteed by the performance of appropriate rites—the blood, in short, of sacrificial victim—can accomplish this feat. Behind this astonishing paradox, the menace of all violent action can be discerned ... the sacrifice is designed to redirect the violence onto inconsequential victims. The idea of ritual purification is far more than mere shadow play or illusion. The function of ritual is to "purify" violence; that is, to "trick" violence into spending itself on victims whose death will provoke no reprisals.[7,8]

Let us pay attention to the neck, for the Hebrew term for that particular calf is called the "*egla arufah*," or the beheaded or broken necked heifer, or literally, *the-calf-that-got-it-in-the-neck*.[9] This links this calf to several narratives of failure, of course, and one is meant to think of the Golden Calf that the Israelites construct while they wait for Moses to return from receiving Law after Revelation at Mount Sinai (Exodus) and of the calves that pull the grain of Joseph as a gift to his father (Exodus), and of the back of the neck that names "Orpah," the daughter in law of Naomi who, unlike the good girl Ruth, turns from her and of course, and finally to the people Israel who are frequently described as "the stiff-necked people" (Exodus). All of these referents pulled in at once! There is a deep weirdness to the killing as well: This calf is killed out of the carefully enacted order of the usual ritual for slaughter, the one that renders the animal kosher, because that is done in exactly the opposite manner, by cutting the jugular vein in the front, not bludgeoning or hacking the head off from behind. We are meant to attend to this ritual upheaval: The one-who-got-it-in-the-neck, the calf, will atone for the one-who-got-it-in-the-neck, the nameless stranger. We kill the calf because we cannot kill, eye for an eye, life for a life, the unknown murderer.

The ground is hard. We are meant to be standing in a harsh riverbed, a wadi, and it will never again be used as a field. Food will not emerge from that place; it is now a place covered in the blood and ash of the sacrifice, and only dirty work can be done there, where dirty work was done.

"The site may never be sown or tilled, but it is permitted to comb flax and chisel rocks."

The ritual has defiled the place.

The elders of that city then wash their hands with water in the place where the heifer's neck was broken and they say, "Our hands have not shed this blood, neither have our eyes seen it" (Deuteronomy 21:7). But did we really think that the elders of a court of justice are shedders of blood! Rather, [the intention of their statement is that the man found dead] did not come to us [for help] and we dismissed him without supplying him with food and we did not see him and let him go without escort. Then the priests exclaim, "Absolve, O Lord, Your people Israel, whom You redeemed, and do not let guilt for the blood of the innocent remain among your people Israel" (vs. They did not need to say, "And they will be absolved of bloodguilt" (ibid), rather the Holy Spirit announces to them, "When you act in this way, the blood is forgiven you.")[10]

Now we are at the center of the rabbinic anxiety, and the text is structured as if we are watching the biblically proscribed ritual from offstage. We returned to the first premise of the Mishnah, the clarification that the ritual phrase must be said in Hebrew:

"The declaration over the heifer whose neck is to be broken must be in the holy tongue."

But why, a voice is recorded as saying as aside, to us the reader, is this ritual happening at all? It looks like the elders are expiating guilt, they are doing a ritual done by guilty people, but clearly, they are not killers of the corpse in the field by the road.

"But did we really think that the elders of a court of justice are shedders of blood?!"

These are the nice fellows, well dressed, civil servants and judges, the powerful leaders. But they are, in fact, understood as murderers. Whatever their "intention," whatever they say, they did not see a man in need of help. Perhaps he did not even show up to their nicely kept lawns and clean shuttered porches, for he knew he was in a place where he would not be welcomed; perhaps he did come and was not seen, perhaps they averted their gaze and walked right by. But they have let a man leave their city and their order and walk alone to his death, perhaps a hungry, thirsty, desperate man, so desperate as to be out without caution, to walk alone after nightfall, to have no place to go, and so, took to the road, a homeless man, he was unseen, like the hundreds who live on the margins of our cities, who sleep by the railroad tracks.

> Rather, [the intention of their statement is that the man found dead] did not come to us [for help] and we dismissed him without supplying him with food and we did not see him and let him go without escort. Then the priests exclaim, "Absolve, O Lord, Your people Israel, whom You redeemed, and do not let guilt for the blood of the innocent remain among your people Israel" (vs. They did not need to say, "And they will be absolved of blood-guilt" (ibid), rather the Holy Spirit announces to them, "When you act in this way, the blood is forgiven you.")

The Cohanim, the priests, now central to the story, now implore God for absolution, and they do so in the name of the entire people. Let us note that the participation of the priests does not render them impure, as death usually does, because the burial of the abandoned one is a *met mitvah*, a dead person to whom we have a specific duty, another overturning of the usual order of the world. Here is the term as it is used in the talmudic tractate Semachot:

> If he found a *met mizwah*, he must attend to him and bury him. Which is a *met mizwah*? When [he who finds the body] cries out and the inhabitants of the city cannot hear his voice; but if they can hear his voice, it is not a *met mizwah*. 57 Yeb. 89b (Sonc. ed., p. 610), Nazir 43b (Sonc. ed., p. 158)[11]

Something terrible has happened and an innocent person is dead, the murderer loose in the world, and there is no one to pursue, so while no one is guilty of the killing, all are responsible for the abandonment:

Notice how large is this responsibility—it takes in everyone! All "your people Israel," not only the elders or the judges, or the priests, not only the people of the city who sent the man by the road out alone, who turned away did not see him. Everyone who is alive has been a part of a society that allows the homeless one to be on the road at night, the hunger and thirsty one to be alone, vulnerable, death coming up unseen behind him, and we are all a part of it.

The Mishnah wants the reader to know that is not the magic ritual, not even the incantation in Hebrew, but the acceptance of responsibility that is valorized, after which it is accepted, God approves and forgives:

> When you act in this way, the blood is forgiven you.

There must have been a great deal of blood. The abandoned person must have called out in vain, desperate. The idea of a body out of place unseen, unheard, evokes horror and reading this text, centuries later, one can feel it shifting beneath us, tense with rabbinic anxiety about disordered death.

There are many comments on this story in the later texts of the Gemara, and the example is referred to repeatedly, in aggada and bariatas. In Sotah, the conversation that is recorded in the text circles back over and over to the story. In one version, Soteh 44–47, several issues are raised and considered and compared: the rules about hiddenness, and references to the rules about hidden sheaves of wheat left for the poor; then the question about the unworked calf and the issue of whether labor disqualifies sacrifice; then a discussion of exactly how long one must accompany a traveler based on a prior relationship and the organization of the power dynamics. Teachers are accorded the longest accompaniment by their students.

The other is our responsibility, reminds Levinas, and his face calls us to this responsibility:

> The face speaks . . . the first word of the face is the "Thou shalt not kill." It is an order. There is a commandment in the appearance of the face, as if a master spoke to me. However, at the same time, the face of the Other is destitute, it is the poor for whom I can do all and to whom I owe all. And me, whoever I may be, but as a "first person," I am he who finds the resources to respond to the call.

But one has to see the Other; that is the trick. And now we are back from the fields outside Jerusalem, and the fields outside of Salinas, California, and I want us to return to this problem of unseen faces, and the rush of the train, and the question of guilt, especially for all the people of Israel, the people whom the priests are considering, and that for which God absolves.

One of the problems with a changing climate is precisely this: we cannot see the faces of the people who will be first affected, and most affected. In other chapters of this book, I detailed the situation of immigrants, and of the women in the poorest regions, and closer still, in every city of the world, at the margins of every place, town, village, and the spaces between, there will be people who are violently killed by the daily violence that is climate change, their death linked to our lives, the line measured from the center of their broken faces to our city.

This may seem farfetched, I know. I have told two stories, both about the deaths of the destitute and unknown, both about the problem of guilt for violent murder without assailants. In both cases, I am suggesting a way to think rather than a direct response, or use of the complex biblical and Mishnaic text in a facile manner to create a norm or prove a point. These are discussions about the difficulty of judgment, and they are useful when we consider the difficult problem of responsibility for acts for which one is not directly responsible, in which one is simply "on the train," more than a bystander, but not a perpetrator. But we strangers on the train are implicated; our bodies add that little bit to the weight of a train that cannot stop. The whole of the people of Israel needs the sacrifice of blood to expatiate the blood of the abandoned one; we all, who are not the bad guys, who have not made the vast profits, or ordered the rainforest plowed to rubble, who don't pass laws to allow extraction, but we are, we Westerners, we who only slightly turn our head away, we who are trying to be good, but just a bit too busy, we who participate in the not-seeing of the outcome of the action that we do. We are implicated in the violence.

In the next chapter, I am going to be very clear about who I think the actual perpetrators are in the global warming story, the international energy extraction companies that make huge profits off of the catastrophe and obfuscate and obscure the facts about the effects of their business. They are clearly the murderer who fled the scene of violence. But here I want to think about the complexities of responsibility that we indeed bear. I have spoken of these in earlier chapters—how Emmanuel Levinas compares our situation to manslaughterers who all "live in the cities of refuge" because our casual purchases, our casual consumptions, our casual use of the world leads, inadvertently but inevitably, ends up leading to a series of events that leads to the death of others. This narrative of the Talmud pushes us further—even our inaction, our inability to see, our avoiding the eye of the homeless, hungry man as we rush about the city—needs to be expiated by a blood sacrifice. Our little bits are little, to be sure, even trivial, but they are part of a world that turns away the poor and does not see their deaths. This is a hard problem. For an ethicist, the moral problem of being, the question, as Levinas asks repeatedly: "Is it righteous to be?" when being itself always consumes the world, bit by little bit, always more for me, less for the Other.

Part III: A Third Text

But this is a book about climate change, and we have ranged far afield (trains! Corpses! Jerusalem!), so I will return to a narrative about one aspect of that problem of global warming and consider why thinking about the complexities of responsibility to Others we cannot see is difficult. Consider the problem of tipping points. A tipping point in climate change language refers to one of several possible threshold conditions where a small, final change in a huge system, that we have called a hyperobject in this book, pushes a system into a completely different physical state.[12] The train takes three miles to stop, long after the breaks are applied, and these tipping points, once triggered, would last for years, perhaps take forever, to stop. Their effects will be deadly, violent: floods and fire and famines, corpses in the fields.

142 ETHICS FOR THE COMING STORM

Books about the tipping points[13] always describe the Atlantic Meridional Overturning Circulation (AMOC) change as one of the most important possible systems in which a tipping point could initiate chaos. The AMOC is the ocean circulation system in the North Atlantic, which begins in the warm waters of the Caribbean, the Gulf Stream, which then runs north along the East Coast of the United States, across the top of the Atlantic where the water cools and drops to the ocean bottom and runs along to Africa, where it warms as it travels back to the Caribbean again. This current is part of the thermohaline circulation, a system of current that regulates vast systems of climate dynamics. In 2015, a study suggested that AMOC had weakened by 15%–20% over the last fifty years.[14] Global warming was causing the system to slow. In 2021, this speculation was confirmed in a new paper. Here is the story.

> Never before in over 1000 years the Atlantic Meridional Overturning Circulation (AMOC), also known as Gulf Stream System, has been as weak as in the last decades. This is the result of a new study by scientists from Ireland, Britain and Germany. The researchers compiled so-called proxy data, taken mainly from natural archives like ocean sediments or ice cores, reaching back many hundreds of years to reconstruct the flow history of the AMOC. They found consistent evidence that its slowdown in the 20th century is unprecedented in the past millennium; it is likely linked to human-caused climate change. The giant ocean circulation is relevant for weather patterns in Europe and regional sea-levels in the US; its slowdown is also associated with an observed cold blob in the northern Atlantic.[15,16]

The way the ocean current is internally calibrated to keep the ocean, and thus the seasonal cycles, the water temperature, the migration of mammals, sharks, and fish, the seaweed and microscopic nutrients, all in a stable state is regulated by a steady circular pattern of warming and cooling. The water is warmed at the equator and pushes north from the Caribbean Sea, to Greenland, where it cools and sinks along its journey back to Africa. But the ice in Greenland is melting, pouring warm fresh water into the Gulf Stream.

> Research suggests that the collapse of the AMOC could itself trigger other tipping points. A collapse of the AMOC may induce causal interactions like changes in ENSO [El Niño–Southern Oscillation] characteristics which affect the climate of millions, leading to a dieback of the Amazon rainforest as

rainfall patterns changed, which would cause an alteration in the climate of the Sahara, which would warm the southern current, and lead to a shrinking of the West Antarctic Ice Sheet. Then, due to what scientists call a seesaw effect, would drive changes in the ITCZ [Intertropical Convergence Zone] alter the southern circulation of the water and drive a large warming of the Southern Ocean, which would lead to further reduction in Antarctic sea ice.[17]

The new report was important for two reasons. It showed that the models for climate prediction were then borne out by evidence. And it showed how much closer to disaster the system had come. By 2022, the tipping point seemed closer than ever, for in the summer of 2022, scientists discovered warming water under the Thwaites Glacier, the most at-risk glacier in Antarctica, whose melting would trigger a sea-level rise of feet, not inches, and shift the currents irretrievably.

Already, the melting of Thwaites Glacier, which is roughly the size of Florida, accounts for 4% of global sea level rise on an ongoing basis. And the amount of ice flowing from it and its glacial neighbors has almost doubled in the last 30 years. Current mathematical models illustrate that if it were to collapse, which scientists believe will happen in the coming decades or centuries, much of western Antarctica's remaining ice will become unstable.

If Antarctica were to lose only Thwaites, the Earth's oceans would rise by about two to three feet or more, researchers believe. That's enough to cause major flooding in New York City and completely engulf some low-lying cities like New Orleans and Venice, Italy, with seawater.[18]

And the Thwaites would only be the first to melt. The situation became worse in 2022, happening faster than anticipated:

An analysis published in the journal Nature Climate Change in August found that the larger system that the Gulf Stream is part of, called the Atlantic Meridional Overturning Circulation (AMOC), is approaching a tipping point. Over the last century, this ocean circulation system has "moved closer to a critical threshold, where it may abruptly shift from the current, strong circulation mode to a much weaker one," says study author Niklas Boers, a climate researcher at the Potsdam Institute for Climate Impact Research in Germany.... Boer's results indicate that the strength of the stabilizing current is declining and that an AMOC tipping point—an ecological point of no return that once crossed could take hundreds of years to stabilize—is much closer than previously understood. "The signs of destabilization being visible already is something that I wouldn't have expected and that I find scary,"[19] Boers told The Guardian. "It's something you just can't [allow to] happen."[20]

The entire agricultural productivity of Britain and Europe, as well as the fisheries, meaning the food supply for millions, not to mention the social and cultural productivity of centuries, is based on a stable and, relative to the latitude, mild climate that is dependent on the ocean currents.[21]

We seem to be far away from the Talmudic story. Yet, here again, do you hear the sound of a person you do not know calling to you? I am thinking of this as an example of our situation of the "unseen face and the unheard call" for several reasons. First, because the concept of a changing current is exactly the sort of far away, vast hyperobject that allows each one of us to imagine that it is not our problem.

Second, because the conveyor belt current has stopped before, and therefore could again, and this stop could last for hundreds of year, long after mitigation efforts, and finally, because it is an example of how warming affects melting, which affects the salinity and temperature near Greenland, which affects the entire heat exchange cycle, setting in place a long chain of events, in the Amazon and the Sahel, that will look like contingency, but of course, will not be at all. First, you don't see the hungry man, so you don't offer him food; perhaps he does not even ask, then he walks out of town, then this and that, and then he is in the place when he can be seized and killed, or you don't see the reason this act or that will lead to this act or that, and then to the melting of the Arctic. This is violence that we do not see; the murderer is not on the scene.

The death will happen a long way away, and a long time away from the first act, and someone will say, "How unlucky."

We seem to be so far from the problem, and so small, we are just passengers on the train, we are not driving, or we are just random people who live in a random city. We are not even proximate to the dead guy. We just had the bad luck to be on the train, or living in the city, or busy with our little carbon-emitting life. Why should we need to atone or feel guilty for something we cannot see—a hungry homeless man—and cannot hear—his mortal cries for help?

Margaret Urban Walker, commenting on the Bernard Williams article, notes this complexity:

> The "problem" of moral luck resides in a sense that the persuasive general beliefs about the conditions for moral responsibility are at odds with our actual common practices of moral assessment in cases involving an element of luck. Common belief is said to endorse the principle—a "control condition"—that factors due to luck are "no proper object of moral assessment and no proper determinant of it, either" (Williams, p. 35) or, more simply, that people cannot be morally assessed for what is due to factors beyond their control (Nagel. P. 59). Yet common practice shows that uncontrolled happenstance indeed figures in the assessment of particular sorts of cases.... What is to be said about the differential moral assessment of cases where the difference is an element due to luck?[22]

Walker considers several responses to what Williams and Nagel call "a paradox," including Martha Nussbaum's turn to moral luck in Greek thought (Nussbaum uses the stories of Greek text much as I use the Talmud) to comment on the pervasiveness of the wish to deny or contain moral vulnerability. It is, Nussbaum says, "a philosophical question as old as the Western tradition."[23] For Walker, the problem of luck and will is not a paradox, but a condition of being human. And that means that our condition is mired in moral luck, for we are what she calls " 'impure agents ... agents of, rather than outside the world of space, time, and causality, agents whose histories and actions belong to it."[24]

> It is in this sense, that one can indeed make judgements. For moral agents, impure to the bone, ought to be aware of it. And aware of the "deep and extensive connections between our causal inextricability ... and the moral significance of our response to it."[25]

We are capable of judgment for the full range of responses, including the turning away, for we live in the world of causality, and the tipping points are begun with small, collective, accumulative acts from which we cannot turn away without a deep unease. We are faced, in this understanding, with moral tests. For Walker these are occasional, vivid, and rare, but I would disagree, and argue, rather, that they are the constancy of one's life work. It is always a moral test, every action leaving the trace, the prints of the grasping hand, and this is true even when the agent is unaware of his or her very agency.

Our entanglement in the causality of the world is hard to sort, indeed. As Walker notes, all agents are impure, and we are the sort of impure agents that fail, but have to act in situations of extremely bad luck, and to do so requires "the virtues of impure agency"—namely, integrity, lucidity, grace, and dependability—so that one keeps a "moral core" in the face of bad luck. Whatever the challenge, we consider them worthy of respect if they "are able to stand and respond in terms that embody ongoing moral commitments or such new ones as may be required."[26]

Walker and Williams and Nagel constantly refer to "ordinary life" that is marked by some unlucky challenges. What I am suggesting in this chapter is somewhat more alarming, I think. It is that ordinary life is a fantasy for the way we live now. We are in the middle of a fast-growing crisis, one that threatens to tip over into full-blown tragedy with every act and every refusal to act. It is not my fault, entirely, each of us can say and that will be (sort of) true. You, reader, are likely not the guy with the knife in your hand sneaking around murderously, but you are the one with the very bad luck to take the train that kills people and the very bad luck to be in a society that has precipitated a crisis of the climate so that the skies are filled with smoke, and record rainfall floods your rivers, and record droughts shrivel the corn in the fields to whispering husks, and far away from you a current in the ocean shudders and falters. It is not a philosophical paradox; it is a theo-political reality. This is why it needs a theological response:

> Absolve, O Lord, Your people Israel, whom You redeemed, and do not let guilt for the blood of the innocent remain among your people Israel.

For Hannah Arendt, the capacity for agency that Walker means (and that needs absolution) is created in the most personal space of all, in the private conversation between one's inner selves, the deep inner dialogue she calls "thinking," meaning, judging. Arendt argues:

> The precondition for this kind of judging is not a highly developed intelligence or sophistication in moral matters, but rather disposition to live together explicitly with oneself, to have intercourse with oneself, that is, to be engaged in that silent dialogue between me and myself which, since Socrates and Plato, we usually call thinking. This kind of thinking, though

at the root of all philosophical thought, is not technical and does not concern theoretical problems. The dividing line between those who want to think and therefore have to judge by themselves, and those who do not, strikes across all social and cultural or educational differences.[27]

Arendt is talking about the situation into which she and the Germans of her time found themselves, extremely bad, mortally bad moral luck, the worst luck of the twentieth century. And each person would have to decide how to live, whether to collaborate, or turn away, or resist.

> To put it crudely, they refused to murder, not so much because they still held fast to the command "Thou shalt not kill," but because they were unwilling to live together with a murderer—themselves.[28]

Arendt is not only speaking here of the Germans who ran death camps and ran the apparatus of the state. She is interested in the bystanders who simply did nothing, overwhelmed by the enormity of the risk of speaking out, or just wanting to avoid politics, who simply lived their German lives until the end, not protesting as the death camps rolled on inexorably when they should have found a way to refuse to participate. She reminds us that each one who did not bear their own guilt has failed: it is not the fault of the system or the state, or history, or luck; it is the failure of the individual who has not heard her own conscience, and not seen the face of the other, but sends the other to her death, an unseen, anonymous, abandoned person between two cities.

It is the argument of this that we cannot avoid the gaze of the other without cost, and without "blood guilt" when we do not "refuse to murder." We know that saying "We don't want to be too political," we who live after the Shoah, is not a credible excuse. We know that saying that you did not see the stranger's face, we who have now read the Talmud, is also not a credible excuse, for when near to us and far from us, we are responsible for the Other, the one we do not see and do not hear, the one who lives on the other side of the vast ocean, the one we speed by in our train.

Let me end this chapter by returning to the well-dressed elders, standing in the ditch, calling out for absolution and for a ritual solution to anonymous violence, a violence we can only know by the human corpses wrecked and left behind in pieces. What should we do now?, the Talmud goes on to ask. We no longer preform the ritual of the broken-necked calf, the text continues, to explain to us, because anonymous murder has become too common. There are just too many bad guys, too many murderers, too many corpses:

> The Mishnah further states: From the time when murderers proliferated, the ritual of the heifer whose neck is broken was nullified. The ritual was performed only when the identity of the murderer was completely unknown. Once there were many known murderers, the conditions for the performance of the ritual were no longer present, as the probable identity of the murderer was known. From the time when Eliezer ben Dinai, who was also called Tehina ben Perisha, came, they renamed him: Son of a murderer. This is an example of a publicly known murderer.[29]

Once the identity of the murderer is clear and the land is filled up with known murderers, you need to go after them, and the time when absolution with ritual acts is over. And this is the topic of the next chapter, where we ask the question: What ought we to do when we know the names of the murderers? When we can rename them with their murderous deeds?

How to confront this sort of evil will take far more than the behavior changes that are easy to make, although they are very nice, like taking the train instead of driving. I thought I was doing my little bit, but it was inadequate, and it was not bad luck that made those four people try to run across the tracks: it was systemic neglect, collapsing economies, and the greed of the ones that made the rules, budgets, and decisions. That is what led to their deaths. Sustainable travel will not be enough—we are on the train already, we are not the guys in the limos speeding by, or much less the privileged ones in flight overhead, completely unconnected to the land. But this choice for sustainability, this ride, will not be enough. Ultimately, it is not serious enough, not enough of a risk. It will take turning that train around until the way can be made safe. It will take getting off the train and standing in the hard ditches with the ones who have no choice, with the Other for whom the Torah is written.

7

Bad Guys

Amalek and the Production of Doubt

Introduction

And the Lord said unto Moses: "Write this for a remembrance in the book, and say it over and over in the ears of Joshua: for I will utterly blot out the remembrance of Amalek from under heaven." And Moses built an altar and called the name of the Lord, for he said, because Lord has sworn to have war with Amalek from generation to generation. (Exodus 17:4–17)

Remember what Amalek did unto thee on your journey as you came forth out of Egypt; how he surprised you by the march and cut down the hindmost and the stragglers of you, all that were enfeebled in thy rear, when you were famished and weary; and he feared not God. (Deuteronomy 25:17–18

Therefore, it shall be, when the LORD thy God hath given you safe rest from all your enemies around you, in the land which the LORD thy God gives you for an inheritance to possess it, that you shalt blot out the remembrance of Amalek from under heaven; Do not forget! (Deuteronomy 27:19)

Amalekites are the first enemy of the newly freed Hebrew slaves, attacking them as they fled from Pharaoh's army. They are a persistent enemy, reappearing at intervals in the Hebrew Scripture, and becoming over the centuries, Israel's archetypical enemy. Scholars Elliot Horowitz and Josef Stern suggest that Amalekites have come to represent an "eternally irreconcilable enemy" that wants to murder Jews, and that Jews in postbiblical times sometimes associate their contemporary enemies with them, first with Rome, then the Nazis, and then Stalin, all said to be "descendants of Amalek." For some, this permits killing Amalekites, for they are the ones who are intractably evil, carrying radical evil in their bones and blood.

Ethics for the Coming Storm. Laurie Zoloth, Oxford University Press. © Oxford University Press 2023.
DOI: 10.1093/oso/9780197661345.003.0008

Yet the tribe is mentioned as founded by the grandson of Esau, who is, of course, the twin brother of the founder of the tribe of Israel, Jacob. What does it mean that your greatest historical enemy is also your closest cousin? And what does it mean to "remember to forget"? This, the odd admonition about the Amalekites, draws our attention to the complexity of enemies in religious tradition, others who are formidable, dangerous, yet familiar, both/and. To mirror this doubled problem, the text doubles as well—we must simultaneously "remember" and "forget," just as we simultaneously recognize and resist our enemy. The story of the enemy is careful preserved—it is, of course, famously, not erased. When a new Torah is written, it is officially checked by turning the scroll to the injunction to "remember to forget," and ensuring that that phrase first of all others, is properly written.

This chapter will raise a somewhat different question, in a somewhat different tone. When I write about global warming and a changing climate, I, like other scholars who address this topic, seek to tell you the troubling truth about the effects of this dangerous change. We rehearse the scientific reports and urge you, because of the heritage of Kant, to know the right act, and then of course, you will have the good rational, will to do the right act. In this chapter, I will make the argument that people who seek to stop the use of carbon will find they have powerful enemies, and while the talk of sin and sinners is quite out of fashion, it is a powerful and important part of the language of religion. Faith traditions have enemies. Early Jewish followers of Jesus faced terrible foes. The Prophet Mohammed had to fight his way to Medina, after defeat in Mecca, and Jews have felt the sting of exile, and the gathering hatred and the darkness of fascist hatred, in every era. Say you have another way to live, say you love the stranger, and say that wealth and power mean nothing because they are illusion, and really mean it, and just watch what happens. The truth about climate change is not just uncomfortable; it is dangerous, dangerous like religions are dangers, to the authority of the state and the positions of the kings and princes and CEOs.

In this chapter I am going to write about sinners and enemies and will explore the creation of Amalek as the archetypical enemy by first closely analyzing the biblical verses that surround the enemy narrative and then reflecting on how this story of enemies remembered shape modern concepts of enemies. I will then consider this text in light of my larger project, which is to find a moral language to understand our present crisis, one that is rooted in shared Scriptural theologies, one that will awaken us and allow us to act. We will then return to our central topic, climate change, and to its causes.

I will consider several questions within this chapter. Amalek is a fundamental part of the existence of Israel, tied up in the liberation narrative at the heart of all Scriptural possibility, and then reoccurring with a force that is experienced as a force built into the world, who enters whenever Israel doubts the existence of God. Amalek is the very face of evil but also the very face of a contrary, stochastic universe. Amalek attacks the uncertain—the doubtful in the Exodus narrative, and the weak in the Deuteronomic text—that is his signal characteristic.

Next I will spend some time on the actual command: to remember to not forget. Forgetting is the twin of memory, of course, the darkness to memory's light. The narrative of failure and doubt is written and then erased, and then written as a commandment to both look and look away. I will then return to the history I began in the first chapter, but this time, focus on the extraction companies and their role.

Remembering the Enemy: The Ethics of Memory

Paul Ricoeur, in thinking about the "uses of memory," wrote an essay about the ways that memory functions ethically.[1] Memory is first a relationship of knowledge, rooted in the "pastness of past events," meaning that since we understand the past as fixed, we then relate the past as true; in other words, its pastness is itself a truth claim. (Something happens, and all can see the evidence.) But memory is also a relationship of action—memory is a way of doing things with our words and our minds; it is, then, a kind of embodied moral gesture. So, Ricoeur asks: what are the *ethics* of memory?

To what extent is there a duty to remember? Paul Ricoeur writes of "the duty to remember," which consists not only in having a deep concern for the past but in transmitting the meaning of past events to the next generation, in hopes of shaping future events as yet to emerge. The imperative to tell is a means of fighting against the erosion of traces: because there is a "general trend to destroy" (quoting Aristotle that time destroys more than it constructs). In this sense, all human activity is a countertrend to the ruins—hence, achieving preservation of the past is the work of memory, and the duty to remember is a duty to warn.

The command to "blot out" the name implies a deep and permanent fatality, not only to the immediate perpetrators but to the possibility of their having a human future. It is a terrible command, yet of course, for the knowledgably Jewish reader, it is also oddly ironic, for it seems that these "blotted-out" progeny rise to reoccur "in every generation." Of course, we see the function of the heuristic as it plays out in naming the repeated enemies of the Jewish people: Haman, Hitler. But it also functions in the paradoxical story of the grandchildren of the Amalekites, we are told in a later midrashic text, who study in Bnei Brak, at the heart of the Jewish religious world, for century after century.

Yet the story has resonance for us not only because of the power of the command from God but also because the narrative is so terrible. The Hebrew slaves, after generations of brutal slavery, are fleeing Egypt. Everybody leaves, including elderly people, pregnant women, and toddlers, those who walk out of slavery slowly. It is they who are attacked—the most vulnerable, those who really have no hope of escape. The terror happens only in the telling, "off-camera," as it were, but the reader can imagine what it looks like when children and grandmothers are killed. Who could do such a thing?

It is an instance of pure evil. And we are told that this action is worse than the Pharaonic rule, for after all, we are not told to "blot out" the name of the Egyptians, who had just imprisoned the same toddlers and grandmothers for four hundred years. In part, this may be that we understand slavery as the way of the world, just as that war is the way of the world, simply part of the political economy. But the attack by Amalek looks different, unfair, out of order, even in that brutal world of war and slavery. That is why we remember it and why we recognize it. This recognition is important, for it gives us language for a particular task: recognizing a specific kind of evil, cruel and gratuitous, with havoc in its wake: genocide.

Let us turn to the narrative traces of the theological and political relationship of Israel and its enemy.

Writing the Enemy: Amalek and the Biblical Tradition

Amalek, as a person,[2] is first mentioned in Hebrew Scripture as the offspring of Esau, Jacob's twin. Jacob will bear the (stolen) blessing of his father and the fate of the Jewish people. It is in his name, 'Israel', that the biblical narrative will unfold. The brothers are not alike: Esau is "hairy," desperate, the threat of violence hangs about him; he disappears from the narrative to reemerge as large and wealthy and sinister, encountered on the road as Jacob returns from his own personal exile, back to the Land. Perhaps it is Esau that Jacob wrestles on that return journey, perhaps it is an angel who wounds him and names him. Esau will father a red-faced tribe, and in later rabbinic literature, the tribe, the Edomites, will be associated with Rome, the great enemy of the Second Temple Jews. Amalek, in the text identified as Esau's grandson is, like Ishmael, the child of a concubine.

> These are the generations of Esau the father of the Edomites in Mount Seir; 10 These are the names of Esau's sons; Eliphaz the son of Adah the wife of Esau, Reuel the son of Bashemath the wife of Esau. 11 And the sons of Eliphaz were Teman, Omar, Zepho, and Gatam, and Kenaz. 12 And Timna was concubine to Eliphaz Esau's son; and she bore to Eliphaz Amalek; these were the sons of Adah Esau's wife. (Genesis 36:10–12)

A few verses later, we are reintroduced to the now grown-up boy, Amalek, and like his father, he is a man of war, a chieftain. It is a brief mention here, last on a list of seven:

> The sons of Eliphaz the firstborn son of Esau; chiefs of Teman, of Omar, of Zepho, of Kenaz, the chiefs of Korah, of Gatam, and of Amalek; these are the chiefs who came of Eliphaz in the land of Edom; these were the sons of Adah.[3] (Genesis 36:15–16)

Thus, the power is described, and the warriors left to wait—as it were—in the text. By the next appearance, the person of Amalek has become a tribe. They appear again textually just after the first in what will be a series of episodes in which the newly freed Israelites, miserable and desperate, complain of their great thirst and their first great doubt about the reality of God's existence, to Moses, who has led them into the wilderness of the desert, apparently without water to worship an invisible God. Moses, for his part, is insulted by their anger, but does, following God's instructions, strike a rock and this allows water to flow and be distributed. He names the place "strife" and "testing" and it is at that moment that Amalek's army attacks. It is the first attack since Pharaoh's army was defeated at the Red Sea; they are the first enemy of the freed people.

> And he called the name of the place Massah, and Meribah, because of the chiding of the people of Israel, and because they tempted the Lord, saying, Is the Lord among us, or not? Then came Amalek, and fought with Israel in Rephidim. (Exodus 17:7–8)

It is one line in this section of Hebrew Scripture, but the wording, as eleventh-century medieval Jewish commentator Rashi notes, is unusual—instead of the "went out" phrase usually used, the phrase is "then came." This should alert us to trouble, Rashi tells us.

Moses responds to the attack with a day-long battle.[4]

> And Moses said to Joshua, Choose for us men, and go out, fight with Amalek; tomorrow I will stand on the top of the hill with the rod of God in my hand. So Joshua did as Moses had said to him, and fought with Amalek; and Moses, Aaron, and Hur went up to the top of the hill. And it came to pass, when Moses held up his hand, that Israel prevailed; and when he let down his hand, Amalek prevailed. But Moses' hands were heavy; and they took a stone, and put it under him, and he sat on it; and Aaron and Hur stayed up his hands, the one on the one side, and the other on the other side; and his hands were steady until the going down of the sun. And Joshua discomfited Amalek and his people with the edge of the sword. (Exodus 17:9–13)

After the battle, which ends in victory, though not in a total defeat, this first attack is memorialized. It is the first mention of a book, a scroll, which is to be spoken by God and transcribed by Moses. Of course, this gesture prefigures the giving of the Law, later, at Sinai in its choreography, and it announces the first command to write is a command that is about memory. It is to commemorate the first act in an ongoing war. And the command is stark and strange. The people Amalek are not only to be extinguished but the very memory of their existence obliterated. And yet, you need to write this down and tell it. The book is to remember to not forget, the essential task of the writer.

> And the Lord said to Moses, Write this for a memorial in a book, and recite it in the ears of Joshua; for I will completely put out the remembrance of Amalek from under heaven. And Moses built an altar, and called its name Adonai-Nissi; For he said, Because the Lord has sworn that the Lord will have war with Amalek from generation to generation. (Exodus 17:14–16)

It is, for a close reader of Scripture, somewhat curious. The Amalekites "come" and "fight with," which seems like a general act of war, a logical possible outcome if a band of strangers comes on to your territory (of course, another logical outcome would be to welcome them, thirsty as they are, desert that it is). The permanent, eternal curse seems out of proportion to the event.

To understand this, let us turn to the next textual occurrence of Amalek. It is a moment of the bleakest despair. Moses has sent spies out to explore the Land promised by God to the Hebrew slaves, and they hate and fear what they see.

> And they went and came to Moses, and to Aaron, and to all the congregation of the people of Israel, to the wilderness of Paran, to Kadesh; and brought back word to them, and to all the congregation, and showed them the fruit of the land. And they told him, and said "We came to the land where you sent us, and surely it flows with milk and honey; and this is its fruit. Nevertheless, the people, who live in the land, are strong, and the cities are walled, and very great; and moreover, we saw the children of Anak there. The Amalekites live in the land of the Negev; and the Hittites, and the Jebusites, and the Amorites, live in the mountains; and the Canaanites live by the sea, and by the side of the Jordan. (Numbers 13:29)

Once again, the Amalekites show up at the nadir, when the congregation is most racked by doubt and when doubt drives out promise and derails and confuses the people. It is as if Amalek is called into being by the doubt itself, sees the Israelites' weakness, and potentiates it. Their product is doubt.

And the people's fear and self-doubt seep into the camp like so much fog, like the antithesis of manna, appearing and making them feel empty, instead of full, making them feel small and weak, "they see us as grasshoppers," they say, like insects. It is too large and complex a problem, they say.

And at this point, a muttering, angry God gives up on this generation, and the people who do not fight, but turn away.

> Because all those men which have seen my glory, and my miracles, which I did in Egypt and in the wilderness, and have tempted me now these ten times, and have not listened to my voice; Surely they shall not see the land which I swore to their fathers, nor shall any of them who provoked me see it; But my servant Caleb, because he had another spirit with him, and has followed me fully, him will I bring into the land where he went; and his seed shall possess it. Now the Amalekites and the Canaanites live in the valley. Tomorrow turn and go to the wilderness by the way of the Red Sea. And the Lord spoke to Moses and to Aaron, saying, How long shall I bear with this evil congregation, which murmur against me? (Numbers 14:25)

Ashamed, the people eventually turn and try to fight, but it is "without God's presence" and they fail terribly.[5] Thus begins the forty-year journey in the wilderness.

Amalek appears twice more in the Torah, once, when Balaam, the Edomite priest hired by the Moabites to curse the Hebrews, because his curses really do mean something, and looks on their neatly assembled tents and, seeing their order, and discipline, is impressed, and blesses rather than condemns them. Instead, he curses Amalek, who are, as they always are, circling like black crows, around the Hebrew camp.

> Out of Jacob shall come a ruler and shall destroy he who remains of the city. And when he looked on Amalek, he took up his discourse, and said, Amalek was the first of the nations; but his latter end shall be that of everlasting perdition. (Numbers 24:20)

Finally, in a list about resolving conflict and admonitions of justice in Deuteronomy, comes the command I wrote at the beginning of this chapter: Remember not to forget! Note how in this retelling of the event, the Amalekites are described as attacking from the rear, and attacking the "feeble" trailing behind, something that is not in the earlier text itself. They appear, rather, in a list of prohibitions about daily justice:

> You shall not have in your bag different weights, a large and a small. You shall not have in your house different measures, a large and a small. But you shall have a perfect and just weight, a perfect and just measure shall you have; that your days may be lengthened in the land which the Lord your God gives you. For all who do such things, and all who do unrighteously, are an abomination to the Lord your God.
>
> Remember what Amalek did to you by the way, when you came forth out of Egypt; How he met you by the way, and struck at your rear, all who were feeble behind you, when you were faint and weary; and he did not fear God. Therefore it shall be, when the Lord your God has given you rest from all your enemies around, in the land which the Lord your God gives you for an inheritance to possess, that you shall blot out the remembrance of Amalek from under heaven; you shall not forget it. (Deuteronomy 25:17)

The Amalekites play a consistent role in Judges, where the long wars against them define the fate of kingship. In Judges 6, they appear when Israel "did evil again in the sight of the Lord" and is punished with an attack and enslavement, first by Moab[6] and then again by Midian,[7] with the Amalekites present to join every attack. Amalekites are referenced in Deborah's song (Judges 5)[8] and in the description of a secession of kings, doubts, and war (Judges 7–10).[9]

But of course, it is in the books of Samuel that Amalek brings a complex tragedy (again) into the text. It goes well at first:

> So, Saul took the kingdom over Israel, and fought against all his enemies on every side, against Moab, and against the Ammonites, and against Edom, and against the kings of Zobah, and against the Philistines; and wherever he turned himself, he did them mischief. And he gathered an army, and defeated the Amalekites, and saved Israel from the hands of those who plundered them. (1 Samuel 14:48)

A chapter later, Saul is asked by God (via his Prophet Samuel) to conduct a war of total annihilation against the Amalakite's camp.

> Samuel also said to Saul, The Lord sent me to anoint you to be king over his people, over Israel; now therefore listen to the voice of the words of the Lord. Thus said the Lord of hosts, I remember that which Amalek did to Israel, how he laid wait for him in the way, when he came up from Egypt. And go and strike Amalek, and completely destroy all that they have, and spare them not; but slay both man and woman, infant and suckling, ox, and sheep, camel and ass. (I Samuel 15:3)

And while he manages to kill, apparently, all the men, grandparents, six-year-olds, toddlers, and smiley Amalekite babies, their lips wet with milk, turned from the breast of their mothers, he keeps the cows and the king alive, and this angers Samuel so completely that Saul loses his kingship.

> And he took Agag the king of the Amalekites alive, and completely destroyed all the people with the edge of the sword. But Saul and the people spared Agag, and the best of the sheep, and of the oxen, and of the fatlings, and the lambs, and all that was good, and would not completely destroy them; but everything that was despised and worthless, that they destroyed completely. Then came the word of the Lord to Samuel, saying, I regret that I have set up Saul to be king; for he is turned back from following me, and has not performed my commandments. And it grieved Samuel; and he

cried to the Lord all night. . . . And Samuel came to Saul; and Saul said to him, Blessed be you of the Lord; I have performed the commandment of the Lord. And Samuel said, What is the meaning then of this bleating of the sheep in my ears, and the lowing of the oxen which I hear? And Saul said, they have brought them from the Amalekites; for the people spared the best of the sheep and of the oxen, to sacrifice to the Lord your God; and the rest we have completely destroyed. Then Samuel said to Saul, Stay, and I will tell you what the Lord has said to me this night. And he said to him, Speak. And Samuel said, When you were little in your own sight, were you not made the chief of the tribes of Israel, and the Lord anointed you king over Israel? And the Lord sent you on a journey, and said, Go and completely destroy the sinners the Amalekites, and fight against them until they are consumed. Why then did you not obey the voice of the Lord, but did fly upon the booty, and did evil in the sight of the Lord? . . . Because you have rejected the word of the Lord, he has also rejected you from being king. And Saul said to Samuel, I have sinned; for I have transgressed the commandment of the Lord, and your words; because I feared the people, and obeyed their voice. And therefore, I beg you, pardon my sin, and turn again with me, that I may worship the Lord. And Samuel said to Saul, I will not return with you; for you have rejected the word of the Lord, and the Lord has rejected you from being king over Israel. And as Samuel turned about to go away, he laid hold upon the skirt of his mantle, and it tore.[10] (1 Samuel 15:2–20)

There is much to consider here in this long account (not the least of which is the modern reader's horror at genocidal religious war and the fact that Samuel is not at all upset by the bloody slaughter of civilian babies), but for the purpose of this chapter, let me point out that Saul's disobedience to God parallels earlier moments in which God's command is ignored. The long narrative of rejection, punishment, and loss, with a supine, begging warrior ripping the coat of his holy advisor, focuses on the confusion that Saul, pragmatist, materialist, brings to the narrative. Does God want power? Animal sacrifice? Nope, says Samuel, you have it wrong. You've mistaken your enemy. You failed to recognize.

What Saul cannot do; David, who takes his enemies more seriously, accomplishes, after yet another war with the always present Amalekites. He learns of the deaths of Saul and of Jonathan, from an Amalekite,[11] and restores the order, in which Amalek is the defeated, yet always needing-to-be-defeated foe, remembered to be unremembered.[12]

> And David struck them from twilight until the evening of the next day; and there escaped not a man of them, save four hundred young men, who rode upon camels, and fled. And David recovered all that the Amalekites had carried away; and David rescued his two wives. And, there was nothing lacking to them, neither small nor great, neither sons nor daughters, neither booty, nor any thing that they had taken; David recovered it all. (1 Samuel 30:14)

Psalm 83 mentions Amalek in a formulaic list of enemies:

> They have said, Come, and let us cut them off from being a nation; that the name of Israel may no longer be remembered. For they conspire together with one accord; they make an alliance against you: 7 The tents of Edom, and the Ishmaelites; of Moab, and the Hagarites; Gebal, and Ammon, and Amalek; the Philistines with the inhabitants of Tyre; Assyria also has joined them; they are the strong arm of the children of Lot. Selah.

Chronicles 4:37 ends the biblical account by describing a final battle and escape.

> And some of them, of the sons of Simeon, five hundred men, went to mount Seir, having for their captains Pelatiah, and Neariah, and Rephaiah, and Uzziel, the sons of Ishi. And they destroyed the rest of the Amalekites who had escaped, and lived there to this day.

Postbiblical Accounts

In later Talmudic and medieval accounts, one sees Amalek thematized, with the invocations of that name as an imprecation—one might as well say "bad guys." Amalek is absolute, irredeemable evil, generationally evil. There are a dozen references in which the term functions this way.

In tractate Sanhedrin, there is a discussion about the timing of conquest, killing, and the building of the Temple, and it is decided that conquest and killing come first by the ever-eager Rabbi Jose, who works it out with his own Scriptural logic. You need, these narratives tell us, to eliminate doubt by seeing it as a war you must wage.

> Judah said: Three commandments were given to Israel when they entered the land: [i] to appoint a king, [ii] to cut off the seed of Amalek, and [iii]

to build themselves the chosen house. While R. Nehorai said: This section was spoken only in anticipation of their future murmurings, as it is written, And shalt say, I will set a king over me etc.

It has been taught: R. Jose said: Three commandments were given to Israel when they entered the land; [i] to appoint a king; [ii] to cut off the seed of Amalek; [iii] and to build themselves the chosen house [i.e. the Temple] and I do not know which of them has priority. But, when it is said: The hand upon the throne of the Lord, the Lord will have war with Amalek from generation to generation, we must infer that they had first to set up a king, for 'throne' implies a king, as it is written, Then Solomon sat on the throne of the Lord as king. Yet I still do not know which [of the other two] comes first, the building of the chosen Temple or the cutting off of the seed of Amalek. Hence, when it is written, And when He giveth you rest from all your enemies round about etc., and then [Scripture proceeds], Then it shall come to pass that the place which the Lord your God shall choose, it is to be inferred that the extermination of Amalek is first. (Sanhedrin 20b)

In another section, the rabbis consider the provenance of the child Amalek, hinting at the idea that his mother has royal blood, but was drawn to the Jews, who reject her for unknown reason, but which somehow begins the entire cycle.

Desiring to become a proselyte, she went to Abraham, Isaac and Jacob, but they did not accept her. So she went and became a concubine to Eliphaz the son of Esau, saying, "I had rather be a servant to this people than a mistress of another nation." From her Amalek was descended who afflicted Israel. Why so?—Because they should not have repulsed her. (Sanhedrin 99b)

By the time of commentary on the book of Esther, a fantastical narrative of revenge set in Persia, Haman, the king's anti-Jewish chief of staff, tries to order the slaughter of all the Jews, but the Jews, warned in time by Queen Esther, the insider Jew in the palace, fight back and kill all their enemies. In this narrative, one sees the extrapolations of the linkage between Amalek and absolute evil—Haman and his sons are said to be Amalekites and thus their treachery and thus the justification for their deaths.[13] Here, too, despite what looks like a successful elimination of the entire family, they persist, giving rise to that odd offshoot tale in which Haman's grandchildren study in Bnei Brak, the heart of the Talmudic world.[14] We will return to this oddity—another doubling—later.

Amalek becomes associated more clearly with doubt by the *gematria*, a numerical system in which every Hebrew letter is associated with a number, and meaning is derived from the numerical sum of the added letters. Thus:

> The numerical value (gematria) of the Hebrew letters that spell *Amalek* (240) is equivalent to that of the letters that spell *safek*, "doubt." All things holy are certain and absolute.... Amalek is doubt; baseless, irrational doubt that cools the fervor of holiness with nothing more than a cynical shrug.[15]

Of course, there is also the similarity in the Hebrew words phonically as well and, of course, the persistent presence of Amalek when Israel is most doubtful and confused at Meribah, the place of the spies' return, surely makes the linkage satisfying. In this view, Amalek represents the great narrative of secularity: that there is no justice or order in the world, that random events and random chance render morality futile. This is echoed in the game of chance played by characters in the Purim story. The opposite of goodness, chosenness, the sense that God's mercy exists in the world, is the game of chance. It echoes the problem we saw in the last chapter of this book, when justice seems to be luck, seen as a matter of chance: in the Leviticus text (16:8), in Chronicles (1:2431), in which the land you get is based on the lot you throw, and in the Purim text, in a sort of a mocking intertextuality.

This rich account of evil, opportunism, and aggression played out in the doubt, instability, and the weakness of the people of Israel deepens in the medieval period, and in the worsening of violent anti-Semitism in early modern Europe: Rome is Amalek, then the Inquisition is run by Amaleks, finally culminating in the naming of Hitler as Amalek and the Nazis as his violent tribe.

Thinking of the Enemy: Hannah Arendt and the Responsibility to Judge

When we speak of Hitler as Amalek, we need to reflect on how doubt or confusion or fear creates the opportunity for Amalek to "come." Our text is the collection of essays in *Responsibility and Judgement*, by Hannah Arendt, gathered posthumously. Arendt is interested in several concepts here. First, she considers two moral actions that

> continu(e) in spite of death: forgiving and promising. Only a human being is capable of being unbound through forgiveness and bound through promising—rapprochement, untying and tying.[16]

Memory's task is to preserve: "the relation of the present to the past—and in so doing we become heirs of the past guilt and debt" and to remember the importance of keeping promises over time. "All utopias would be empty were it not for the reactivation of unkempt promises."[17]

Remembering[18] the enemy as an enemy is important for moral clarity, to foreground the importance of the history of suffering:

> over the general tendency of history to celebrate the victors. We could say that the whole philosophy of history... is concerned with the culmination of advantage, progress, and victory. All that is left behind is lost. We need therefore, a kind of parallel history... which would counter the history.... To memorize the victims of history... should be a task for all of us at the end of this century.[19]

Her second point moves us closer to our task: that of judging actions as immoral as we return to the necessity of judging that I raised in the last chapter.

> There exists in our society a widespread fear of judging that has nothing whatever to do with the biblical "Judge not, that ye be not judged," and if this fear speaks in terms of "casting the first stone," it takes this word in vain. For behind the unwillingness to judge lurks the suspicion that no one is a free agent, and hence the doubt that anyone is responsible or could be expected to answer for what he has done. The moment moral issues are raised, even in passing, he who raises them will be confronted with this frightful lack of self-confidence and hence of pride, and also with a kind of mock-modesty that in saying, Who am I to judge? actually means We're all alike, equally bad, and those who try, or pretend that they try, to remain halfway decent are either saints or hypocrites, and in either case should leave us alone. Hence the huge outcry the moment anyone fixes specific blame on some particular person instead of blaming all deeds or events on historical trends and dialectical movements, in short on some mysterious necessity

that works behind the backs of men and bestows upon everything they do some kind of deeper meaning.[20]

In particular, of course, this is a problem with the Amalek Hitler:

> As long as one traces the roots of what Hitler did back to Plato or Gioacchino da Fiore or Hegel or Nietzsche, or to modern science and technology, or to nihilism or the French Revolution, everything is all right. The point I want to raise here goes beyond the well-known fallacy of the concept of collective guilt as first applied to the German people and its collective past—all of Germany stands accused and the whole of German history from Luther to Hitler—which in practice turned into a highly effective whitewash of all those who had actually done something, for where all are guilty, no one is.[21]

"When all are guilty, no one is." I will return to this claim.

> Remember (*zachor*) what the Amalekites did to you when you left Egypt
> How, not fearing God, they surprised you on the way, and cut down the vulnerable who were in your rear.
> And you were weary and famished.
> Therefore when God gives you safety and rest from all your enemies around you
> In the Land which Adonai is given you as a portion
> You must wipe out the memory (*zecher*) of Amalek
> From under Heaven.
> Do not forget!

Seeing the Enemy: Bad Guys and the Production of Doubt

In other chapters in this book, I have asked you, as reader, to consider how renegotiating texts from the classic traditions of Jewish thought might help us better understand the crisis of global warming and climate change. Every day, we read about the worsening news: scientists across dozens of countries publishing data that describe ever grimmer scenarios for humanity, and in this book thus far, I have suggested ways to use traditional narratives to understand and respond justly to this reality: we have perhaps only a decade now to act to avoid the worst aspects of a changing climate.

Perhaps most alarming is the steady fact that predictions made about the timeline of our fate are coming true and at a faster pace than predicted. When I turned my attention to the effects of global warming, there were predictions about species extinction, and now, fully half of all species that were alive when I was a child are gone. There were predictions of more powerful hurricanes, more severe droughts, floods, and mass migration, and in 2023, migrants crowded the borders of the countries of the global north, and Hurricane Ian devastated Florida and Cuba, the deadliest since 1935, and Hurricane Fiona set records as strongest storm in Canadian history. There were predictions about increasing deadly wildfires in the American West, and the year that I first completed this manuscript, in 2019, I was evacuated from fires north of Los Angeles when I was there to visit my family: the ridge of fire and the cloud of rising smoke were so intense they could be seen from space. All of these things are happening around us, happening now.

And what have we said? Largely, to change our ways. Many scholars, citing the lessons from religious traditions, urge us to welcome our neighbors fleeing from danger; or teach us the lesson of debt; or remind us to limit our desire. I have done exactly that in the chapters you have just read. So familiar are these admonitions that arguments from Jewish ethics—and from religious ethics in general—can seem passive, compromising, often shifting blame for the crisis to an amorphous "all of us." It is exactly what Arendt fiercely tells us is wrong.

In this chapter, I want to do something else: I want to lay blame. I want to point the finger.

For instead of making the problem one in which useless and careless consumptive Americans simply take too much for themselves, although of course that is also true, let me make it clear that global warming is a business decision. It is not made as a moral decision; it is just that you can make a great deal of money selling gas and oil. Some people (usually not middle-class families in America, whose real wages have stayed the same since 1980) are doing very well by global warming. They are oil, coal, and gas companies, and they are not only selling, at a vast profit, the carbon sources poisoning the air, they are also selling a far more sinister product. They are producing, promoting, and selling doubt. And it is this doubt that has, for three decades, made it extraordinarily difficult to allow the public to understand and act on the problem of the global warming that drives climate change.

Doubtfulness, and uncertainty, the idea that there were "two sides" to the reality of the scientific reality of global warming, has been a well-documented campaign strategy of the energy industry.

> In case after case . . . a handful of scientists joined forces with think tanks and private corporations to challenge scientific evidence on a host of contemporary issues. In the early years, much of the money for this effort came from the tobacco industry; in later years, it came from foundations, think tanks, and the fossil fuel industry. They claimed the link between smoking and cancer remained unproven. . . . They argued that acid rain was caused by volcanos and so was the ozone hole. They charged that the Environmental Protection Agency had rigged the science surrounding second hand smoke. Most recently—over the course of nearly two decades and against the face of mounting evidence—they dismissed the reality of global warming . . . in case after case, they steadfastly denied the existence of scientific agreement, even though they, themselves, were pretty much the only ones who disagreed.[22]

Because most of the scientists were physicists who had participated in the building of the atom bomb and had played key roles in the immediate postwar creation of the new alliances between government and science, they had long been close to power. Many have served as leaders of elite science associations and advisory boards for nuclear regulation. And several had been president of the National Academy of Sciences. They were men who were used to giving counsel to presidents and senior policymakers, often in the high-stakes world of war: life and death. Thus, despite the fact that they had done no original research, had taken no observations, or collected data, they took positions against the emerging consensus that global warming was driven by the burning of fossil fuels, and against their colleagues in the earth sciences. When oil, coal, and gas companies hired "experts" to defend their business, it was to this handful of people they turned. They engaged the public relations firm who had been used by the American tobacco companies, who had told them: "Your product is not tobacco. Doubt is your product." And thus, while in the early 1970s, as we have seen in early chapters of this book, most of the world's population who knew about global warming agreed that it was a significant issue, and moreover, that humans had the capacity to stop its probable effects, nothing was done to curtail their production, profits, or the tax breaks that enabled it, and nothing was done to alert the rest of the polity to the danger. Even George H. W. Bush who famously ran as a Republican on a slogan "Don't worry about the greenhouse effect because you will have the White House Effect," promising swift action on greenhouse gas emissions, which of course did not happen, was unable to change the unceasing extraction, nor could he affect the geopolitical forces that, larger than any one government, shaped the structure of the world's largest global industry. The issue of climate change became contentious and fell into the increasingly politicized, media-driven, semiotics of civic life. Global warming became something liberal and left-wing parties cared about, while right-wing parties cared about the way in which any regulation on industry would lessen the profit made. Media began to structure the issue as a "debate" as if the basic science on this question was a matter of opinion. Doubt replaced consensus and blocked effective political action. Personal, privatized marketplace choices, in which the little social choices made by moral agents, acting as consumers, replaced the hope of larger civic choices, made by moral agents acting as citizens.

Let's return to the history I began to describe in the introduction to this book, how the early curiosity about fossils and the Ice Age started a quest to figure out how global temperature changed, and how more and more knowledge and more and more iterative science over decades had alerted scientists, politicians, and policymakers to the magnitude of the problem. It is the contention that the forces lining up against climate change science began to win political victories just as the world was organizing the Intergovernmental Panel on Climate Change (IPCC) in 1988 and planning for the first Earth Summit. Nathaniel Rich details how close the world came to addressing the problem in time to have mitigated the worst effects of global warming and kept the global temperature below 1.5°C, something that is now impossible even if every machine, airplane, toaster oven, steel mill, and agrobusiness farm stopped dead in its tracks, for the forces at play, the melting of ice, the loss of albedo, the release of methane from melted permafrost, all of this will continue.

> If the United States had endorsed the proposal broadly supported at the end of the eighties—a freezing of carbon emissions, with a reduction of 20 percent by 2005—warming could have been held to less than 1.5 degrees. A broad international consensus had agreed on a mechanism to achieve this: a binding global treaty. The idea began to coalesce as early as February 1979, at the First World Climate Conference in Geneva, when

scientists from fifty nations agreed unanimously that it was "urgently necessary" to act.[23]

The Group of Seven, which is a meeting of the world's richest nations, called for such a treaty in 1988. In 1989, after a decade of research, yet another global climate meeting was held, with representatives from sixty nations, politicians, and a growing number of very worried scientists, and approved a framework for a treaty, and called for another meeting with the capacity to enforce the needed norms. In 1997, the Kyoto Protocol was signed and was initially approved by the United States. In it, all developed nations pledged to reduce emissions by an average of 5% by the period 2008–2012, with wide variations on targets for individual countries, to ensure that the developing world would still be able to industrialize, while slowly proposing to wean developed countries to alternative sources. It was a deep compromise, far less rigorous that what had been proposed twenty years earlier, and when the atmospheric carbon was far less, yet even this was too much for the United States. The Senate immediately declared it would not ratify the treaty. This was despite the fact that Bill Clinton was U.S. President, and Al Gore was Vice President. It was a spectacular failure. And so was the U.S.'s failure to ratify every ensuing climate change treaty: in Bali, in Copenhagen, in Mexico, and finally, in Paris, when all parties in the United Nations (UN) approved it, as well as the United States, until the Trump administration reversed the approval, which was reversed again in the first days of the Biden administration. The treaty was only voluntary in the first place, for since Kyoto, no treaty had put enforcement mechanisms in place. The treaties also became less optimistic: the climate temperature goal was now 2°C. Atmospheric carbon was higher than at any time in human history: over 400 parts per million (ppm), and, of course, rising every single year, as was the amount of carbon burned by humanity, every single year. The later UN reports and the Paris treaty began to have language about carbon dioxide removal, imagining enormous technologies that did not yet exist as the way to save the earth: creating a global, permanent cloud cover under which humanity would operate; digging huge wells and putting extracted carbon back in the earth where it came from in a rather desperate attempt to avert disaster. But of course, even this strategy creates other problems:

> The technology remains costly and energy-intensive. It is often difficult to pin down costs for new technologies, but one recent study estimates that it would cost about $94–$232 per metric ton. Previous estimates were

higher. Direct air capture also requires substantial heat and power inputs—scrubbing 1 gigaton of carbon dioxide from the air would require about 7 percent of all projected U.S. energy production in 2050.[24]

When the world met again in Glasgow, it was to recognize the failure of the Paris accords, and when in 2022, another summit was held, it was still to understand how far we were from the optimism of the Paris agreements. The new U.S. plans passed by the Biden administration and the Democratic majority, may inch America closer to the standards promised, but given the uncertainty of the economy and the divisiveness of American political life, this is certainly not a secure path.

Of course, reading this history is incomplete without also understanding what the energy companies and their lobbyists were doing when the scientists were out measuring carbon. They were busy. They had been paid to be. Let us consider the case of Exxon, which of course, used to be called Standard Oil.

Standard Oil was the largest American oil-producing, oil-transporting, oil-refining, oil-marketing company on the planet, and it was a complete vertical monopoly. It was established in 1870 by John D. Rockefeller and Henry Flagler. Flagler would become known as the founder of the first railroad to Florida and the developer of Florida as a vacation destination, transforming mosquito-ridden swamps into beachside property for his wealthy friends.[25] (Ironically enough, his fabulous mansion right on the beach is regularly now threatened by floods as sea-level rise threatens to flood most of the state.) Rockefeller invented a new way to extract oil from Pennsylvania and then Texas oil fields, called the "combine," which extracts the crude oil he shipped (and got special rebates for, unavailable to others) to his refinery in Ohio. It was the largest oil refinery in the world of its time, and John D. Rockefeller was the world's richest man.[26] This happened in part because he dominated every single aspect of energy production and swept it all into a novel business entity called "the trust." The trust meant that from the milling of the machines that dug the oil, to the freight lines, to the refineries, and for each product—petroleum, kerosene, motor oil for every engine, synthetic rubber for every gasket,—and all the logistics to make this all run were under Rockefeller's control, fixing price at every stage, and generating enough money to make his name a synonym for wealth and power.

They pumped so much oil, the thick black slick of it pouring out over the rigs, over the soil, that even the growing American industrial market could not buy it all, and Standard Oil became the first multinational company. First, they expanded to China. In 1890, Standard Oil's plan was to first distribute free tin lanterns, stamped with the company name, that could not work with vegetable oil, the standard fuel at the time, but burned brightly with kerosene, which was only available from the Standard Oil company salesmen who returned to each village new oil in hand. Production and sales of kerosene increased so rapidly it soon exceeded even Chinese demand, and the company began viewing other export markets. China had became Standard Oil's largest market in Asia, and it was the largest single U.S. investment in all of Asia. By 1903, Standard Oil was in Orville and Wilbur Wright's Kitty Hawk airplane, and in Henry Ford's new "quadricycle." By 1906, it had begun to operate in the British-controlled Middle East. Standard Oil controlled 91% of all oil production and 85% of all final sales of oil. Henry Ford's "Model T" began production, upping the need for petroleum in every city in the world.

By 1909, the U.S. Justice Department finally had enough and sued Standard Oil for illegal monopoly practices under the newly crafted Sherman Act. The case went all the way to the Supreme Court:

> On May 15, 1911, the US Supreme Court upheld the lower court judgment and declared the Standard Oil group to be an "unreasonable" monopoly under the Sherman Antitrust Act, Section II. It ordered Standard to break up into 34 independent companies with different boards of directors, the biggest two of the companies were Standard Oil of New Jersey (which became Exxon) and Standard Oil of New York (which became Mobil). Standard's president, John D. Rockefeller, had long since retired from any management role. But, as he owned a quarter of the shares of the resultant companies, and those share values mostly doubled, he emerged from the dissolution as the richest man in the world. The dissolution had actually propelled Rockefeller's personal wealth.[27]

Rockefeller solidified his position as the richest man in the world, as the initial income of these individual enterprises proved to be much bigger than that of a single larger company. Its successors such as ExxonMobil or Chevron are still among the companies with the largest revenues in the world. The chairman, Darren Woods, made $1.7 million (base pay) and $15,800,290 (benefits and perks) in 2021, and Exxon profits are up again for a third year in 2022.[28] To put that number in perspective, let's use the metrics of this book: it would fund digging and maintaining a well, providing fresh, clean water and hygiene education to 2,000 villages, or clean water for 3,950,072 people a year, which means that all the women and girls who had been spending their day walking to get water could go to school, and some the babies that died from infant diarrheal disease might, perhaps, have a chance at growing up.[29] This is not to mention that gas and oil prices have risen dramatically, so that the profit is built on the backs of people shuddering with cold because they cannot afford to heat their homes. In 2022, ExxonMobil gave him a 10 percent base pay salary increase to $1.88 million, and an increase of his total package to $23.6 million, according to the Security and Exchange Commission, as oil companies made record profits. One man.[30]

While you, reader, consider that, let us move on to the role his company played in our history of climate change, which as you recall, took a major turn in 1988, when there was enough consensus among nations to form the UN IPCC. That summer, James Hanson, the NASA scientist in charge of the Earth Science division at the Goddard Space Institute, a NASA section, had given testimony to the U.S. Congress about global warming. Hanson is a serious and quiet man. His testimony and the hearing, which took place, famously, on one of the hottest days yet recorded in Washington DC, was the result of a decade of accumulating research by environmentalists, scientists, and policymakers, but it was Hanson's authority and earnestness that won the day. (I would later witness this when he gave a presentation to the NASA National Advisory Board, of which I was a member, about the melting of the permafrost and ice that had defined Inuit villages in Alaska, and how entire villages had to be rescued and moved away from the shore. All that he had forecasted in 1988 had come to pass for them, facts on the ground.)

> Exxon had been tracking the carbon dioxide problem since before it was Exxon. In 1957, scientists from its predecessor, Humble Oil, published a study analyzing "the enormous quantity of carbon dioxide" contributed to the atmosphere since the Industrial Revolution "from the combustion of fossil fuels."[31]

This was studied by the American Petroleum Institute (API) in 1955, which found that fossil fuel combustion had increased the atmospheric carbon by 5%, by Edward Teller, the scientist responsible for America's nuclear weapons program and a confidant of presidents, in 1967 and 1959 in major speeches to the API, and to the American Chemical Society:

> When the temperature does rise by a few degrees over the whole globe there is a possibility that the icecaps will start melting and the level of the oceans will begin to rise.[32]

In 1968, the API did another report, informing all its members, all the energy companies, that we would face "significant temperature changes by the year 2000." In 1972, the National Petroleum Council, another industry group, agreed with that timing, and in 1978, Exxon scientists wrote a memo, saying that humanity then had only five to ten years "before hard decisions regarding changes in energy strategies might become critical."[33] Ten years later, after at yet another Congressional hearing, Exxon's Duane LeVine began to raise a new sort of alarm—that a global treaty to regulate carbon emission seemed imminent, perhaps as soon as 1992, and he was worried.

"Such a treaty should avoid adopting a Draconian policy that might lead to premature limitations on fossil fuel." More importantly for our story, he had consulted with a public relations officer and came to say—despite what the API and his own scientists knew—that there was uncertainty on the science itself.[34]

The API followed soon after with a "Position on Global Climate Change" that called the scientific research a "limited understanding" and, along with Exxon, sent these policy statements to the young UN IPCC, joined by Shell, Texaco, BP, and the Saudi Aramco.[35] As Naomi Oreskes and Erik Conway document in their work:

> Meanwhile, the companies began to attack Hansen's testimony and what looked like governmental consensus for change with a veritable dust storm of doubt. They established a lobbying organization called "The Global Climate Coalition." They took as their logo a green colored earth, and as their mission statement on their website "The GCC was established to coordinate business participation in the international policy debate on the issue of global climate change and global warming."[36]

> Its motto: "growth in a global environment." But of course, a green earth was the furthest thing from its collective mind. Designed to look vaguely like an environmental NGO, the group presented itself that way and was granted NGO status not only at the Kyoto meeting but at every single climate change gathering between 1989 and 2001. The founding members were ExxonMobil, Phillips Petroleum, API, the National Coal Association, the United States Chamber of Commerce, the American Forest and Paper Association and Edison Electric.[37]

GCC was the largest industry group—it included virtually every industry that would be impacted by regulation of fossil fuel consumption, eventually representing over 230,000 businesses. Industry sectors represented included aluminum, paper, transportation, power generation, petroleum, chemical, and all the major oil companies. It spent over $1 million a year on lobbying, on paying scientists who they could find to agree with them $2,000 per op-ed, on funding local "grassroots" groups to lobby Congress, renting buses for them, bringing them to Washington, DC. The Koch Industry Group, now awakened to the serious risk that their trillion-dollar integrated energy and manufacturing project could be threatened by global carbon constrained, poured money into GCC and, later, other groups.

> Koch Industries realized early on that it would be a financial disaster for the firm if the American government regulated carbon emissions or made companies pay a price for releasing carbon into the atmosphere. The effects of such a policy would be measured over decades for Koch. The company has billions of dollars sunk into the complex and expensive infrastructure of crude-oil processing. If a limit on greenhouse gas emissions were imposed, it could dampen demand for oil and diminish the value of those assets and their future sales. The total dollar losses would likely be measured in trillions over a period of 30 years or more. In the face of this political problem, David Koch and his brother Charles built a political influence machine that is arguably unrivaled by any in corporate America. Construction on the Koch political machine began in the 1970s, after Charles Koch took over the family company. He and David began funding and orchestrating a political project to restrain government power in the United States through lobbying, think tanks and political donations. The machine is so effective because it is multifaceted. In addition to one of the largest registered corporate lobbying offices in the country, located about two blocks from the White House, there is a constellation of Koch-funded think tanks and university centers. They all convey a consistent message: that government programs can only cause more harm than good and that market forces alone must shape human society. And their work is bolstered by a private network of donors that David and Charles Koch assembled over the years, a network that gives donations at levels rivaling a political party. Finally, Koch controls a "boots on the ground" army in the form of Americans for Prosperity, a network of employees and volunteers who knock on doors, attend rallies to protest climate change legislation, and visit the offices of any lawmakers who seem likely to cross Koch Industries on the issue.[38]

They used front groups, paid by industry with parodic names like Citizens for the Environment or the Information Council on the Environment—which sounded so convincingly "green," or the Advancement of Sound Science Coalition, meant to sound like the actual scientific group, the American Academy for the Advancement of Science.[39]

A $1.8 million disinformation campaign was launched by GCC to defeat tax increases on oil companies, and even the Republic "cap and trade" plan was considered, eventually, too regulatory. And that Kyoto treaty? The GCC spent $13 million just on a single ad campaign to defeat it.[40] Even after the Bush and Cheney administration made climate change denial the de facto policy of the government, industry-led groups hired actors to attend town hall meetings pretending to be "concerned citizens" designed to confuse the issues,[41] or support construction of new power plants.

Meanwhile, the Marshall Institute—member of GCC—began an aggressive campaign against the growing scientific consensus circulating a "white paper" called "Global Warming: What Does the Science Say?" and the authors, physicists who had done none of their own research in the field, nevertheless had strong political clout, and they briefed members of powerful offices in the U.S. government, the Office of Management and Budget; the Office of Policy Development; and the Council of Economic Advisors. What did the "science" say? You can watch the 2007 film made with interviews from this period—2.5 million people viewed it in the United Kingdom, with an audience share of 11.5%,[42] in which old clips of the Cold War physicists, Fred Singer and Fred Steitz, among others, deploy their various strategies to cast doubt: First, they say that the warming is not so bad—there was actually a decline, as temperature goes up and down "naturally." Next, they say that even if there is warming, well, it is because of the sun.

> The central claim of the Marshall Institute was that the warming that Hansen and others had found didn't track the historical increase in CO2. The majority of the warming had been prior to 1940—prior to the majority of the carbon dioxide emissions. Then there was a cooling trend through 1975, and a return to warming. Since the warming didn't parallel the increase in CO2, it must have been caused, they claimed, by the Sun. Drawing on sunspot and carbon-14 data from tree rings, they argued that the Sun had entered into a period of higher energy output during the 19th century, and that this solar output increase (of about 0.3 percent) was responsible for the climate warming to date.[43]

This sounds (and, in the movie they made later, looks) extremely persuasive, like a normal scientific dispute. However, it is not. The "data" they present are only a cherry-picked piece of a larger graph; they claim volcanos emit as much greenhouse gas as human industry, and this is simply untrue, as the British Antarctic Survey notes:

> Current annual emissions from fossil fuel burning and cement production are estimated to be around 100 times greater than average annual volcanic emissions of CO_2. Large volcanoes cannot significantly perturb the CO2, concentration of the atmosphere is apparent from the ice core and atmospheric record of CO_2 concentrations, which shows a steady rise during the industrial period, with no unusual changes after large eruptions.[44]

But while scientists objected, the Marshall Institute report not only affected administration policy but was covered in the *Wall Street Journal*. Now, when the press wanted to do a story about the odd observable changes in the climate, they saw two sides to a story, in which the sides neatly seemed to match up with the increasingly polarized political debates. Unlike, say, the discovery of new elements, or new treatments for childhood leukemia, discoveries in this one field of science were suddenly "doubted" as true. As Naomi Oreskes and Eric Conway point out, the public relations firms behind campaigns to discredit any science that might impact on profits—tobacco, ozone, or oil—had a playbook. The same voices that opposed government regulation on one industry—tobacco—show up to oppose government regulations on carbon emissions. Some also opposed the teaching of evolution. Journalist Christopher Booker, who denies climate change, also is concerned about the theory of evolution, stating that Darwinists "rest their case on nothing more than blind faith and unexamined a priori assumptions"[45] a steady attack on science gained strength. Some other deniers have clear conflicts of interests:

> Australian geologist Professor Ian Plimer is the director of three Australian mining companies—listed by www.sourcewatch.org as Ivanhoe Mines, CBH Resources and Kefi Minerals—and a prominent climate-change denier in Australia and globally. With these lucrative interests, it is unsurprising that his 2009 book "Heaven and Earth" has been labeled the "denier's bible." Guardian journalist George Monbiot, in a highly publicized debate with Plimer, described the book as "filled with fabrication after fabrication, simple untruths, repeated again and again."[46]

Others dislike regulations on the market per se and are willing (and given the platform to) simply create fake facts. Here, Lord Nigel Lawson, chair of his foundation the Global Warming Policy Foundations, invited to write op-eds in leading papers in the United Kingdom, and invited to be the "other side" against a scientist, claims in an interview:

> What is interesting is that in the second half of the 20th century, when there were huge increase [sic] in carbon emissions, so far from there being a greater increase in sea level, the official figures show that, if anything, there was a slightly smaller increase in sea level in the second half of the 20th century than in the first half.[47]

This is complete nonsense. Sea levels have steadily risen, and according to the latest UNIPCC report:

> Between 1901 and 2010, global sea levels rose by 19 centimeters—an average of about 1.7 millimeters per year. But looking at the last few decades, it's clear sea level rise is speeding up. Between 1993 and 2010, sea levels rose by 3.2 mm per year—almost twice the long-term average.[48]

It would be terrible enough if one just considered the net effect of global warming, but as we have seen in earlier chapters, the effects of paralyzing doubt that drives inaction affects the poor disproportionally. It is the vulnerable, the "ones at the back" of human civilization, the ones on the sand ridge surrounded by rising seawater in Bangladesh, the straggling chain of migrants, toddlers and grandparents, fleeing from drought-ravaged places in Central America, that are at mortal risk. Amalek comes in situations of doubt and confusion, but this time, the people cannot turn away for forty years, because we do not have forty years left.

Global warming is caused by a handful of practices, largely the wildly lucrative practice of pulling oil and gas out of the ground and refining and selling it. The extraction companies have created a false debate; they have marginalized scientists and in many cases acted to gin up opposition that has tried to destroy scientific careers. This is so lucrative and so profitable, and so firmly in the hands of a tiny group of billionaires, that it will be extraordinarily difficult, this time, to stop such a tribe of Amalekites—but they must be seen clearly for who they are. They are digging up and selling five times what scientists say will destroy our planet and they will keep digging and selling and digging and selling until every last drop of oil is gone, as if in a frenzy, no matter how much money they have, no matter how much they are driving the earth to collapse; they are spending millions to cast doubt over possible solutions. They have come to make money, and their project will destroy the lives of the poor. The word for this can only be sin. To really stop, in the next decade, honestly, will mean the end of this enterprise. And while it is nice to make personal changes, and of course important, my call to understand the evil at the heart of the enterprise of energy extraction is a serious matter, and it will take a significant, serious, and global civic movement that is just as determined as they are to stop them. Such a change will need to draw on many sources, far harder than recycling, and even significant personal sacrifice, and it will take at the very least all of that as well. We will need much courage and many arguments, of which these texts are one.

In this book, I have argued that we are exiles on this earth, whose resources and land are on loan from God. We have been expelled from Eden to this place, we have survived the Flood and the folly to come to this moment, and if we sin, if we are tempted by the powerful who sin, we deepen the exile. The rabbinic texts were written in the long period of powerlessness, but they remembered that justice would at some point be restored, and at times, thinking of exile and its end, they imagined that sinfulness would be exposed:

> And when the exiles are assembled, judgment will be visited on the wicked, as it says, And I will turn my hand upon thee and purge away thy dross as with lye, and it is written further, And I will restore thy judges as at the first. And when judgment is visited on the wicked, transgressors cease, and presumptuous sinners are included with them, as it is written. But the destruction of the transgressors and of the sinners shall be together, and they that forsake the Lord shall be consumed. And when the transgressors have disappeared, the horn of the righteous is exalted, as it is written, All the horns of the wicked also will I cut off, but the horns of the righteous shall be lifted up. (Megillah 17b)

Let me end by forestalling the obvious, horrifying question: Do I mean we are justified in actually harming the sinning CEOs? Heaven forfend, that is not the job of the philosopher; we are not the ones with the armies. But we do need to do the philosophically equivalent thing: we need to name them: son of murderers, bad guys. We cannot mistake our enemies: we need to recognize them and we need to blame them. We need to erase their terrible lies. We need to remove doubt.

In my final chapter, I will consider the implications of such a claim. What do we do when we wait for judgment of history? What can one do as a scholar, or a reader or a citizen?

8
You Must Interrupt Your Life

The UN Intergovernmental Panel on Climate Change (IPCC) issued a report today that says the effects of climate change are already occurring on all continents and across the oceans. The world, in many cases, is ill-prepared for risks from a changing climate. The report also concludes that there are opportunities to respond to such risks, though the risks will be difficult to manage with high levels of warming.

The UNIPCC issued a final report, saying human influence on the climate system is clear and growing, with impacts observed on all continents. If left unchecked, climate change will increase the likelihood of severe, pervasive and irreversible impacts for people and ecosystems. The gathering risks of climate change are so profound that they could stall or even reverse generations of progress against poverty and hunger if greenhouse gas emissions continue at a runaway pace. Failure to reduce emission, the groups of scientists and other experts found, could threaten everyone. Society faces food shortages, refugee crises, the flooding of major cities and entire island nations, the mass extinction of plants and animals and a climate so drastically altered it might become dangerous for people to work or play outside. (*New York Times*, International Edition, November 3, 2014)

Nations need to move away much faster from fossil fuels to retain any hope of preventing a perilous future on an overheated planet, according to a major new report on climate change released on Monday, although they have made some progress because of the falling costs of clean energy. The report by the Intergovernmental Panel on Climate Change, a body of experts convened by the United Nations, warns that unless countries drastically accelerate efforts over the next few years to slash their emissions from coal, oil and natural gas, the goal of limiting global warming to 1.5 degrees Celsius, or 2.7 degrees Fahrenheit, will likely be out of reach by the end of this decade. That's the threshold beyond which scientists say the dangers of global warming—including worsening floods, droughts, wildfires and ecosystem collapse—grow considerably. Humans have already heated the planet by an average of 1.1 degrees Celsius since the 19th century, largely by burning fossil fuels for energy.

But the task is daunting: Holding warming to just 1.5 degrees Celsius would require nations to collectively reduce their planet-warming emissions roughly 43 percent by 2030 and to stop adding carbon dioxide to the atmosphere altogether by the early 2050s, the report found. By contrast, current policies by governments are only expected to reduce global emissions by a few percentage points this decade. Last year, fossil fuel emissions worldwide rebounded to near-record highs after a brief dip as a result of the coronavirus pandemic.

"This is a climate emergency," said United Nations Secretary General António Guterres, adding that wealthy economies and corporations "are not just turning a blind eye; they are adding fuel to the flames. They are choking our planet, based on their vested interests and historic investments in fossil fuels, when cheaper, renewable solutions provide green jobs, energy security and greater price stability." (*New York Times*, April 4, 2022)

As global warming passes certain limits, dire changes will probably become irreversible, the researchers said, including the loss of polar ice sheets and the death of coral reefs. The researchers said that even at the current level of warming, about 1.1 degrees Celsius (2 degrees Fahrenheit) above preindustrial levels, some of these self-sustaining changes might have already begun. (*New York Times*, September 8, 2022)

The Last Place

We are living in the Last Place. There is no other world for us, no second chance. This one world is so beautiful, with the sweet green willows shushing in the August breeze, and the halting, diamond turns of water from small plastic sprinklers, the ordinary grace of a swerve of bright white birds and the spun net of high, floating clouds. The blue-green weed called miner's lettuce, abundant in the sidewalks of the city, the first snow on the black iron railings, the wet tear and tear of it, and the shocking shimmer: the yellow of oak in October. The trailing guitar from a block away, the way that wood rubs dark gold and soft from use, the crack of a hammer, clear and high, the sway of each of us on the train, in wet wool coats, the bodies of others in the soft black coats, elbows, the downward glancing grin, the way the old man down the alley whistles a song he learned as a boy. *Seedtime and harvest time, cold and heat, summer and winter, day and night, always and again* (Genesis 8:22).

We have covered the earth, so we can drive the buses and the cars, made the last place we have a good place for driving around, for working. We need to work, and so much of the work is good. We have made the Last Place with wide white streets. And here are all the usual things we know: this is a world so clean and easy for people with wealth, so hard and dirty for the poor; that the seas are polluted with the nitrogen we use to fertilize the fields; the forests are chopped for paper; species are blinkering out; we know this. We sound the depths, we dig up what is left of life crushed to carbon beneath us, and we burn it: to make important things, really—hospital intensive care units, high school libraries, synthetically derived insulin, ambulances and steel beams for the new clinic, the high school library. But we burn it for nothing, too, really, for vanity and emptiness, and the tracing of that smoke lies over us now, invisible, warming the oceans, then the air, then all of the Last Place. Nothing about the usual things we know, the essential, terrible, injustice of it all, has stopped the burning. In fact, in the year those article were published, we loaded up the air with more carbon than ever and every year since, we have escalated our use of fossil fuels, barely pausing for a global pandemic. We have been told clearly that this burning is deadly, and it has not made us change a thing. Our lives continue, seamlessly, lucky.

But we have gotten that Intergovernmental Panel on Climate Change (IPCC) warning letter, and for scholars of religion, and for you, reader, we hear this as a prophecy: A storm is coming, it is already on our own horizon; it has been coming for years. The first mention of the fact that human beings might be changing the "nature of the air," the term for "weather" in Hebrew, came in 1957, written exactly at the place in which the American Academy of Religion (AAR) had gathered for our 2014 annual meeting, during which I delivered the address that became this chapter. There in San Diego, Professor Roger Revelle, founder of the University of California San Diego and of the Scripps Institute of Oceanography, first published his data. Now it is clear he was prescient. Let me first say it in the words of the large and serious consensus body of the scientists who have been researching the issue for the last thirty years, the IPCC, whose chairman came to speak to that AAR gathering in 2014: "Human influence on the climate system is unequivocal. Greenhouse gases are at the highest level in human history. The changes are unprecedented and will cause long-lasting changes in all components of the climate system, increasing severe, pervasive, and irreversible impacts for people and ecosystems."[1]

I rewrote this chapter five years ago now, and finished the editing of that speech nearly a decade after that meeting of the AAR, and the reports from the IPCC are only grimmer, for many of the things we were warned about have come to pass. In the summer of 2019, we were told not to go outside unless we must, for it was too hot. I have a snapshot of my littlest granddaughter at eighteen months old, in a turquoise surgical mask as she and her sister, four years old, also in her surgical mask, were packed into a car because Oakland, and the San Francisco Bay Area, had become so smoky from the Paradise fire, 500 miles away in the Sierra foothills, upwind, that they had to leave. Cities have flooded; Miami floods now on a regular basis. The beach I wrote about only a few years ago is smaller now, the ends of the beach where rocks tumble down to the sea closed by the tides almost all the time, not just at high tide. One does not have to go on an investigative trip to exotic places to see dying corals reefs, or melting Arctic glaciers, from a private plane, for an ordinary season on your own porch will tell you what is occurring now.

In 2022, Pakistan was inundated with terrible floods, and over one-third of the country was covered in water. In Kentucky, and in Germany, rivers flooded towns and simply swept them away. Winters meant floods, and summers now, impossible heat waves; the summer and fall of 2022 had story after story about drought and entrapping heat, and in Europe and in California, reservoirs and rivers sunk away, their last water puddling and vanishing into mist. First the hunger stones, called because they had despairing messages hacked into their sides in medieval droughts, appeared and then the rivers sank lower. Navigation ceased.

Let me say it plainly in this chapter: Everything we count on, everything we know, every formula, and story, and Scripture takes place in a world in which the climate has been essentially stable and predictable for ten thousand years. Every text written, every idea about faith, every song sung, or harvest planted, has been created in this Last Place. Because of the amount of greenhouse gases burned and extracted, humans have already changed the world for the next thousand years. Now at stake is only how very bad it will be. This means that the global temperature has already risen to 1.0°C, which is .2°C more than the first time I wrote this speech, and the already extracted energy (oil and gas), if burned, as is likely, may raise the global temperature to close to 3°C.[2]

I want to be clear, for no one reading this book can say: I did not know. And that was my goal in undertaking this research, and my goal as a president of the world's largest organization of scholars of religion, and one of America's largest scholarly organizations. As an American bioethicist, I wanted us to face the most important issue in bioethics and the central moral imperative of our time. Climate change, and the way that it threatens the lives of the most vulnerable, ought to be a critical focus of scholarship, I thought, and more: it ought to be a critical focus of ordinary speech and, finally, of action. I wrote this chapter as a speech to the scholars of the AAR. But that was not enough, and they are not enough. So, I write now, to you, to mark this time, this day, this moment and because if you read it, you might be able to consider the urgency with which I call to you. I wanted to say, when I gave that talk to my colleagues: Here we stopped, and here we started to think differently about what we could do. We stopped acting as if we were grasshoppers, terrified Israelites on a journey home, but overwhelmed and already defeated. I write now to overcome doubt, and I write, because like many others, I do not want to be ashamed of doing nothing when my grandchildren ask me why I did not know. In my talk, I asked my colleagues and friends to do something very simple, just to stop once every seven years, instead of coming to our big annual meeting, with its huge carbon burden and unsustainable practices. And while they rose to their feet in applause, nobody really did want to miss the annual meeting after all. It is very hard to stop doing something you love, that you do every year, hard to stop your life, I know. So that talk seemed to deliver little. I will return to this.

But—what would make you halt? What would stop your busy life? What would be so important that you would sacrifice that trip you feel you must take? What would interrupt you?

Being Interrupted

What do I mean by "interruption"? I begin in an ordinary definitional way. The concept of interruption signifies both "betweenness" (inter) and brokenness (rupture.) To interrupt is, according to the *New American Dictionary*, "to stop the continuous progress of action; to stop (someone speaking) by saying or doing something or, to break the continuity of a line; or to obstruct (something, especially block a view)."

To be a being is to be a being living in the illusion of a life that is a continuous, busy process. We are committed to continuity, to historicity, to plans and prospects, to the order of things, their repetitions, patterns, and sequences. We expect, rather touchingly, that we live in a consistent, progressive narrative, and the interruption of being is a break in the story that we want to resume—we have made promises, we have bought tickets, we have a book contract, we are on the way to salvation, we need quiet for our mindfulness and not that noisy kid, or that cry in the dark.

To some extent, we resent interruption because of this narrative ideal. We have an important product to produce, we tell ourselves, and even if the product is some unit of reflection or some ephemeral conference paper, to be interrupted is to be taken, snatched from our work to some other call, some other's need. To be interrupted is to be broken in to. It is to have one's view blocked by something one does not want to see—say the beggar, say the warming air, the acidifying ocean—to have one's talk stopped, the speech act, the professing, a declaration in your own voice, your own needs, your own story, stopped: a disagreement, perhaps, or someone calling out for help, a question, a story orthogonal to your own.

But if we are to understand the character of our being as temporal and located, and if we are to create a theory that can ground a decent response to the question of how we ought to live, how we ought to live in a world that is burning, it cannot be based on this idea of the pristine journey, or the next new thing. "The arc of the moral universe is long but it bends toward justice," we learn from Martin Luther King, who learned it from the 19th century cleric Theodore Parker, but it is not a smooth resolve: it is a very sturdy line, and our pulling makes cracks and fissures—we live in the spaces between the rupture, and if we are to do anything as scholars or as citizens it is that we work always in light of that arc but that we know it needs repair.

The world as we know it is not flat, yet it is altogether flattened into a series of ceaseless falsities that present as actual challenges, and, in their quotidian necessity, make us despair. It is a world of totality, to take a term from Levinas, and we are told and we tell ourselves a story of seamless, totalizing desire, each little event, each little trial, each little flattery presenting as if we were the only one in the room with our particular victory just ahead. Here is what it means to be modern: we believe that everything can be under control, ordered in advance, the costs and the benefits weighed up. But into our lives, and utterly out of our control or our will, comes the complete otherness of interruption. Is it a surprise that we understand interruption as a problem, the distraction of being within a world of necessity, and not, for example, as we would if we were medieval scholars—as the voice of God? Is it surprising we do not see the necessity of disorder? The chaos of the utter otherness of being—all that is not-self coming knocking at the door; all that is not-work come calling, just when you are writing your big idea.

For what are we interrupted? There are the thousand small serious interruptions; there are the questions of students, and their needs; there is the constant interruption of cleaning and clearing, which goes by the name of "administration" in institutions; there are the petty calls of email, the cascade of media noise, the sense of news constantly on a crawl beneath the actual work of our lives. There are bodies that need ordinal tending: children, the old, everyone who needs us to look at the drawing, to attend to the wound, to lift them up in our arms, right *now*.

For what are we interrupted? For the grandest dramas and greatest joys of human life. For the befallenness of illness, the birth of children, for true love, for desperate need, and, of course, for death itself. This is the deep praxis of interruption, and if you are a moral being, you will have done well to be a being who has broken off, who has stopped. This is so vividly true about our lives that it is obvious, but unseen, "something that we know when no one asks us, but no longer know when we are supposed to give an account of it is something we need to *remind* ourselves of,"[3] as Ludwig Wittgenstein noted in describing the task of philosophy.

Interruption as Theology

Here is what a theologian might say: We are interrupted by the insistent call of God, and when we respond rightly, it is prayer, it is action for the widow and the orphan, it is standing and saying—*hineni*, I am here. Yet it is hard to respond rightly, and from this we flee in terror, not, as moderns, to be sure, into Great Fish, or toward Tarshish, or into deserts, but into work, meetings, parking applications, email, Netflix, grant achievable goals in a list. In my field, bioethicists seek out ever more unlikely cases or misguided desires. We consider obscure fears, cool movies, read the *New Yorker* about improbable technologies—all the places we go when we are in flight. We are in flight and the world is tiny, distant, far away. Here is the image I mean: it is George Bush, staring at the wreckage and flooding after hurricane Katrina, that great climate disaster, from his airplane window, and we know it, because it is our own gaze. We are in flight, even people who know better, people who actually read the Prophets; we are off to the metaphorical caves. Who wants this interruption, this reminder, this challenge, this *politics*?

A theology of interruption demands that we attend to the interruption in a different way, which is of course to say, to act as if the interruption were the

Real, and the other stuff of our lives the Distraction. How to live such a theological ethics—attention to the call of the Other, and alert, always, to the call of God, without seeming like a madwoman or a religious fanatic? What would such a life look like?

For a Jew, of course, there is Shabbat, made ever more absolute a stop in time because of the constancy of the machines that we admire and pet and constantly speak into. In the interruption of the Sabbath, we turn only to one another, to Torah, to the grammar of prayer. We turn to actual faces, speak to actual friends, see their eyes and hands. This is perhaps too romanticized a version, for we also eat and complain, but it is not a trivial act, in modernity, to make a Shabbat, as a sign, to honor by the gesture and the interruption. And for any reader of Hebrew Scripture, there is the commanded interruption of the *Shmita* year—the sabbatical year, the year of release, when after every six years all agricultural work stops, and a sabbatical year begins, the fields are left fallow, and every living creature, animal, and person can eat from the field and the vineyard and the wide open world, when the boundaries of ownership and possession are broken so that the poor can take what they need, when all debts are released. It is a practice that is not metaphysical, but describes an actual theo-political economy—in fact the year of the meeting when this presidential address was written, 5775 in the Jewish calendar, a Sabbatical year, practiced and observed in Israel and throughout the Jewish community.

These acts of praxis, the acts of attention within lived communities of faith, these interruptions, are signifiers that the human person, each of us, a person within a people, living in actual places and standing next to actual others, is willing to act—even partially, even briefly. You can act if you hear something, someone, as if something that is not sold, not portrayed quantitatively, measured, displayed, or advertised, actually matters to being. This something heard is a part of one's self. It is not the only possibility for how to hear, but religions structure the practice of interruption, which is a moment of justice, or beauty, or compassion, or grace, in such an unjust world. And thus, to interrupt your life is a theological claim.

Let me argue that the text of many Scriptures, surely Hebrew Scripture, the New Testament, and the Quran, is written as a sort of argument, with in-between narratives and a chance to answer back. The Quran is written in the second-person address: "Have you heard?" There are breaks, discontinuations, lacunae, ruptures of people speaking back, leaving room for centuries of *responsa*, commentary, rupture, public reception and fierce public fights, and of course academic scholarship. As scriptural readers, as

I explain in a previous chapter, we have the texts, in which in narrative after narrative the given, stable, hierarchies of power, the truth claim, the natural order of the empirical world, the dark and steady pull of cultural customs, even the sequence of narrative, is interrupted by God. Let me turn to some examples of the story, interrupted. There are many in the Torah which I ask you to consider: first, the Great Flood texts and then the pivotal story of Abraham—who interrupts, according to the medieval commentator Rashi, a conversation with God to attend to the three strangers who show up, hungry, at his tent—and of course, the story of the Daughters of Zelephophad, women who interrupt the biblical narrative of the allocation of property to insist on their inheritance.

Texts of Interruption

For the rabbis of the Talmud, the question of interruption is one of fascinated concern: in repeated, different, and prolonged discussions, the rabbis debate when interruption is permitted: on the Sabbath, on public reading of Torah, on a Nazirite vow, or in study, work, or prayer. Interruption is, of course, the very method of teaching and learning and ethical decision-making in Jewish thought, and one interrupts with story on story on story, each disagreement challenging the half-finished sentence of the previous argument. Perhaps a life lived in the midst of interruption is exactly the point of such a theological discourse.

But the Talmud, when it speaks of interruption, has something very specific in mind, a specific story, called the Great Interruption. Consider the scene of the Great Interruption, described in rabbinic literature: One day, the house of study was suddenly opened to all. To everyone: the poor, the ugly, the uncertain, a great interruption of the hierarchy of learning that was the very center of the imaginary of rabbinic Jewish life, carefully crafted and described, after the Roman destruction of the Second Temple:

> A Tanna taught: On that day the doorkeeper was removed, and permission was given to the disciples to enter. For Rabban Gamaliel had issued a proclamation [saying]. No disciple whose character does not correspond to his exterior may enter the Beth ha-Midrash. On that day many stools were added. R. Johanan said: There is a difference of opinion on this matter between Abba Joseph b. Dosethai and the Rabbis: one [authority] says that

four hundred stools were added, and the other says seven hundred. Rabban Gamaliel became alarmed and said: Perhaps, God forbid, I withheld Torah from Israel! . . .

A Tanna taught: *Eduyyoth* was formulated on that day—and wherever the expression "on that day" is used, it refers to *that* day—and there was no halacha about which any doubt existed in the Beth ha-Midrash which was not fully elucidated. . . . On that day Judah, an Ammonite proselyte, came before them in the Beth ha-Midrash. He said to them: Am I permitted to enter the assembly?

R. Joshua said to him: You are permitted to enter the congregation. Said Rabban Gamaliel to him: Is it not already laid down: "an Ammonite or Moabite shall not enter into the assembly of the Lord?" R. Joshua replied to him: Do Ammon and Moab still reside in their original homes? Sennacherib, King of Assyria long ago went up and mixed up all the nations, as it says, "I have removed the bounds of the peoples and have robbed their treasures and have brought down as one their mighty inhabitants." . . . Said Rabban Gamaliel to him: But has it not been said: "But afterward I will bring back the captivity of the children of Ammon, says the Lord," so that they have already returned? To which R. Joshua replied: And has it not been said, "And I will turn the captivity of My people Israel," and they have not yet returned? Forthwith they permitted him to enter the congregation. Rabban Gamaliel thereupon said: This being the case, I will go and apologize to R. Joshua. When he reached his house he saw that the walls were black. He said to him: From the walls of your house it is apparent that you are a charcoal-burner. He replied: Alas for the generation of which you are the leader, seeing that you know nothing of the troubles of the scholars, their struggles to support and sustain themselves! He said to him: I apologize. Forgive me. (Brachot 28a)

What is happening in this narrative, which describes the strange day? This is a complex text, with side references to other biblical narratives and characters the original readers would have known. What is this text teaching us? Who is that tanna that appears in the middle?

Here is a lesson about the enormous interruption. On one day, the rules of the language game and the admission standards of the rabbinic study hall were upended. "On that day" the halls of the academy were opened to everyone—so many came—was it four hundred or seven hundred? Despite the shocked response of Rabbi Gamaliel, the wealthy putative leader, an entire tractate of the Talmud is created that day, and every question of the law was answered with certainty—the closest thing to a miraculous event for Jews. Even the terms of "race" are undone—an Ammonite can enter the hall of study, for colonialization has interrupted fixed biological lineage, insists this text. A tanna, an unnamed teacher, a compiler of the first generation, during the two hundred years from 10 CE. Usually from Palestine, they are of the generation of the Mishah, and he begins the story. But he is interrupted in the telling with a second story, for something else happens "on that day." There has been a dispute between the wealthy and powerful Rabbi Gamaliel and another rabbinic teacher, Rabbi Joshua, about allowing a convert into the house of study, one with a mixed racial background, and one from a tribe that it is impermissible to marry. Joshua points out that colonialization, war, and subjugation has created something like stateless people from all the tribes, destroying their nations, their fortunes, and their patrimony. Empires fall. Gamaliel insists on racial purity but he is wrong, and he needs to apologize. Gamaliel goes to ask for forgiveness, for he has not fully understood the depths of these changes and when he goes to Joshua's workplace, he sees the terrible poverty of his colleague, Rabbi Joshua, who works at that most desperate of jobs—burning wood into carbon, making charcoal—and the story ends with the critical claim about study itself, that teachers must understand the lives of the poor, and interrupt their professing with these facts: look at the blackened walls of the workplaces of the poor, learn from the poorest, who are also scholars.

The passion for interruption on behalf of the poor continues in later medieval texts, in which prayer can be interrupted for a claim of injustice. In a ninth-century text of interruption, a narrative is preserved in which the leadership of the Ashkenazi community, deep within the long exile in Western Europe, hears a case and decides a particular matter. But the woman who is the subject of the decision is unhappy, and she is determined, even when no one in power will listen to her, to appeal her judgment. And she can. She can take her claim to the synagogue and interrupt the prayer to demand: *Listen to me.*

This is a remarkable moment in Jewish law, a method by which a judgment can be challenged by an interruption in a holy place, of a holy act. What is suggested is an astonishing moral gesture, especially given the elaborate rabbinic limits on interruption of the communal speech act of prayer. But clearly, there is tension between prayer and the needs of others. In the medieval text, it is suggested that the act of justice, the interruption for justice is also a part of the service. It is a radical claim—but it is a clear echo of the day of the Great Interruption: attend to the situation of the poor, see her.

Acts of Interruption

What do narratives and practices tell us about how to be good, about the worth of our lives in a burning time? Why do the rabbis worry about interruption and its protection? Why do I say: *You must interrupt your life?*

To be interrupted is to acknowledge the power of the Other over your being, to see the interrupting, messy, needy Other as entitled to your full attention. But because we do not have a clear account of how one ought to live, to live as a good person at a time of climate chaos, and because full attention is so hard, we struggle to defend what looks like a series of affections or hobbies—we recycle, we bike. Is there a way to articulate a foundational theory behind actions of this sort?

To argue for the need for interruption is to advocate for a moral chronology. We are beings who not only live in particular locations; we live within a time that we order and sort, another sort of accountancy. How we order time, how we understand ourselves as having a past that leads to a present that promises a future, is always an interpretive moral choice, albeit one that seems to us utterly invisible, given. The clearest advocate for this recognition is Walter Benjamin, who alerts us to how we see time, how we experience it as "empty space" along which we endlessly travel, which aligns us with a sort of secular passivity.

Progress, economic growth, more units of things, the storm catches up to our desires and our stuff. Benjamin sees that empty time exists as an homogeneous continuum of moments which have no goal and finally no subject... this sort of time has to be arrested; the thinking that it enables, indeed, necessitates, has to be interrupted.[4]

How unlike the radical breaks of religious texts—the sun that stops in the center of the sky, the Prophets who unmake history and its narrative of subjugation. How unlike the Jewish view of time, Benjamin argues, where "every second was the straight gate through which the Messiah entered." Empty time colludes with institutions that say "it has always been like this; this is impossible to change." It creates people who only yearn for things to stay precisely like they have always been. Or people who want stuff to fill the void. Yet we know that sustaining a world of endless, repeated injustice, an always unthinking movement ahead, is problematic. Argues Benjamin, uninterrupted time "expels any substantive expectation and thus engenders that fatalism that eats at the souls of modern women and men."[5]

That fatalism, and the acceptance. But time can be interrupted at any point by redemption—an exodus can begin, slavery end, a bush can burn, a Messiah can be revealed at the gates of the city, hanging about with the lepers. This is not only a Jewish assertion. A former AAR president, Otto Maduro, argued it from the very podium where I delivered this address. Scripture calls us to live as if at any moment, we could be surprised, awed, ready to rise to action and to grace, ready to welcome the Messiah, ready to appear to one another, in public, because our interruption could alter what we have come to think of as "the course" of history. Moral chronicity is an account of interruption as cessation, and redirection, and of ourselves as creatures with pasts, presents, futures, and as moral agents with the capacity to be ready.

The premise then, is larger than acting well as an individual, for I am responsible for my neighbors' pledge, reminds Levinas in "The Pact"—responsible for her responsibility. We act in this manner not out of fear of the future, although any rational person should at this point be quite sobered by the scientific accounts. The premise is that interruption of time, in the sense that Benjamin meant, leads to the creation of a sort of person with the virtues to which we aspire, but also to an argument that might convince others. And it is that sort of person that is capable of being a moral citizen.

The storm is coming and we are not a discipline of engineers, I told my scholar colleagues then. All we have is words, and the capacity to think, as Hannah Arendt insists, and every citizen is capable of thinking. We must think quite clearly now, about our situation. To "do," to perform "ethics," is to think about how to be good. All of the complex work we do, all the research, is to know the story of how people struggled, spoke, wrote, and heard of the question: How are we, how am I, to live a good life? Now, how ought I to live when the world is burning? Reader, this is true not only for scholars of religion but for any of us.

How to reclaim this sort of thinking from stupid trivialities, or caricature? One way might be to avoid the easy tropes: both the rainbow promises and the apocalyptic threats. And another might be to consider the problem of evil, and how we have so thin a modern theory of evil, and this leaves us uncertain.

But the one direction I want to suggest is to think about interruption as an ethical choice: based in the actualities of our human lives, lives in this time, when, always, there is the knock at the door, and despite all our fears, to be good is to open that door and welcome the stranger. Thinking about interruption, the stopping, the hearing, leads to thinking about hospitality, the act of speech and welcome. Because climate change transforms the world, there will be exile, and there will be strangers on the move. This is vividly true now, when thousands crowd the roads. We must think about welcome, and we must stop, get up, and make the move to answer, for we are the only ones left, and this our home is the Last Place for the traveler. So: a theology of interruption as an ethics for the coming storm. This is the theological basis for the structure of response—but now what do I do?

Consider this case: August 2019

The earthmovers arrived to begin construction during the last monsoon, accompanied by the police. Coconut palms were uprooted. Paddy fields and a mango orchard were removed. A cellphone video taken at the time shows local women screaming, pulling their saris over their heads in deference and falling at the feet of a company representative, begging him to spare their land. Soon, a concrete boundary wall went up. Then, makeshift offices. Then, a chilling message went out to locals who dared protest: The police charged five men, who did not want to give up their land, with criminal trespassing.[6]

What is happening in the text of this case?
The $14 billion Adani Group—a sprawling conglomerate with interests in energy, agribusiness, real estate, and defense, among other sectors—leveraged both business acumen and politics to realize a plan to buy the rich paddy land of Godda, a desperately poor village in India and with the generous support from the Indian government, to build its latest coal-fired power plant there. Godda's famers are not the only ones to have their land used in a coal power energy scheme. Australians, despite warning about the corruption of groundwater by coal mining, were told that if they did not let the Adani group mine, they would miss out on a chance for wealth:

Company representatives made the case to rural Queenslanders that they could gain from opening up the Galilee Basin, the vast coal seam that the Adani Group wanted to exploit. Adani's people held public meetings to explain how India's thirst for coal could lift the area's fortunes. They donated to community organizations, gave money to a basketball arena, made campaign contributions to politicians and hired former political aides to lobby on the company's behalf.[7]

Like Rockefeller, Adani himself owns the entire vertical and horizontal structure of his coal empire. He received vast subsidies from an Indian state that does not have a robust system of support for the poor—including the ones who lost their land in a perfectly legal, but morally questionable swap that allowed Adani to take it. The Western world has largely abandoned coal in favor of natural gas and other energy sources, including of course, clean sources which if people like Adani were appropriately taxed, would make clean energy simple business sense. But Adani is going, because he still can, to suck the last bit of profit, whatever harm he creates.

> "If you just looked at the social costs of air pollution, coal is so bad that, if those are added in as a tax, no coal plant would make economic sense," said Anant Sudarshan, an economist at the University of Chicago who studies energy policy.[8]

This is despite the decades of science I have described in this book, despite all the arguments and meetings. Can you yet see that it is time to interrupt this?

When I returned to the essay that has become this chapter, I was worried. I was concerned that my arguments were unduly emotive, not as scholarly as I would want. I am too haunted by the image of a woman with her sari over her face, begging the man on the tractor to stop. I began to feel like it was an image for all of us, supplicant, our faces in our clothes. I was worried that this book was too trivial. I have summarized the arguments and good work of others and given you some reasons, in the form of religious texts to make an argument and I know that a good argument must stop the tractors. Yet, even as I write that, it can seem absurdly naïve, or too thin a claim. I too, wonder if my arguments will be seen as grasshoppers.

I think that Scripture presents extremely powerful arguments for human action, indeed they have for over two thousand years. These texts offered arguments for justice in the face of human slavery, and in the face of monumental imperial systems. When no other argument worked, when failure was everywhere asserting its logical answer, these narrative, carried in the arms of the losing side, still spoke to the possibility of restoration, even victory. Amalek is a terrible enemy, because he gets inside the mind; in our time, doubt reads as skepticism, irony, or smarts, and who doesn't want to go along with a crowd? But doubt can be defeated, I know this, mine as well as yours, and I hope that this book helps.

We need to act to interrupt because now that humans have loosed one hundred times more carbon every year since the Industrial Age, the planet will do what biological and physical systems do: it will get warmer on the land and the air and the sea, and there is no reason to think it will stop until our civilization itself stops, [9] which of course it will, and how mournful the image of an empty place, our last place, spinning, a world without us.

Three Ways We Interrupt: As Moral Individuals, as Citizens, and as Scholars

When I gave this talk, I wanted to end on a note of possibility, so I suggest a set of tasks for my colleagues in the scholarly field of religion. It is my hope that not everyone who reads this book will be an academic, so let me address these ideas with this in mind, with you in mind, reader. First, we must think and then act as individuals. It will not be enough, and when we act as individuals, with our little ordinal choices, it will feel futile against the scale of icebergs and thousand-year floods. It is true that the scale of our individual action, even if every one of us refuses meat, abandons our car, insulates, and recycles, will not be enough. But how are we to live unless we stop, one by one, and stand like objects of resistance, like interruptions, in the flow of the river of history, breaking the rushing lines, and disrupt? If I don't, who do I imagine will?

There are many reasons to act beyond the calculation of benefit or payoff, of course, beyond some sort of cheap grace or virtue signaling. We are shaped by our acts, our bodies, our homes, our organizations, and one reason we act is to create a life worth living, a life of meaning and courage. This act of stopping will shape me, and the act of unthinking consumption—that will shape me, too. I am a Californian, and I grew up in a curl of the Pacific coast, a cove called La Costa, which means "the home," where the sea has risen and the storms are newly terrible, and the rocks are now bleached acid white. Each time I act, I act for that childhood home, and this is true for each one of us.

What I do, how I live, is a moral act: every single gesture as I have said in an earlier chapter. And while the gestures seem innocent, they are cumulative, and they set in motion a chain of action that, given the structures of exchange, is part of the systemic order of the world. And the world is so shaped, in the production and exchange and consumption of the goods, that the wealthiest have garnered the vast majority of wealth, burning the vast majority of carbon at the expense of the lives and the health of the poor. I repeat this because it is the central moral point of this work.

And we are the sort of creatures with a plight into which we are each born, which is that we cannot *not* act. There is no "doing nothing," for the doing of nothing is a something, a moral act, one in which you support the existing constructs of carbon use and the policies of the energy companies, and it looks for all the world like you are then acting as if you have a duty to them, one that you enact every time you get into the car.

Second, we must think and then we must speak as citizens. For Hannah Arendt, the public speech—the speech to one another that disturbs and breaks into the power of totality, the unthinking acceptance of the loss of agency—is both political and ontological. It is the act of civil disobedience that creates the institutions of a larger democracy. Consent, freedom, all of this, is contingent on the fact that we *could* protest, we could enter the event of the polis, and we could speak to stop it. The reverse is, of course, also the case. If we do not speak, if we do not stop, then we partake of what is being said, we sustain the givenness of this order, an order so convenient for us, so terrible for too many, terrible one by one in too many places, child by child. Can you not hear them at your door?

We must act. It will not be enough. But let me expand this idea of civil interruption, for we must act as citizens in addition to acting as individuals. I now turn to a distinction made by Arendt in her consideration of civil disobedience. Individual acts, she argues—Socrates's refusals and Thoreau's protest—while infinitely appealing are ultimately subjective. Thoreau himself is happy with his conscience being clear and his one day in jail, when he refuses to pay taxes to a state that allows slavery and war. This is noble, but personal (and his buddies bail him out and quietly pay the tax). Thoreau writes that "we come into this world, not chiefly to make it a good place to live in, but to live in it be it good or bad." And Arendt understands the limits of his personal choice theory this way: "Indeed, this is how we all come into the world, lucky if the world and the part of it we arrive in is a good place at the time of our arrival."[10]

But what if it is a place where the wrongs committed are of such a nature that it requires you to be an agent of injustice to one another, she asks. "For if this is the case, then I say, break the law."[11]

This idea, this tension between being a good person and being a good citizen, between morality and politics, is as old as the idea of the state, Arendt notes; as old as the city in which, as Socrates teaches, one must avoid evil "because you would then have to live together with the wrongdoer." The thinking person—the philosopher, the critical, alive-to-others person—must think not only of the judgment of others but also of the interior integrity of the self. But there is a problem with this strategy, and it is why if we only each recycle our cups and bike to work, we are not finished with our duties in this burning time. Ultimately, she argues, individual acts remain subjective and self-interested, for they have as a justification only individual and private directions, which can look strangely like opinions or choices in the marketplace, and it is hard to know which choice is more justified. And such personal acts are evoked only in times of emergency, such times when, as in her time, the "good person" emerged from anywhere, (a few) to oppose fascism with their conscience, lives, bodies.

Arendt wants more that even this: she wants more than the individual interruption; she wants public action. She wants civil disobedience, meaning organization. It is when "minorities band together, make a decision and take a stand" that the state can be changed. And here, in her beloved America, in the decades of the 1770s, the 1860s, and the 1960s about which she was writing, when "the defiance of established authority . . . can be the outstanding event," when persons act as citizens in the "name of and for a group . . . on the ground of basic dissent, not as individuals."

To be a citizen, to actually change things in a democracy, is to seize the deadly serious duty of continuing participation in" all matters of public interest." This participation, this voice, this interruption of the business taking place in the public square: this is all that free people have. But we must act as if participation matters, beyond a noble loneliness, and that requires a great deal from us, especially if we are the sort of citizens that are not used to thinking in this way, the sort of scholars who are worried about being political, who are willing to forego some comforts, to be sure, but not entirely sure we want to risk what is so dear to us, our work, our profession, our professing, to do well, *politics*?

Third, we must act in accordance with our moral aspirations. If you believe that you have a good moral code, then act in accordance with it. I think and then teach as a scholar of religion. For me, the question of the Other, the one who has not arrived in a lucky place, emerges from my own scholarship. Isn't that the point of knowing that the stranger, widow, and orphan are at the door, that the mendicant needs alms, that the land needs a year of release? We must live as if ready, say the texts we teach, we must live as if we were chosen to uphold the Law, to be the persons who come in love, who ask even about the city of Sodom. Who will do this, if not the teacher that I am? Letting the danger, the power, and the endless mercy of religion be excellently told is the task of the scholar of religion. To teach religion excellently is to engage in "the public examination of things," the task of the scholar since Socrates spoke public truth—*parrhesia*—to his Academy, notes Arendt, "which doubtless spread uncertainty about established customs and beliefs." And my teaching, if it is actually *parrhesia*, telling the public truth, should raise the questions that will doubtless interrupt the usual way of things, which would mean disruption of the institutions that govern us in the absence of a vivid, democratic, civil participation: the *ratio* and the *episteme* of the marketplace, a marketplace devoted to continuous expansion, whatever the cost.

Finally, I have a duty as a scholar that emerges from the blunt fact that in Scriptural texts I think important, the point is made over and over again: Your moral activities can affect the rain, the harvest, and the health of everything you love. If you are a person who also believes in religion, you will know this as well. If you are a person who has other moral or ethical commitments, you will find in them that the link between moral choices and material outcomes is made continually, and it is received and studied toward normative action. Ethics suggests the interruption of desire, of consumption, and of acquisition, linking that interruption to the order of the natural world, of harvest time and planting. Our behavior is a part of this, for unless we see the world of the charcoal burner, of the women with her sari over her face, on her knees on the ground, our ethics and our faith will be lacking.

What Can I Do to Interrupt Your Life?

What can I do to interrupt your life? To pull you over and make you attend to this crisis? Consider this scene: Lunch with friendly fellow scholars, who happily are munching their hamburgers all around me, and all agree that climate change is coming, that it will be terrible, and that is it foolish to deny this. Yet no one is ready to change their lives, to give up meat on their plate, or to abandon the car for a bike, to change habits of air travel to conferences that we zip in and out of on jet planes. Around us the world changes, but it can seem so far away from this particular lunch, this particular choice.

There is nothing I can say that anyone who reads the daily news does not already know, except this: *We must be interrupted; we must stop.* To make the future possible, we need to stop what we are doing, what we are making, what we are consuming, what we think we need, what makes us comfortable. We need to interrupt our work—even our good work—to attend to the urgency of this question. For it is, as yet, only a question, one that needs a coherent answer, an answer we have not yet seen. Is our society unable to stop careening toward the deep trouble of the coming storm because we have not fully attended, because we cannot stop?

We should be quite sobered by the scientific accounts. Listen to the language of the IPCC (2013) report:

> The mass die-offs of forests, including those in the American West, the melting of land ice around the world, an accelerating rise of the seas that is leading to increased coastal flooding, and heat waves that have devastated crops and killed tens of thousands of people: all happening already, not a generation from now, but now.[12]

The scenes of flooding are familiar if you live in the wake of Hurricane Sandy or the hurricane that wiped out thousands in the Philippine Islands. But they are familiar and resonate to all of us as well. We should know the language of flood. So let me turn to the texts of flood.

The text begins as if in the middle of the story, in despair, the thoughts "of the heart" of a watching God:

> And he saw that all the very imaginations—of the heart of humans are nothing but evil, every single day. So much evil by the humans, the earth and by every shape of being . . . And He regretted that he made the human in the earth and He grieved to the very heart of Him. And He said I shall obliterate the human whom I created from off the faces of the ground. From human to beasts to every moving animal and to the flyer of the heavens that flies. I regret that I made them.
>
> The very earth, His Last Place, "she is ruined," says He-who-regrets, in the text. "She is ruined by men." It is done in front of His face, *m' panim*, violently.
>
> And, look, I, even I, will bring a flood of waters upon the earth, to destroy every living, breathing being from under heaven. Everything in the earth shall die. (Genesis 6:5)

Let me continue in the Quran. In the Quran, the account of the flood is different—there is a chance, a warning, an invitation to truth:

> Surah 71: We sent Noah to his people, and said to him, "Warn thou thy people 'ere there come on them an afflictive punishment." He said, "O my people, indeed I am to you a clear warner, worship Allah, fear Him and obey me."

It is not only Abrahamic texts that tell a story of a vast flood that destroys some great wickedness or chaos, but in Gilgamesh; in Plato, in the Theology of Bibliotea; in the Irish story of the Cessair; in the Finnish Kavevala; in the Kwaya, Mbuti, Maasai, and Yoruba narratives. In India the flood is told; in China, it is called Gun Yo; in Malaysia, the Celav; for the Thai, Khun Borom. There is a great flood told by the Hopi, the Mayan, the Incas; in Chile it is Trentren Vilu, in Peru a flood and a rainbow and the waters running out in the huge waterfalls of Bogota.

Let me be frank: in the tradition of the Hebrew Bible, it is not a happy or redemptive tale. And after the catastrophe, the narrative ends exactly as it began: God watching, the words *b'Levo* in his heart. "I will not kill the living beings as I did."

We are left with the faintest of hope, a rainbow that vanishes, that barely lasts until we turn, a few lines later, to the prophet Noah naked, drunk, and silent, and a world which will continue endlessly, ceaselessly and without interruption, wrapped in its own spiral.

> Until all—of days—of the earth, seed and harvest and cold and warmth and summer and winter and day and night no, they shall not cease, *lo shabbato*.

And this world, full of tempted, broken people, where not even childhood is innocent, is the one in which we live. It is not Eden, we are told, and we who believe in science believe in this, that carbon thrown into the cycle of summer and winter will cause a spiral in predictable unceasing physical realities of this place.

The word "will not cease" in Hebrew is *lo shabbato*, "not *Shabbat*, meaning to actively stop. *Shabbas* actively ceases the marketplace exchanges and all the frenetic, mechanical action of the world, all the digital zinging, all the traveling, all the writing, all the finishing of things into other things. One interrupts the natural order, the ceaseless cycle—to cease, to make an in-between—*rupting* or breaking the totalizing cycle of events. Break the six-day week, and make a Shabbat, an event that is exactly not in the natural order, the people are commanded from Sinai. And every six years, break the bonds to the field and the seed time and harvest time and make a stop for justice, make a Sabbatical Year. If we do not, imagine the relentless earth, spinning, the waves washing up, the birdless sky full of stars, not ceasing, but seasons coming and going, the physical world without our civilizations because it is too warm, too wet a place. God promises not to cease the world, but of course, we are another matter.

This is a task of humans, not a divine task—*lo shabbato*—and it is a moral choice, this active, human *shabbato*, that could stop this inexorable temperature rise. And we humans, we need to stop; we can make an argument to stop and start, to understand the link from behavior to the turning world. But it will take the sort of argument that is made in the many, many flood stories: there is a moment, just before the flood, when it could be otherwise. Listen to the prophets' warning, say the texts, allow even a corner of goodness to survive and the world could be otherwise than destroyed. We could stop here, attentive, thinking.

What Time Is It?

Let me say a word about why what I am asking is so hard. To be present in your place: *hineni*, to God's asking, "Where are you?" is not only the event of attendance. We understand—how could we not, with our Google maps and our PDAs—where we are, we feel like we can own and possess place and territory, but we are uncertain *where we are* in time, "when" it is that we exist. We don't have the time, sorry. We do not have time, we cannot grasp it. And so we think we have, if not forever, later.

It is this essential miscalculation that is the point. As Ban Ki-moon noted on November 2, 2014: "Science has spoken. There is no ambiguity about the message. Leaders must act. Time is not on our side."

Of course, as I write now, in 2023, that call seems impossibly optimistic. It was, of course, ignored by most of the leaders to whom he was speaking.

We think that the great interruption of climate chaos is an event of the far future and, look, we are busy, we are worried about ISIS and Ebola and tenure committees and the poor in our own cities and actually, tenure committees. We think that, while we need to play the long game—after all, what is religion if not the long game?—we can think about the issue some other time. And here is a fundamental problem. For the climate has already changed, as the UN IPCC has told us. This information interrupted: Time is not on our side.

> The report contained the group's most explicit warning yet about the food supply, saying that climate change has already become a small drag on overall global production... the world's food supply had shown signs of instability... factors like high food prices and intensified weather conditions would most likely leave poor people worse off. In fact, the report said, that has already happened to a degree.[13]

Why can this occur in our faces, this hunger, and yet we do not stop, we who worry about missing lunch because we stop and talk? Why, knowing everything, having proof texts and data, do I still act without real urgency?

There is something more. There is something else that makes it easy to flee from our duty as we confront climate chaos. We find it impossible, as moderns who live in the always-present, to imagine our own death. Our version of climate denial is about the great flight and our denial of our death; that is the real denial. Only a distortion this central to the event of our being can *possibly* explain why rational scholars, rational political leaders, even rational capitalists can act as we act, as if the good American life will be stable. As if we did not have to stop in our tracks. Why is our denial of death a particular problem in this catastrophe?

A few months ago, speaking to my son about the terrible paradox of evil people flourishing, the rewards for mendacity, for greed, for simple carelessness, he reminded me that the essential premise of one rabbinic argument is that evil people have no share in *olam haba*, the afterlife, or "the world that will come," and I told him that this argument was entirely unconvincing, overly pious. But in fact, my doubts about *olam haba*, my modern lack of simple faith in a cosmic system of reward and punishment, is a symptom of a far larger issue. The modern inability to imagine an afterlife, in the comforting way the people living in earlier periods of history could, is linked to our inability to imagine a life after us—any sort of world to come, either to conceptualize a divine afterlife, or even to imagine a future in which the world continues without us. If we cannot confront the facticity of our own death, and we cannot then imagine a time in which we will not be here, in our present, with our stuff and our loves, our temperature control, our airline travel, our oceans nicely in their place, then we cannot possibly imagine the world that our grandchildren will face. But we must imagine it, for if not, they will face it alone, stunned by the thought that we, if we had acted as if we were mortal moral agents, could have made it better.

The world, the coming one, is a place we can already see if we look, but only if we look at the lives of the most marginalized, the border dwellers, the women on the ridges of the sand in Bangladesh, the Chinese herders in the great dust storm, the men who burn charcoal to sell. But we cannot see them if the world is full of, well, me, and my immortal, continuing happiness. So we flee, we are fleeing, we are trying to outrun the coming storm.

But, reader, we do not have to run. We can stand, in our place, in this place, and in our work and our citizenship, we can claim our power. Let me explain. Religions, we who study them, have many liabilities and in too many ways have made some things worse, to be sure. But we might agree that religions have at least four powerful capacities.

First, religions confront the enormous terror of each as we face death, with narratives that allow us to imagine our good life as a part of a larger story, in which we are mortal, broken, old, and yet beloved.

Second, religions allow ordinary people to believe in their own power to change unjust situations, despite all odds and everything arrayed against them. This idea, of the beauty and crystalline brilliance of action, of the value of compassion and repentance and of the power of humility, is so unlike the tropes of our American culture, and of our academic culture as well, that it is hard to even teach. But it is a vivid truth of our texts and our traditions. There is power here, dangerous and vivid. It is the power to see the most ordinary, the smallest, the most degraded one, the remnant, the lost, the desperate hungry stranger, as your sister who is next to you at Sinai, as the center of the teeming world. Religious language fights for values beyond the marketplace exchange; it holds the last, lost tongue of justice.

Third, religious traditions allow for prophecy. To imagine the future, to call for repentance, to see a day coming that can be imagined, changed, redeemed, all of this is possible: the road to the impossible is open. Calling and wild, or rational with charts and graphs, come now the activists and the scientists, comes the guy in the lab coat, comes the farmer: if you teach religious studies, you will know them as prophets, and within the traditions that attend to dreamers, they can be heard.

Fourth, religious are without borders. Just as medicine can be *sans frontier*, religions allow us to consider ourselves to be global members of covenants far deeper and far broader than national boundaries. Religious are often strongest in the places where the climate is worst—the global South, where the land lies close to the sea, and where clean water is a day's walk away. Understanding the borderless nature of the problem is the first step toward solidarity. I am not going to claim that only religious systems do these things, because I know the power of philosophy, but I do think that only religious communities do all of them, over many years, and in many geographies.

As a scholar of religion, who loves the power of faith, I understand that we may see the words of desperate warning burned or discarded by the powerful who deny a link between moral behavior and the actual word. We know what it is to walk around like Jonah in Nineveh and despair of change; or to be the smartest outsider like Daniel, in the King's Court, the ones who are taught to speak Chaldean, or science, or politics; or to be Joseph, the interpreter of the terrifying visions of the future. We know what it is to speak against the marketplace and the soldier's order, Rabbi Akiba, Jesus, the Buddha, all stories of resistance that we humans treasure. As a scholar who reads the texts that show how a human life might be lived in view of faith, I am used to disbelief and used to the idea that religion is trivial or naïve, or simply unrealistic.

What Time Is It?

What time is it? Let that question interrupt you. What the scientists are saying is that the time is right now.

All we have are words—we have no armies, only friends, family, colleagues, and neighbors. All we can do is teach one another—to act as moral agents, to live out our work.[14] We live in a time, we teach at a time, when religions are in center stage of history, have marched into the center stage, and, in the center of the stage, enact and speak. Of course, because all real moral agency is based on the idea that real, deep evil is a possible choice, enacted there is both peace and violent war; both attention to the climate and the display of wealth and power that destroys the climate.[15]

We must stop, and we must start, to do whatever it is that can be done. If you care about the lives of the poor, now, you need to care about the climate. If you care about women, now, you need to care about the climate. If you care about children, this is what you need to think about: the world to come. Do not think for a minute that you are powerless. Our scientists are already in motion; engineers are already working in projects about mitigation, or new energy. What they need is a clear moral argument that is understood by millions. We need to move toward collective action, to evoke resources for cultural and political change, and to be sure that the one great foe of even the most apolitical person—ignorance—is defeated.

Conclusion

I told you in the previous chapter that I would tell you the implications of understanding the enemies and friends in the struggle to contain global warming, and I will. I am not the kind of ethicist who merely describes the issues, or throws up her hands to say, "Oh gee whiz, that is awful."[16] We must make real decisions in this actual world: To whom do you listen? For whom do you work? Who stands with you? So, armed with this concept, I suggested very concrete ideas, as one does in climate change scholarship. Here are some pragmatic signs and acts, I argued, at the intermediate scale—here are acts in public that may make a public space, ways to stop and then start: tithing and the sabbatical year. Both of these ideas come from Hebrew Scripture, but are present in many other religions. You will find your own ideas. But do not think there is nothing to be done. There are hundreds of books about small changes you can make, and you should read them, and make the changes. When you are really ready to take the problem seriously, you can make big changes: you can give up eating meat, give up your car, rarely fly in an airplane, and work as a citizen in every possible way, from letter writing to street demonstrations. Suggesting this does not make you popular, which only means that we are largely still denying the starkness of the issues and the cost of actually doing what will be needed to make real changes. In the meantime, I suggested two ideas to my peers, other scholars of religion.

First, I suggested that we ought to let science interrupt enough to "tithe" enough time to respond. Every time you have a serious discussion, for me, in every semester I taught, I urged them to bring up the issue, to make it a subject of conversation, to pay attention to this problem of climate change.[17]

Second, I suggested that our meetings themselves, our big national gathering, created an unjustifiable carbon burden, for we are ten thousand people, the size of a small city. I suggested one idea, from my Jewish tradition; I hoped a good one among the many that would emerge-- to create an AAR Sabbatical Year. What would this mean? It means that once in every six years, we would pause. Following the biblical cycle, we could choose to not meet at a huge annual meeting in which we take over a city. Every year, each participant going to the meeting uses a quantity of carbon that is more than considerable. Air travel, staying in hotels, all of this creates a way of living on the earth that is carbon intensive. It could be otherwise. What if instead of coming together, I suggested, we spread out over the land, as it were, and read out papers to one another at our own universities and institutions? What if we could meet, each of us in our own city, and turn to the faces and the needs of our fellow citizens? What if, *on that day*, we taught the poor, volunteered in local high schools or community colleges, or the prison, the hospital, the church, mosque, synagogue, or temple, at a place that is not your own, worked at planting an orchard or a garden, served food to the poor, offered our teaching, offered to learn? What if we turned to our neighbor—the woman who cleans the toilets, the man who sweeps the sidewalks—and included them in the university to which we are responsible? We would then be actively making an interruption in our lives, saying by this act: I will sacrifice to save my planet. I am not suggesting—far from it—I said at the time, that we do more than try this, in seven years when the sabbatical year comes again—2021. We can go happily back the other years. But remember, I argued then, time is not on our side, and there will come a time, in seven, or fourteen, or twenty-one or twenty-eight years, when we will not be able to fly to this coast of California unless we radically change the course of history. I thought then that if the AAR began a sabbatical year, others might follow. Perhaps other organizations, institutions, and individuals would also say "No more flying for business," and that would be one very clear act—Shabbat, stopping, *shabbato*. Of course, it will be hard, I told them, and you might be thinking now how hard, how costly, how—as they say—how *inconvenient*. But we had seven years to figure out the details and they are a very, very clever group of scholars, I argued. Do you want more government action? Think big business has not done enough? Then let us start with a dramatic and definitive action ourselves, I said at the time. It was 2014. I ended this talk, and I end this chapter nearly a decade later, with this claim—for I still believe it is true: To live an interrupted life, to live a life of moral attention, is the first duty not only of the scholar but of all of us.

I wanted to be a scholar who took seriously the prophetic duty of my field, bioethics, to warn, to speak of the possibility of our power and our responsibility, and who interrupted you and told you to let the call of the stranger stop you in your tracks and the brokenness of the earth call you to action. I wanted to be the one who said to you, stop. Stop and start. And now all of this, this world, I said in 2014, this, the greatest moral question of our time, it is completely in your hands.

And in the coming months and years that followed, I was constantly told that it was impossible. People would be upset! People needed to all be in one place! People needed the meeting so that scholarship would continue! And the AAR needed the revenue. And we had contracts. And we would lose money.

I am sorry to say that my idea for stopping the conference as a physical event came true, tragically enough as we all know now and not only for my organization. In the Covid plague year of 2020, the annual meeting of the AAR—which so many had insisted could *never* come to a halt, could *never* be given up, for a thousand reasons—was entirely virtual. In the sabbatical year of 2021, the world still beset by pandemic, it was again. As it happened, many people liked a meeting on line. Possibilities opened up for disabled members, and for people for whom the entire event, which costs well over a thousand dollars for travel, hotel stays for a week, food, and registration, was too expensive, it became a meeting they were now able to attend. Many international scholars "came" to the meeting for the first time. In a pandemic, suddenly, it seemed scholarship could indeed continue and allow all of us a new way to think. We lived our lives, interrupted, but not broken, and found ways to be full of curiosity and grace.

Conclusion

Conversations

In an interesting coincidence, I happened to have gone to a big California public high school with a tall, red-haired clever boy who, when he grew up, has turned out to be a leading national figure in the small band of professionals who make a living writing and speaking about climate change, although in his case, he speaks about why it is not really happening, or why, if it is happening, it is not caused by humans, and it might not be so bad.[1,2] He works as a scholar-in-residence at one of America's most conservative, pro-business think tanks, and he is a serious man, just like he was a serious boy. He regularly gives talks at places like the Heartland Institute, and because we are friends, he sends me his PowerPoints, full of complex formulas about gases in the stratosphere. So on the internet chat room for our high school class, he regularly interrupts our sweetly meandering discussions about our old teachers, or what it is like to be fifty-five years out of high school, or good places to eat in our old hometown, with articles he has written for their newsletter about the why climate change is not a "crisis" or that the data are incorrect and the ice is really not melting, or, somehow unbelievably, in a state wracked with fires, that wildfires are occurring less often.

In a way, for a scholar like me, it is rather a gift, these postings, which are full of the latest ideas from the most conservative people in the United States, and it tells me what they are thinking about climate change.[3] He is my personal interlocutor, and while I don't think either he or I will change our respective views on climate change, one of us will be proved incorrect. It is only a matter of time.

"Think about volcanoes," he urges his audience, he tells me. Of course, I have thought about volcanos. Peer-reviewed articles have tracked volcanic emissions, both from the fossil record and from observational data. On average, volcanos emit between 65 and 319 tons of CO_2 annually. No scientific data contradict this.[4] Compare volcanic emissions to human emissions, and you will see why the volcanos are not the culprit in global warming.[5]

The burning of fossil fuels and changes in land use results in the emission into the atmosphere of approximately 34 *billion* tonnes of carbon dioxide per year worldwide, according to the U.S. Energy Information Administration (EIA).[6]

This means that human fossil fuels emissions numbers are about one hundred times bigger than even the maximum estimated volcanic CO_2 fluxes. My friend thinks it is silly to call this a climate "crisis." Have you seen other evidence that is? No, he says:

> But there is little evidence of serious climate impacts attendant upon increasing GHG concentrations. Temperatures are rising, but as the Little Ice Age ended around 1850, it is not easy to separate natural from anthropogenic effects on temperatures. The latest research in the peer-reviewed literature suggests that mankind is responsible for about half a degree of the global temperature increase of about 1.5 degrees since 1850. There is little trend in the number of "hot" days for 1895–2017; 11 of the 12 hottest years occurred before 1960. Global mean sea level has been increasing for thousands of years; it may or may not be accelerating.[7]

My friend feels it is not fair that minority voices are not heard, but it is extremely difficult when the facts are at stake. Here are the facts:

> Earth's global surface temperatures in 2018 were the fourth warmest since 1880, according to independent analyses by NASA and the National Oceanic and Atmospheric Administration (NOAA). Global temperatures in 2018 were 1.5 degrees Fahrenheit (0.83 degrees Celsius) warmer than the 1951 to 1980 mean, according to scientists at NASA's Goddard Institute for Space Studies (GISS) in New York. Globally, 2018's temperatures rank behind those of 2016, 2017 and 2015. The past five years are, collectively, the warmest years in the modern record. "2018 is yet again an extremely warm year on top of a long-term global warming trend," said GISS Director Gavin Schmidt. Since the 1880s, the average global surface temperature has risen about 2 degrees Fahrenheit (1 degree Celsius). This warming has been driven in large part by increased emissions into the atmosphere of carbon dioxide and other greenhouse gases caused by human activities, according to Schmidt.[8]

And effects are showing up already, contrary to his claim of "no visible effects." The Pew Center reports a 40% increase in North Atlantic tropical storms over the historic maximum of the mid-1950s, which at the time was considered extreme.[9]

One of the leading researchers of hurricanes, Kerry Emanuel, of MIT, happens to be a politically conservative scientist. What he has found is that global warming because it warms the oceans, and a warm ocean is the most important driver of hurricane, increases the intensity of hurricanes. As sea levels rise, the storm surges that are the most dangerous part of hurricane damage get closer to inland areas, and warmer, moister air causes an increase in torrential rain, both of which cause flooding. When people talk about a crisis, they are talking about the impact of events that are now occurring with just 1°C of global temperature rise, and thinking ahead about the impact of a half a degree, or the fact that the temperature would simply keep increasing until human activity ceased.

Let's remember the scientists from the first chapter of this book, who establish how the temperature cycle worked in the first place. The global temperature mainly depends on how much energy the planet gets from the sun and how much it radiates back into space—quantities that change very little. The amount of energy radiated by the Earth depends significantly on the chemical composition of the atmosphere, particularly the amount of heat-trapping greenhouse gases. A 1°C *global* change is significant because it takes a vast amount of heat to warm all the oceans, atmosphere, and land by that much.

And of course, effects are already being seen. Here is a short list of effects published in peer-reviewed literature:

> Increased deaths to heatwaves—5.74% increase to heatwaves compared to 1.59% to cold snaps (Medina-Ramon 2007); increased heat stress in humans and other mammals (Sherwood 2010); spread in mosquito-borne diseases such as malaria and dengue fever (Epstein 1998); increase in occurrence of allergic symptoms due to rise in allergenic pollen (Rogers 2006); decreasing human water supplies, increased fire frequency, ecosystem change and expanded deserts (Solomon 2009); decline in rice yields due to warmer nighttime minimum temperatures (Peng 2004; Tao 2008); increase of Western United States wildfire activity, associated with higher temperatures and earlier spring snowmelt

(Westerling 2006); encroachment of shrubs into grasslands, rendering rangeland unsuitable for domestic livestock grazing (Morgan 2007); decreased water supply in the Colorado River Basin (McCabe 2007); decreasing water supply to the Murray-Darling Basin (Cai 2008); less compacted ice, hazardous floes and more mobile icebergs posing increased risk to shipping (IICWG 2009); drying of arctic ponds with subsequent damage to ecosystem (Smol 2007); melting of Arctic lakes leading methane bubbling (Walter 2007); leakage of methane from the East Siberian Shelf seabed sediments (Shakhova 2008); escape of methane gas from the seabed along the West Spitsbergen continental margin (Westbrook 2009).[10]

Against this, we have what will be a temporary greening effect. The very article in which the "greening effect" is praised by my friend as evidence that CO_2 is beneficial, is careful to point out that any positive consequence of CO_2 is outweighed by the negative consequences, moreover:

> The beneficial impacts of carbon dioxide on plants may also be limited, said co-author Dr. Philippe Ciais, associate director of the Laboratory of Climate and Environmental Sciences, Gif-suv-Yvette, France. "Studies have shown that plants acclimatize, or adjust, to rising carbon dioxide concentration and the fertilization effect diminishes over time.[11]

And paradoxically, some researchers attribute CO_2-fueled growth spurts as one of the climate change impacts, along with rising temperatures, and decreased water, and lack of nutrients, that has led to the decline of the Amazon rainforest's ability to absorb CO_2:

> The combination of flat growth rate and increasing tree deaths means the amount of carbon the Amazon stores has declined by around 30% since the 1990s, the researchers say. So what is causing more trees to die? Co-author Prof Oliver Phillips from the University of Leeds tells Carbon Brief it could be down to the growth spurt fueled by rising carbon dioxide levels: "The faster trees grow, the sooner they reach maturity, and the sooner they may eventually age. "As tall trees are more vulnerable to high winds and drought, faster growth may also be putting trees at risk from weather extremes.[12]

Climate change in the Midwestern states caused massive flooding as soil saturated by increasing rainfall froze and, in the spring of 2019, could not absorb more water.[13]

> Climate change has made wet weather more common in the area. Since 1991, annual precipitation in the Midwest has increased, according to the Fourth National Climate Assessment. Additionally, intense rainstorms have become more common.[14]

Sometimes my interlocutor says that the earth is not warming, and sometimes he says it is but that it is just part of a "natural cycle." I hear this a lot. But it is a misunderstanding of how the climate of a whole planetary system changes. The climate does not swing back and forth. However, there is viability in the short term: for example, some years are La Nina, and the ocean surface is cooler, and other years are El Nino, and the ocean warms. Even events like the European Warm Period were not planet-wide. To change the entire planet's climate requires something the scientists call a "forcing event," like meteor strikes, or the amount of solar energy changing, or the changing of enormous ocean currents. It is thought that external forcing events caused the Ice Ages, and this changed the total albedo.

> Scientists keep track of natural forcings, but the observed warming of the planet over the second half of the 20th century can only be explained by adding in anthropogenic radiative forcings, namely increases in greenhouse gases such as carbon dioxide.[15]

My interlocutor sometimes says that there is a sort of conspiracy to keep scientists who disagree away from policymakers, and he advocates a "red team–blue team" approach. This is such an appealing argument—we all like to hear all opinions on various matters. But science is not a matter of "teams." It is a matter of data, observations, quantitive not qualitative measurements. Scientists explore a problem—how does the atmosphere work? And they come up with an hypothesis: the atmosphere absorbs sunlight and reflects it back, and the more it absorbs, the hotter the atmosphere gets. The more CO_2, the hotter it is. This hypothesis was tested from the eighteenth century onward, researched, and efforts were made to find contrary evidence. Like Darwin's theory of evolution, developed at the same time, or Newton's theory of gravity, or Harvey's account of the circulatory system, at some point, scientists agree that the question is answered and humanity knows something more. It is not a matter of opinion, and there is no need for a debate.

I have spent a fair amount of time answering my climate denier friend's ideas,[16] in part because you, reader, may have questions as well. But the time for doubting is past. Climate scientists, 97.1% of them, write peer-reviewed papers and can say clearly, without doubt, that the earth is heating dangerously, and it is caused by human activity. I actually think that underneath the simply incorrect claims about the scientific fact is the real issue: It will be very costly to cope with the damage that climate change will wreak but it will also be very costly and immediately costly to address the issue seriously. It will be hard to give up cool things we like to do, and meat we like to eat. It will be difficult to give up the major American synecdoche of freedom, a gasoline-driven car. All sorts of small things: out-of-season grapes, cooking on gas flames, fireplaces, will be things we will not have anymore, and these are things that I love. Switching to noncarbon forms of energy will be costly, too, at first.

Even if we stopped now, we would still have to give up on many of our favorite coastal cities, because there is a lag between when CO_2 is added to the atmosphere and the warming effects take place. All this will mean that our generation will have to do the sacrificing to protect the next one, and that will be hard. Of course, our lives as Westerners will still be vastly superior to most generations of the past, if we do this, and still we will live far more comfortably than many ordinary people in the developing world do now. But daily life will be different. My interlocutor is not convinced. He thinks the future generation would rather have the money, which means that he does not yet fully understand what our grandchildren will be facing, nor does he count as social good the world beyond money because that is largely how he argues, we measure worth.

What is interesting about climate change research, among other social realities, is the way that most Americans have understood both that climate change is happening (71%) and that it is caused by human activity (56%), and more than half (54%) believe it will affect the United States, and yet they cannot act to change it. Why should this be the case?

First of all, the numbers as an aggregate obscure the fact that numbers about the belief in climate change as a real, human-driven phenomena represent a very large partisan gap. Democrats and Republicans progressives and conservatives, differ in ways that reveal other, fundamental concerns.

Because climate change is a collective action problem, to change things will need both millions of individual choices, and the actions of large state actors, thinking like states think. For many right-wing conservatives, this represents a clear market threat and a direct challenge to individual responsibility for one's own actions, and for the disturbing 17%, who believe that global warming is a hoax perpetuated by the liberal media, it is far worse—it is a delusion.

For Dale Jamieson, the problem is somehow biological as well as philosophical: we are evolved to cope with immediate threats, fast-moving objects, something like a rapidly approaching firestorm, or a large predator, and climate change is subtle, incremental, and largely invisible. We fail—we have failed to act as if our lives are at stake because we are good at accommodation; we cannot visualize other people thousands of miles away; we have a difficult time thinking about the future in general.

Timothy Morton has argued that climate change is a "hyperobject." It is very large and difficult to grasp all at once, like ordinary objects, which can be held in the hand, and this means we cannot ever fully know it, for, like all very large, unexaminable objects, it has a dark side that is not in play, at every moment that we interact with it. Because hyperobjects seem to exist beyond or outside of time, and yet, because we are also "within" the object, we cannot grasp it fully and are paralyzed into inaction. Anand Ghosh speaks of a "great derangement" which makes it impossible to think clearly about global warming, for it is so out of character for our planet.

In many essays, the tone is simply of despair. Reading the sobering reports of the UN IPCC, where 194 countries have carefully agreed that the only way to avert disaster will need to include as yet undiscovered ways of capturing CO_2 out of the air and sequestering it, is to feel overwhelmed.

What is "history?" History is more than memory, more than a gaze backward, for it is curated, not every single event told. But telling the story of the recent history of climate change, as I did in this book, does allow for some facts, some undisputed facts to emerge: the people that denied climate change were wrong.

In the chapter on Bad Guys, I promised to reflect on the implications of understanding that oil and gas extraction companies, the billionaires that run them, and the states that give them legal advantages are best understood as sinners, in the classical sense of the term, as doing evil with deliberation. It was not some mistakenness, some error or wrong path taken, that these business and political leaders made the big bets with our environment and thus our lives. They chose to do it because it made them very rich. If in 1973, these leaders had received the science that was newly understood with something other than obfuscation, if they had said: "Here is a real problem—let's turn our research toward finding new ways to generate power," it would have been possible to have a solution, after thirty-five years of well-funded research, or at least to know that no technical solution was yet possible.

What makes their behavior actionable is that they have harmed humanity. This is more than an abrogation of duty. It is a direct harm, done by identifiable people to other identifiable people, a harm against humanity, even though it was all perfectly legal. Thus, the implications are that they need to be tried, and they need to be judged, and if they have done this dreadful thing, they need to take responsibility for this harm. Of course, all of their ill-gotten gains will not be enough—we will all have to pay, we are already paying, and our children and theirs, too, even if we are to stop emitting carbon right now, but it will be a beginning, of remediation, and most of all, of justice.

But to enact this will require the creation of a strong, true, and understandable argument, one that moves people toward action. That is the purpose of moral philosophy and my field of ethics, making a good argument, finding new language, and reclaiming the powerful language of justice that is embedded in scriptures and traditions of religion, for it is clear that all the brilliant science in the world has not moved people toward action quite yet. We need more compelling reasons, we need to be clear about the enemies, yes enemies, and we need to make sense. If books help toward creating political movements, and if these political movements work, then it will be of some consequence to write books. But the task of moving from thinking to politics, reader, is your work.

The Principle of Fidelity

Can we fix what we have broken?

In the last decade, the pace of climate change has accelerated. In the long summer, as I write this chapter, new records for heat, especially in places where summer heat is quite odd, Sweden, Ireland, are being created. Irish citizens are carefully instructed in how sleep in the heat ("Now, take a bowl of ice, put it by your bed . . .") on public radio.

It is an unprecedented problem. For the majority of human beings, the coming of modernity, industry, and the liberal state was an extraordinary event, changing the life situation of peasants and farmers. There was, sanitation, clean water, antibiotics, vaccinations, and the entire industrial structure to make them, pavement, electricity, rationality, civil rights, women's liberation, intensive care units, beta blockers, refrigeration. It is important to remember how much was gained when we lament what was lost. My grandmother, living in Los Angeles, would tell me about her nineteenth-century world: a small shetl, mud up to her knees in spring, dust in the air all summer, deep snow in the winter, turned into slush by the horses' hooves, the horses' waste. When we bemoan the catastrophic wasting of our oceans, our forests, our air, we need also to remember that industry, and the carbon that runs it, was embraced, not only by capitalists and kings, but by millions, billions of our fellows. Cheap food, mobility, refrigeration, plastic IV tubing for rehydration, surgical suites are not wasteful or trivial commodities. It is unimaginable to think of rolling back these advances. I spent a decade of my life as a nurse in a neonatal intensive care unit, caring for the bodies of the babies of the poor of Oakland, and when we speak of new ways of living, or of giving up fossil fuel, I think of that unit: the technology, the plastic isolettes, the machines, the tiny needles, the complex pumps, the plastic bags of fluid, the plastic covers on the lights, the disposable ventilator tubing, in bright blue plastic, everything plugged into the electrical sockets in the wall, humming. We are not going to turn away from neonatal intensive care units. We should not.

When my fellow scholars and authors write about climate change, at the end of their books there are often calls for a simpler way of life, a more preindustrial life as a solution to global warming. Then the global warming deniers mock them, for who can live in the eighteenth century? Surely none of the babies in the NICU, for one thing. Yet, there is truth to the narrative of sacrifice, for we surely face an unprecedented reality, and it is a disaster of our own making, of appetites and of desire. In this book, I have spoken of the need for serious sacrifice, in large part as a moral and religious claim, for I argue that sacrifice for the commons ought to be at the heart of human societies. But it is also undoubtedly true that some technological responses will also be needed in addition to an altered way of life, for modernity inescapably requires electricity, at the very least. Alternative sources of energy need to be found and developed, in addition to the growing use of solar and wind energy, and a careful and thoughtful reconsideration of how the rate-limiting factor in nuclear energy—its deadly waste—could be addressed. If, as I have argued in the book, humanity is facing a terrible catastrophe, then every avenue ought to be pursued.

This will include ideas to capture carbon and to control global warming with technology as yet to be tested. And about this, at least, my interrogator and friend agree. As an example, synthetic biologists are researching ways to understand the energy produced by photosynthesis, and how it might be used instead of carbon energy sources. Investigators are curious about processes that break down carbon, or that use carbon, taking it out of the atmosphere. There are more speculative ideas about using engineered particles to darken the sky over the poles, as a desperate plan to reduce the melting of ice caps. Should these be studied? I would argue, without question, studied at least, for there is an essential principle at stake, even if the ideas themselves fail entirely and that is the ethical principle of fidelity.

The engineers of the eighteenth and nineteenth century, who created the Industrial Revolution, were motivated by complex forces: financial success, of course, but also a religious conviction about power, especially the power to transform and order what they saw as God's universe. Critics of these engineering or bioengineering schemes—and at this writing they are no more than theoretical schemes—are concerned that if humanity has a technological reprieve, we will continue our profligate, essentially sinful ways, and even if global warming is somehow slowed, we will move on to cut down every forest, pollute every lake and ocean. There is validity to this critique. Pope Francis has noted that addressing climate change will take a significant shift in our priorities, rather than a only shift in the source of our energy and of course he is entirely correct.

It is correct to be cautious, because of the history of industrial technology. What is worrisome, and perhaps more so now that capital is so concentrated in so few hands, is the lack of fidelity that global energy companies exhibit. By "fidelity" I mean that the creators of technology ought to have responsibility for the effects that their industry creates, beyond their profits, they must be faithful to the communities when there are losses. Consider the coal executive I told you about, whose profits will be won regardless of the tragic loss of land faced by the women in a small Indian village. He won't see them, or meet them, or have to account to them, because he lives in another city, and jets to New York and Paris. Consider an earlier time, when a mine owner lived near his mining shafts, when he attended the same church as his foreman, when his family drank from the same wells as his workers, when it was still in his interest to make sure the place he lived was essentially safe. This is no longer the case. But fidelity to one's place and one's neighbors is an enduring virtue. Like sacrifice, it is at the heart of religious traditions and at the heart of well-ordered societies.

When you suggest this, of course, you will be told it is impractical. Please remember that this sort of impracticality has animated our world for generation.

For ethicists, words like *fidelity* and *sacrifice* are the words that describe what is possible for states and societies, and it is time we turned to these ideas instead of to our endless competition for money and power and attention.

So what is "ethics?" Emmanuel Kant teaches us to consider three questions: What can I know? What ought I to do? I have spent time in this book telling you things about climate change you can know, and I have spent some time in the last chapter telling you what we need to do. Kant's last questions was: For what can I hope?

Finally, we need to know for what it is we hope.

I want to end this on a note of hope, a note, perhaps of prayer, a lovely additional prayer, discussed in a Talmudic section about adding prayers after one had said the obligatory She'ma prayer, about the link between human moral action and environmental order, the one I have discussed in my earlier chapter. Here is one from a discussion about the need for "good companions" in addition to moral action.[17]

> R. Eleazar on concluding his prayer used to say the following: May it be Thy will, O Lord our God, to cause to dwell among us love and brotherhood and peace and friendship, and may Thou make our borders rich in students and prosper our old age with good prospect and hope, and set our portion in Paradise, and confirm us with a good companion and a good impulse in Thy world, and may we rise early and obtain the yearning of our heart to fear Thy name, and mayest Thou be pleased to grant the satisfaction of our desires!.

To enact our duties as commanded beings, the obligations of religious life, will also take "good companions". Is your task impossible? I do not think so, but it cannot be done alone.

We have experience in creating mass movements that are both political and force legal and legislative changes and create new cultural imaginaries. Consider the student-led protests of 1966–1970. While focused on ending the war in Vietnam, this movement also led to changes in the limits on presidential power; on the draft itself; on ideologies of "the domino theory" and the Cold War; on national liberation movements worldwide; as well as women's rights, sexual norms, and cultural values. Not only were our laws different, but the way we thought it best to live changed.

For people of faith, not one of these ideas should seem odd. Consider how small the group of Iron Age wonderers who became Hebrews, telling the story of a God who liberated them from slavery and brought them to Sinai, and gave them the Law of the Torah. Think of how few people must have heard the words of the prophet Amos, and how many have heard them today: "let justice roll down like water and righteousness like a mighty stream" (Amos 5:24).

Or consider the small group of Jews who heard Paul speak of Jesus as the Christ, who were hunted by the enormity of Roman imperial power, and how far the Gospels have traveled and how they have changed history. Muhammed was one man, Siddhartha, who became the Buddha, one man. (Now, it does not always work out, for example, consider the Mani of Manicheism who was murdered, his canon destroyed and his followers silenced.) No one who thinks of themselves as a believer should doubt the power of small movements to change the course of events or to bring goodness and grace into the world. And you do not have to believe in any faith at all to consider how the way the world is organized is still influenced by these traditions. The idea that a few students in a few universities could stand up to the American government and stop a war in Vietnam seemed absurd. The idea that something as entrenched as the exclusion of African Americans from Southern voting rolls, or from public places and restaurants could end; or that places like the University of Mississippi could be changed and routinely admit African American students, was at first, a crazy, unrealistic idea. When people moan about what a "wicked problem" climate change seems to be, or how big and complicated it all is, we must consider the scope and depth of the problems that humans have addressed successfully.

We have experience in thinking about public health and the barriers to it and taking on the most powerful lobbyists in the country and winning. Consider the role smoking and tobacco companies played both in our culture—what was "cool," what was adult—and in our laws by their lobbying. Look at video of Hannah Arendt, or Humphrey Bogart in interviews, smoking away happily. When people began to think carefully about the science that told them smoking was harmful, they quit in the millions. Here, too, the way we thought it best to live changed rather rapidly, as did the laws about where one could smoke legally. This seemed impossible in the 1950s of my childhood, for all rooms, all airplanes, and all public meeting were smoke-filled. The idea that a combination of very difficult personal choices and far-reaching legislation could change that seemed a fantasy. Yet here we are.

This, too, should be familiar to people of faith. Christians long have practiced Lent through laws of dietary restriction. The laws of Jewish life are many and considerable. Maimonides spent time reflecting on and admonishing about the need for moderation in personal habits, especially in diet. The dietary laws of kashrut set limits on all sorts of things: what can be eaten, what can be eaten together, and in what order. To some extent, the rules on personal choice are all enacted to keep human behavior within limits, and to restrict unlimited consumption of any commodity. The rules vary between faith traditions, but all religions dislike gluttony, and all have rituals that make the act of eating special, even sacred, at times. Religions limit insatiable human desire, and many laws are linked to ideas about what a healthy physical life should entail. Jewish law advises living only in cities, for example, that have basic decent standards for health care, baths, and clean water. Rules for behavior in epidemics appear in many religious texts, not only in Jewish thought. Finally, contemporary religious communities made rulings on vaccinations, the use of prenatal genetic screening for Tay Sachs disease, and about smoking. The health of communities is not only supported and constrained by civil law, but by religious law as well.

Every American city has a building code. We accept that some individual choices present a threat to the common good, and we prohibit them. Places where children go to school, or where people congregate, have stricter codes. In some cities, you cannot build on dangerous ground. Everyone may grumble at inspections, but everyone wants their neighbor to comply, and this is widely understood. In my city, trees and bushes have to be trimmed back to a certain height, and trash cannot accumulate in the alley. To raise a flock of chickens, surely an individual choice, you need to get a permit and license from the city, just as you would for a dog. Rules about our private choices are simply a part of living in a democracy where the personal is understood as also political.

There are several discussions about building codes in the Talmud. Prominent here is the rule on building railings around parapets (Bava Batra 6) and the many complicated discussions on balconies. Rules about how much a house could impose on a public street, or how close together they could be (Eruvin 66–67b), were a synecdoche for the relationship of private property owners and the public in the street. And the Jewish texts are not the only places where religious communities limit the scope of the market or of individual reach. Laws about usury, rules about slavery, limits on deception, all represent familiar, ordinal ways that communities accept the fact that free choice needs to be limited for the good of all.

Americans have acted for the next generation, even against immediate market-based interests. Consider the National Park system. In 1889, ranchers used the deep grass of the alpine meadows to graze cattle in the summer, sheep whose grazing and whose waste threatened to destroy the entire ecosystem. Despite their insistence that they needed these grasslands, Yosemite was founded to protect the meadowlands for future generations. The California Giant Sequoias, later the redwoods, the Grand Canyon—all of these are protected for the next generation. On a familial level, we see this all the time. Families save for their children; ordinary houses are passed down, not just huge estates. No farmer in her right mind would waste her land in one generation. The concept of sacrifice for the children of the future is a part of every immigrant dream, not some nutty or extraordinary idea.

And one of the most powerful locations of hope for the next generation is in the language of the Scripture and traditions themselves. We need it now because we may well be capable of ignoring the warnings that everything we know is at risk.

Here are the headlines—it might as well be a quote from the prophet Amos:

> For half a century, climate scientists have seen the West Antarctic ice sheet, a remnant of the last ice age, as a sword of Damocles hanging over human civilization. The great ice sheet, larger than Mexico, is thought to be potentially vulnerable to disintegration from a relatively small amount of global warming, and capable of raising the sea level by 12 feet or more should it break up. But researchers long assumed the worst effects would take hundreds—if not thousands—of years to occur. Now, new research suggests the disaster scenario could play out much sooner. Continued high emissions of heat-trapping gases could launch a disintegration of the ice sheet within decades, according to a study (this last) March, heaving enough water into the ocean to raise the sea level as much as three feet by the end of this century. (*New York Times*, front page, March 30, 2016)

Quotes like this can terrify, and that is not my intent. I know that the course of history can change. I know it because I am part of a community that reads about how an enslaved people were freed from a Pharaoh, and because I know that while it can be costly to stand against power, it is possible. As a young student, I was a part of a large and potent movement that supported civil rights, that supported a farmworkers union, and that stopped a war in Vietnam. I know what it is to turn from the path you are supposed to follow—in my case, to college—and to stop, because you can no longer go on as a part of a country that is waging an unjust war. In 1960, the war was conducted without much American notice. But as the war grew, it became what we now would call "a wicked problem" or a "hyperobject." The war was complex, eventually involving several countries: North and South Vietnam, Laos, Cambodia, and

Burma. Troops were housed in Thailand, and each country presented its own dynamics. It had ecological consequence, as Agent Orange was deployed to destroy the jungles that hid North Vietnamese troops; there was the legacy of French colonialism, there was the "domino theory," there was money, and there were legacies, and there were American ideas about manhood, and it was just the way it seemed naturally to proceed, war after war. But a student movement which had a good argument built and built until the streets were full and no one could stand aside.

It is not only this movement. In my lifetime, I saw the single most entrenched adult habit, smoking, go from being cool to being disgusting. As people learned about the science, and as the federal government took action to expose the deceit of the tobacco companies, people in their millions made a personal decision that changed agriculture, business, and public space. In both instances, there was a mix of deeply private decisions—not to smoke after years of the habit; not to register for the draft or not to go into the Armed Services—and a movement that supported and valorized these changes and insisted on government policy. This is what a democracy is built for.

Of all the examples of how a great moral change was accomplished, even though it shook the foundations of the economic system, is the struggle against slavery in America. Opposition to slavery began in religious communities eighty years after the first slaves from Africa were brought to the British colonies. It was a Mennonite meeting in Germantown, Pennsylvania, where the question was taken up in 1688. Aware of their own persecution and flight to America, they wrote a letter of protest and sent it to their governing body, which was the Society of Friends, the Quakers.

> There is a saying that we shall doe to all men like as we will be done ourselves; making no difference of what generation, descent or colour they are. And those who steal or robb men, and those who buy or purchase them, are they not all alike? Here is liberty of conscience wch is right and reasonable; here ought to be liberty of ye body, except of evil-doers, wch is an other case. But to bring men hither, or to rob and sell them against their will, we stand against.[18]

The Quakers ignored the congregation's logic for another ninety years.

In the First Great Awakening of 1730–1740, evangelical preachers began to link salvation with the abolitionist cause, and by the time of American debates about making a revolution which was justified because all men were endowed by their Creator with certain unalienable rights, finally focused on the moral problem of slavery they were able to draw on a tradition of resistance. And Washington, Jefferson, and the others both understood the contradiction but did not free their slaves and built their wealth by a practice they knew was immoral.[19] Slowly, after the Second Great Awakening, and the growth of an abolitionist movement, people began to consider slavery morally horrific, at least in the North. By the time of the Civil War, half of all the wealth of the South was tied up in human slaves, and the entire agriculture system of wealth was dependent on their unpaid labor. It had been two hundred years of justification, denial, and defense of this wealth that allowed what was slowly understood to be a moral outrage to continue. America had two hundred years and a bloody Civil War to fight before the ideal that slavery had to be stopped was finally made real.[20] It took over two hundred years of religious arguments, political changes, and a change in the power of the economy of the North. If you were a slave during that time, the cruel and unjust wait for liberation while free white men made up their minds, was a moral horror, and we see this now. But we do not have two hundred years to decide to do the difficult but morally necessary change. We do not have generations and generations of time, of leaders and martyrs to make our point. We have, perhaps, says the UN IPCC, ten years. In the end, justice flowed down like a river and righteousness, like a mighty stream, which we should remember, and while the victory of the Voting Rights Act was imperfect, it was a turn for history, from totality, to the possibility of change, and we must do this as well.[21]

What would it take to stop your life?

I cannot convince my family to change their lives, so, reader, how can I convince you? My sister and brother like meat, my sons like meat, everybody feels they need their car, and it seems like they do, given how the world is structured.

Of course, we need to do every single thing we can as individuals to change our behavior. This will not mean small lifestyle changes, but serious changes that will make our life more difficult, serious sacrifices. I am sorry that this is the case but, in fact, sacrifice at a very serious level—one's firstborn animal, a tenth of one's crop—was the moral expectation imagined in Hebrew Scripture.

But "doing somethiing" must also mean something more. It must mean long-term political action. In 2022, we had what are called "glimmers of hope," in several news articles. The Biden bill, formerly called "Build Back Better," and now "The Inflation Reduction Act," moves to address climate change by creating a series of incentives for citizens and corporations to act responsibly in our use of carbon. The Office of Management and Budget has anticipated a 40% reduction in greenhouse gas emission below 2005, by 2030, reducing levels dramatically and allowing America to finally meet the Paris goals. This happened because of decades of political action, and it is just a beginning.[22]

I am going to end this book with an ordinary prayer. I have described this prayer in my first chapter on Jewish thought, and it is the one after which Rabbi Eleazar adds his extra prayer of hope, and I will repeat it and my argument here, because of its centrality.

"If you will" thus begins the Sh'ma, the prayer Jews are liturgically commanded to call out two times a day, every morning and every evening. This is a daily prophecy, and it could not be clearer:

> if you will listen constantly and diligently to My commandments that I command you this day, to love HaShem your God and to serve God with all your heart and with all your soul, then I will give the rain of your land in its right season, the early rains and the late rains, so that you may gather in your grain, and your wine, and your oil. And I will give grass in your fields for your cattle, and you shall eat and be satisfied. Watch yourselves, beware, because your heart can be deceived and seduced, and you will turn away astray, and serve other gods, and bow down them;
>
> Then the anger of HaShem be blaze against you! And He will shut up the heavens, so that there shall be no rain, and the ground shall not yield her fruit; and you will quickly be banished, starving, from off the good land which HaShem gives you.

It could not be clearer or more forthright: justice, the Sabbath, the care of the stranger, the ordering law, and the narrative of exile—you must repeat this all, for it is your covenant that keeps the world a good world.

"The heaven will shut its skies and there will be no rain" is the punishment for injustice to the poor. We are obligated by Hebrew Scripture to care for the poor, the marginal, the desperate, the hungry ones. When we do this, it is not because we are nice, or charitable, or that it is tax deductible. We do this because we have bound the words of Torah to our bodies, flat-out right between our eyes—*tzedakah*, the word for charity is the same word for justice, *tzedek*, and we give it because it is a public act that means we understand that we live in a theo-political economy, an imperative moral economy, that is far more important than the marketplace which deceives and seduces and tells the enormous lie that the earth can be destroyed, its energy sucked off and burned for profit. We don't say: Look at me, I am so kind. We ought to say: Look at God's world, in which the poor are central actors in the working out of moral order, look how abundant are the corners of the field, which belong to the poor, look at the richness of the second harvest, which belongs to them. And in Jerusalem, Rome, and Medina: Look at our awesome God who cares for the land so we can care for the poor, so we can steward the land so that it will be abundant, green, and golden to the corners. And if we do not, says Deuteronomy, the entire productive cycle will stop—because what is it all for, the abundance of it, the way it returns, really despite everything and all our petty sins, if not for the poor?

We face a moment when our own denial blinds us. We forget the great concern with sacrifice at the heart of Torah, pages and pages of blood and fire, our favorite lamb, the first one, our only cow, given to the glory of God, to the priests without land, to the poor without bread. Every single person, beggar to king, lives in a world of deep sacrifice. But we forget the loss, the Temple and the Cross, at the heart of faith. That is why we can so easily forget how hard the world is if you live in Northern Syria, where when the drought came there was no choice but to walk into the most uncertain of futures, or how hard it is to be poor, pregnant, and living in a favela ridden with Zika mosquitos, or along the Silk Road, when the Gobi Desert has encroached so steadily that the Chinese government has already had to move 1.14 million people out of the way of disaster. We read now, we read daily, of the end of the worlds of others, but still we do not act.

The summer that I wrote this book was astonishingly hot, so much so that many people began to understand that their lives have already begun to change. In the north of Finland, on July 18, temperatures were the highest ever recorded. In Sweden, unprecedented fires swept through Arctic forests because of unusually hot, dry, windy conditions. Weather records were broken all over Europe. Already, forest fires had killed over eighty people in Athens, Greece, and this summer, the heat threatened again. Then the far north began to burn and over 80,000 acres of forest were alight in Siberia. In Britain, France, and the Netherlands, lawns dried to a crisp brown. In Japan, heat so intense and persistent swept across the islands, that government officials declared a natural disaster.[23] Summers like this, noted Peter Stott of Britain's Met Office (the National Meteorological office) as well as many others, was unusual—now it is not. The likelihood of exceptionally hot summers and of very cold ones used to be about equal. Now, it is not. That summer, the worse hurricane in the history of the Bahamas (and now we are used to this elocution) savaged the islands.

When fall came that year, the heat continued, and in California, where I had gone to visit my family, there was no rain, and the hills above Los Angeles silently turned to the golden brown that delights visitors and worries native Californians. Every year, the winds from the desert just east of the San Bernadino and San Gabriel mountains of California rise and blow due west, hard and strong, whistling through the canyons and spinning the sand by the Pacific into small, sharp, circles—the Santa Ana winds. The Santa Ana winds were desiccating the already dry vegetation and pushing brush against power lines. When they spark, and a fire begins, the embers are blown along the ridges, and into the canyons. It is fire season.

Usually, the season peaks in October, for by November, the rains begin, and the winds stop, and the vegetation dies back. But since the climate has changed, each summer is hotter, the winds are hotter and fiercer as well, and the rain does not come. That year, as I worked on this book, I sat in a westside hotel with my family, evacuated from the Woolsey Fire like nearly 200,000 others in the Los Angeles area, during the worst fires in the state's history. Ten of the worst fires have occurred in the last fourteen years, which is why my friends from out of state ask me, "Wasn't there just a fire in California?" They mean the fire season of 2017, which was the most destructive until 2018. Then in 2020, the very worse yet. Then in 2022, as I re-edited the manuscript, the heat in California got worse, and the heat was suddenly worse everywhere that summer, and the entire Western United states faced record-breaking new fires, and as I write, record-breaking heat, so that every year as I write, things become more dire and the world still releases record-breaking amounts of carbon and every year, the extraction companies pump more fossil fuel out of the ground, making larger and larger profits.

It is my contention that we need bold and courageous action, the sort of action called for by the prophets of so many traditions and the sort of action needed if we actually understand that humanity is facing the greatest moral challenge of our time. We are forewarned—liturgy, Scripture history, narratives, scientists shouting, Look at this!

And each of us, you, me, the neighbor by your side, the stranger at the door, we need to understand that this chance, it may be our last chance to live "with love and brotherhood and peace and friendship" in this fragile and beautiful and only world, our Last Place.

Notes

Acknowledgments

1. Oppenhimer Mark, "Setting Aside a Scholarly Gathering for the Planet's Sake." New York Times, December 5, 2014.

Introduction

1. Emmanuel Levinas, "On the Jewish Reading of Scriptures," in *Beyond the Verse* (London: The Anthlone Press, 1994), p. 102.
2. Timothy Morton, *Philosophy and Ecology after Ecological Crisis* (Minneapolis: University of Minnesota Press, 2013)..
3. Ephraim Urbach, *The Sages* (Cambridge, MA: Harvard University Press, 1987), p. 348.
4. Emmanuel Levinas, "Demanding Judaism," in *Beyond the Verse* (Bloomington: Indiana University Press, 1998), pp. 4–6.
5. Emmanuel Levinas, "A Religion for Adults," in *Difficult Freedom* (Bloomington: Indiana University Press, 1997), p. 21.
6. ART. XXXI.—Circumstances affecting the Heat of the Sun's Rays;: (Read before the American Association, August 23d, 1856.) APSFoote, Eunice. American Journal of Science and Arts (1820–1879); New Haven Vol. 22, Iss. 66, (Nov)

Chapter 1

1. Nathaniel Rich, *Losing Earth: A Recent History* (New York: Farrar, Straus and Giroux, 2019), pp. 8–10.
2. Baruch Brody was my first teacher in bioethics, and this truism was a phrase he used often in teaching. Brody, Baruch, lectures in bioethics, Kaiser National Bioethics Conference, 1990.
3. https://www.bbc.co.uk/news/science-environment-15874560
4. A note on Agassi. Like many of the men and some of the women of his time as well, Agassi held incorrect and racially biased views. This is a fact of scientific history. My use of his and their work in gas exchange is not an endorsement. Others, such as Joseph Priestly, were known for their deeply democratic commitments.
5. Rich, *Losing Earth*, p. 12.
6. Kyla Mandel, wikipedia, Eunice Newton Foote May 18, 2018: "This woman fundamentally changed climate science—and you've probably never heard of her."
7. Ibid.
8. Rich, *Losing Earth*, p. 21.

9. Mount Tambura erupted in 1813 and caused a European cold spell for the next year, as ash from the eruption caused "the year with no summer." But this was unusual, which is why we know about it. In an aside, it was during this cold Genevan summer that Mary Shelley wrote her masterpiece, *Frankenstein*, so beloved by bioethicists who see it as the foretelling of a technological age that has gone beyond human virtue.
10. Rich, *Losing Earth*, p. 32.
11. https://history.aip.org/climate/Revelle.htm
12. Gilbert Plass, "Carbon Dioxide and the Climate," *American Scientist* 98, no. 1 (January–February 2010): 58–67. Reprinted as a "Classic" from the 1953 edition.
13. https://history.aip.org/climate/Revelle.htm
14. The International Geophysical Year (IGY), as it was called, was modeled on the International Polar Years of 1882–1883 and 1932–1933 and was intended to allow scientists from around the world to take part in a series of coordinated observations of various geophysical phenomena. Although representatives of forty-six countries originally agreed to participate in the IGY, by the close of the activity, sixty-seven countries had become involved.International organization and funding of the IGY were overseen by the International Council of Scientific Unions (ICSU), an independent federation of international scientific unions. A Special Committee for the IGY (CSAGI, an acronym derived from the French) was formed to act as the governing body for all IGY activities. Care had been taken to ensure that CSAGI would remain non-nationalistic, apolitical, and geared toward a scientific agenda.
15. https://history.aip.org/climate/Revelle.htm
16. Jimmy Carter, *The Global 2000 Report to the President* (New York: Penguin Books, 1980), Preface.
17. Bryon Daynes, "Global Climate Change and Presidential Leadership: Has There Been Any Significant Response by U. S. Presidents to This Vexing Global Threat," Western Political Science Association Annual Meeting, 2013.
18. With Zoloth, at the American Academy of Religion, 2014, on a special plenary on climate change.
19. Carter, *The Global 2000 Report*, p. 51.
20. Private conversation, 2014, American Academy of Religion meeting. San Diego, California.
21. Carter, *The Global 2000 Report*, pp. 52–53, 257, 259.
22. Daynes, "Global Climate Change and Presidential Leadership."
23. https//www.eenews.net/stories/1060105233/print
24. https://www.bbc.co.uk/news/science-environment-15874560
25. https://www.ipcc.ch/about/history/
26. https://www.bbc.co.uk/news/science-environment-15874560
27. Since 1988, the IPCC has had five assessment cycles and delivered five Assessment Reports, the most comprehensive scientific reports about climate change produced worldwide. It has also produced a range of Methodology Reports, Special Reports, and Technical Papers, in response to requests for information on specific scientific and technical matters from the United Nations Framework Convention on Climate Change (UNFCCC), governments, and international organizations.

28. https://www.eenews.net/stories/1060105233/print
29. Rich, *Losing Earth*.
30. Ibid.
31. https://www.nature.com/articles/d41586-021-00090-3#:~:text=After%20rising%20steadily%20for%20decades,on%20daily%20fossil%20fuel%20emissions
32. Not that the weather was always benign, of course. But with the exception of the Little Ice Age of 1300–1850, which was not a global phenomenon, but a feature of Europe medieval history. In our present situation, the climate changes will affect the entire human population.
33. Karen Lebacqz, *Justice in an Unjust World* (Minneapolis: Fortress Press, 1987).
34. Giridharadas, Anand, "*Winners Take All*: The Elite Charade of Changing the World" Penguin Random House, Press, New York, 2018
35. It could be argued, in fact, that Jewish thought can have only the faintest of impacts. (Even in American terms, Jews are only 2% of the population.)

Chapter 2

1. Lynn White, "The Historical Roots of Our Ecologic Crisis," *Science* 155, no. 3767 (March 10, 1967): 234.
2. Ibid., 234.
3. Ibid.
4. Ibid.
5. Ibid.
6. Willemein Otten, *Thinking of Nature and the Nature of Thinking* (Stanford, CA: Stanford University Press, 2020).
7. Stanford Encyclopedia of Philosophy, https://plato.stanford.edu/entries/natural-law-ethics/#SubNatLawVie
8. Thomas Aquinas, Summa Theologica, IaIIae 94, 4.
9. James Keenen, Geron Stem cell seminar on religion and stem cells, and discussions, Palo Alto, California, 2000.
10. John Locke, Second Treatise, §§ 25–51, 123–126, 1689.
11. For Anad Ghosh, climate change is "the great derangement," for normally, nature is well arranged; it is one's Mother, both predicable and welcoming—but human beings have created a monstrous, enormous thing, a non-mother, instead.
12. There is also a series of books about global warming, in which reporters and writers jet, ironically enough, to distant places, often to watch scientists at work, and sometimes to scuba dive, or go caving in exotic and rare venues, which are threatened by a changing climate. The places are beautiful, virginal, yet threatened, for the truth of the violation is more vivid there. Even as I deplore the carbon burden spent on these trips.
13. Elliott Dorff, *Modern Jewish Ethics* (Oxford: Oxford University Press, 1997).
14. https://www.questia.com/magazine/1G1-17379708/one-walking-and-studying-nature-vs-torah

15. Charlotte Fonrobert and Martin Jaffee, *The Talmud and Rabbinic Literature* (Cambridge: Cambridge University Press, 2007), p. 3.
16. The terms of Greek analysis do not precisely fit the Jewish system. As Levinas says, the Law needs to be translated into Greek.
17. Saul Berman, "The Ethical Commandments," scholar in residence, paper at Berkeley, California, 1992.
18. Barry Wimpfheimer, *Narrating the Law*, introduction.
19. Fonrobert and Jaffee, *The Talmud and Rabbinic Literature*.
20. Laurie Zoloth, "Face to Face but Not Eye to Eye," *The Journal of Clinical Ethics* (Winter 1995).
21. Herb Basser, as noted on the Post-Modern Jewish Philosophy Network.
22. John Puddefoot, from a discussion on the Post-Modern Jewish Philosophy Network. In this posting, Puddefoot reminds us that authoritative texts ought to be regarded as living texts carried along by a tradition which simultaneously qualifies them and is itself qualified by them.
23. The concept of *tzedakah*, or justice, is expressed by the same word as the word that means charity; the term for the fitness of food, *kosher*, is also the term for a person of high character. How this works, in fact, reads even more clearly than in principle. It is often the daily blessing and the daily disciplines that bring the entire sacred world into the simplest home setting. Note how this acts as a feminist corrective to a religion that is, of course, patriarchal by historical definition.
24. The first procedural question that the system of Jewish ethics addresses is the problem of how to achieve good ends in a nonteleological system. How are the norms in a "modified deontological" system evaluated and enforced over time if neither classic consequentialist nor classic deontological ethics is part of the tradition? Judaism answers this in a way that is the unique hallmark of the method. The basic procedure for the evaluation of norms is the mode of argumentation, commentary, debate, and discussion. Essentially casuistic, the halachic system uses the encounter with the Torah text, and the encounter with the Other's encounter with the text, to create a continuous discursive community. Cases are raised to illustrate points of law and then to illustrate alternate interpretations of the law. Narrative, in a variety of literary forms (metaphor, allegory, historical reference, intertextual mirroring) called *aggadah*, are embedded in the text. While the details of the aggadah did not create binding laws, the form was used to grapple with and embellish the discussion of the details of the halachah.
25. In fact, it is essential to remember that much of the case law turns on elaborate constructs that never happened, or could never be expected to happen. Much of the law concerning the role of the court in judging a murderer can be seen in this way (which, by the way, needs to be understood wherever the text is used to understand actual historical circumstance: this is one of the major sources of confusion in some traditional interpretations of Jewish tradition by Christians, especially relative to the Christian understanding of the "trial of Jesus").
26. When confronted with a contemporary problem, a question of how to behave in the face of the AIDS crisis, for example, halakhists go first to the text and commentary to seek solutions.

27. It is this vagueness that Peter Ochs claims is another name for multivocity. Internet posting, Thursday, May 18, 1995, Post Modern Jewish Philosophy Network.
28. Emmanuel Levinas, "The Pact."
29. Emmanuel Levinas, "Ethics and Spirit," in *Difficult Freedoms* (Baltimore: John Hopkins University Press, 1990), p. 7.
30. Consider: August 11, 1996, marked the total collapse of the Western grid power system in six of fifty states for several hours. This event shut down all uses of electrical power for four hours. No matter how wealthy or how close to the trillion-dollar marketplace one was, the electricity that worked the world was absent. That day was Shabbat. And on that day, my family, in my community, was oblivious to the event which dominated the front page of every Western state newspaper. We walked to synagogue, ate a shared meal, sang, prayed, read the Torah, studied together, walked home, slept, played with the children, shared another meal with friends, and sang. That night we noticed the clocks had stopped. We had, as a community, stepped out of the crisis itself—a model for what a conscious community might be able to do, a metaphor.
31. Levinas, Emmanual, "As Old as the World," in *Nine Talmudic Readings* (Indiana University Press) republished as an ebook in 2019.
32. Levinas, "The Pact," in *Nine Talmudic Readings* (Indiana University Press).
33. Ibid.
34. This original article raised the issue of population because it was written for a book about population and the environment. This continues as a critical part of my thinking, so I include it here: the growth of the population in a world described as "full." The world is in a period of the most rapid population increase in history. Nearly 88 million people are born each year, nearly 1 billion born every eleven years. But Jews have a history that is decidedly at odds with this surge in growth: it is a history that renders it ironic. It was at precisely the moment of rapid population increase that Jews were counting their losses, 6 million, 30% of the total population, dead after 1948. The entire discourse on population in Jewish life is haunted at the margins by the specter of the Shoah. In a real and specific sense, European Jews had already experienced life in a period of total environmental collapse, a near species extinction. This frames our Jewish reflections on the limits on population. Consequently, many Jews in the immediate generation post Shoah feel an obligation to restore the terrible losses to Jewish population that occurred at the hands of the Nazis, or are at the very least wary of external suggestions to limit Jewish population. The most recent figures attest to the complexity of the issue. The Jewish population continues to plummet around the world, except in Israel, and countries affected by the immigration of Jews from Russia into a small population (Canada, Germany, Panama, and Hong Kong). Only 13 million Jews are alive worldwide. In the United States, the population has dropped from 4% to 2.3%, a result of a consistently low birthrate and an intermarriage rate of 50%, with 75% of those families not raising their children as Jews, resulting in an unprecedented loss of identification and affiliation. It is not only the lessons of recent history that cast a tragic light on the question of population control and ecological justice, but the entire textual account of biblical history as well. Despite the injunction from God to be fruitful, and despite the promises to Abraham that "your descendants will as numerous as the stars" (Genesis 15:5), the account of Jewish history is framed by narrow escapes from total annihilation. The Exodus story

is an account of the outwitting of the decree to destroy all male children, the subversion of the midwives (who are the textual represeentors of fertility itself) at the heart of the drama. The skirmishes in Canaan always have complete annihilation at stake.
35. The commands of Bal Taschit, in the view of Maimonides, seem to be about property, not saving trees in particular, for any ecological reason. Here is his comment on that verse: "And not only trees, but whoever breaks vessels, tears clothing, wrecks that which is built up, stops fountains, or wastes food in a destructive manner, transgresses the commandment of *Bal Taschit*, but his punishment is only flogging by rabbinic edict" (Maimonides, *Sefer Ha-mitzvot*, Positive Commandment #6).
36. A classic case is this. I have said that the law is made in the house of study, and this is in general true of the rabbinical period. In one classic text, an argument cannot be settled by reliance on heavenly signs or a "bat kol" or voice from heaven. This text—Baba Metzia 59a, is happily cited in many liberal circles, but in many other texts (see Eruvin 13b, when a bat kol decides for Hillel over Shamai) often uncited, a bat kol makes many final decisions.
37. Two thousand years of narrative and history yield many moments in the biblical, rabbinic, and medieval texts that are critical to a search for theological language which supports rigorous ecological caution. Hence, many recent and important works have emerged in the last several years that describe an overview of Jewish thought on the environment that isolates one or another of these quotes: the injunction to protect the fruit trees of a city that one is waging war against, for example, or the generally applicable call to seek justice, the calls for a Jubilee, or the mystical prayers for the celebration of Tu b'Shevat, the New Year's holiday for trees and plants. In fact, there has been a renaissance of theology and deeply felt correspondent practice around the issue of ecology. Shromrei Adamah, for example, a national organization within the Jewish renewal movement, is devoted to teaching Jews to make the connection between Jewish tradition and the environment. They publish workbooks for adults and children, run a training camp in New York, and speak nationally on this topic. Arthur Waskow, among others, has long preached and written of the connection between the agricultural base for Jewish holidays and a general sense of commitment to the protection of the peace of the land.
38. There is a long literature about why the Hebrew Scripture begins with Creation and not the story of Abraham, specifically. For medieval commentators Rashi and Nachimonedes answered differed. Rashi tells us it is because telling the story from the beginning would make it clear that the Jews had come honestly to their birthright, but Nachmonedes insists that it is to tell the story of contingency, failure, new effort, and failure of all but the final way of understanding social order.
39. Arnold Eisen, *Galut: Modern Jewish Reflection on Homelessness and Homecoming* (Bloomington: Indiana University Press, 1986), p. 5.
40. Benjamin, Walter, "Thesis on the Concept of History." http://www.arts.yorku.ca/soci/barent/wpcontent/uploads/2008/10/benjaminconcept_of_history1.pdf and http://www.marxists.org/reference/archive/benjamin/1940/history.htm.
41. Eisen, *Galut*.

NOTES

42. Arnold Eisen, "Exile," in *Contemporary Jewish Religious Thought*, ed. Arthur A Cohen and Paul Mendes-Flor (New York: The Free Press, 1972), p. 220.
43. Eisen, *Galut*, p. 49.
44. *Sifre: A Tannaitic Commentary on the Book of Deuteronomy*, ed. and trans. Reuven Hammer (New Haven, CT: Yale University Press, 1986).
45. Eisen, *Galut*, p. 42.
46. Eisen, *Galut*, p. 49.
47. Eisen, *Galut*, p. 49.
48. Elie Wiesel and Philippe-Michael De Saint-Cheron, *Evil and Exile* (London: University of Notre Dame Press, 1990).
49. Max Weber, "Science as a Vocation." The Vocation Lectures, Hackett Publishing Company, p. 31. In the final paragraph of this essay, which is full of random anti-Jewish asides, Weber contrasts the Jew, endlessly waiting, with the proper German, who is "ready to spring forth."
50. Nachmionides (Ramban), Bereishit 12:6.
51. J. Baird Caldicott, "The Search for an Environmental Ethic," in *Matters of Life and Death*, 2nd ed., ed. Tom Regan (New York: Random House, 1980).
52. Further, the rabbinic structure of elaboration of laws about the Land of Israel is a complex theological move. Why is it that large sections of the Talmud might be devoted to an agricultural order that at least some must have suspected was actually, practically far beyond their grasp? Even more curious, why did the rabbis continue to debate the details of the Jubilee year long after its enactment was a possibility? I suggest that this gesture was the moral equivalent to the clothing of the nakedness of Exile itself. The garment of consideration is shaped by a meticulous attention to the problem of limits. It is the correlation between limitedness and law that allows for enormous industry, vision, and productivity with a limit to prideful acquisition.
53. It is a rabbinic truism and a later constant in the work of mystics such as Isaac Luria and Abraham Isaac Kook; theorists such as Buber, Rosensweig, Heschel, and Soleveitchik; and political leaders such as Theodor Hertzl and Henrietta Szold that both spiritual and physical homecoming requires a partnership in the process of *tikkun olam*, world repair.
54. Maimonides, *Guide for the Perplexed*.
55. David Korten, p. 10.
56. United Nations Intergovernmental Panel on Climate Change, *Land Use and Climate Change Report*, August 2019.
57. Eisen, *Galut*, p. 49.
58. United Nations Intergovernmental Panel on Climate Change, *Land Use and Climate Change Report*, August 2019.
59. Eisen, *Galut*, p. 49.
60. United Nations Intergovernmental Panel on Climate Change, *Land Use and Climate Change Report*, Chapter 6.
61. Washington Post, August 2019.

Chapter 3

1. Voltaire, "Les Délices," November 24, 1755.
2. https://earthscienceshistory.org/doi/pdf/10.17704/eshi.2.1.tn14161r6477q554
3. Midrash Rabbah, Sefaria, Judge 2:9.
4. Misnah Berakhot 9:2 and Berakhot 54a:2.
5. Talmud Balvi, Berakhot 59a; 4, Sefaria.org.
6. John Mullin, https://scholarworks.umass.edu/cgi/viewcontent.cgi?article=1044&context=larp_faculty_pubs.
7. Ibid.
8. Anand Giridharadas, *Winners Take All: The Elite Charade of Changing the World* (New York: Knopf, 2019), p. 86.
9. Anna Rosling, Hans Rosling, and Ola Rosling, *Factfullness: Ten Reasons We're Wrong* (New York: Flatiron Books, 2018). Let me spend some time considering this excellent book, which makes the solid case that the world is far better than we think it is—for millions of people are no longer abjectly poor, more women than ever before in history go to school, epidemic disease is waning, clean water is more accessible to more people, more people live in cities with electricity. All of this is true, and reason for optimism, but all of this progress would still be threatened, as indeed middle-class people in America are threatened by climate change.
10. John Mullin, https://scholarworks.umass.edu/cgi/viewcontent.cgi?article=1044&context=larp_faculty_pubs
11. Natan Levy also suggests this final addition, from *The Teacher* by Zvi Kolitz (p. 136), to the Job story, which turns us back to earthquakes: "The teacher raised the question of the daughters of Job—At the conclusion of the book of Job, he said, the Bible tells us that Job's later years where even more blessed than his earlier. The Bible tells us little about the nature of those blessings, except in the case of his daughters, born to him in his latter year. 'And in the entire land,' it says, 'there were no maidens found more fair than the daughters of Job.' . . . The beautiful appears almost as organic to the dreadful, or perhaps dreadful is the wrong word. I would rather evoke the metaphor of earthquake and flowers. In Job's case the flowers, as symbolized by the fair maidens, are not so much consolation for the earthquake as its transformation. The Bible is trying to tell us, in words of visionary poesy, that the beauty bestowed on the daughters of Job did not signify a break with their father's tragic past, but a newly found, marvelous creative ability to let that past mold the nature of their fairness. . . ." For Levy, it is not that there is good in disaster but "that a broken house allows us the opportunity to widen the door a bit to the stranger, or in the words of King David (psalm 25) 'troubles have enlarged my heart.'"
12. I am aware of the critique of narrative ethics: that it is too vague, or that there is no argument and no data. There is a need to count, of course, for it makes public health possible. Ladders are made to a certain height, buildings to be judged strong enough. Normativity has a relationship to quantitative judgments in addition to qualitative ones. Yet it comes at a cost, modernity brings the possibility of the statistical everyman, and chance and contingency can be calculated with precision.

13. Emmanuel Levinas, *'Ethics as First Philosophy': Is It Righteous to Be? Interviews with Emmanuel Levinas* (Stanford: Stanford University Press, 1961).
14. Not merely safe for us, not merely a green, gated community for our other woke friends.

Chapter 4

1. "Syria Climate Study Warned Assad of Drought Dangers in 2010," *Climate Change News*, September 18, 2015.
2. Ibid.
3. David Wallace-Wells, *The Uninhabitable Earth: Life After Warming* (New York: Tim Duggan Books, 2019).
4. A thoughtful reviewer noted the many worlds to which we are obligated: beyond the world of our campus, to our cities, our nation, to the developing world. All of these commitments surround each of our daily acts.
5. Jonathan Blitzer, "How Climate Change Is Fueling the US Border Crisis," *New Yorker*, April 2, 2019.
6. Ibid.
7. Malnutrition in children appears in three ways, and it is most commonly assessed through the measurement of weight and height. A child can be too short for his or her age (stunted), have low weight for his or her height (wasted), or have low weight for his or her age (underweight). A child who is underweight can also be stunted or wasted or both (UNICEF 2009, p. 13).

    Stunting. Stunting affects approximately 195 million children under five years old in the developing world, or about one in three. Africa and Asia have high stunting rates—40% and 36%, respectively—and more than 90% of the world's stunted children live on these two continents (UNICEF 2009, pp. 15–19).

    Wasting. Children who suffer from wasting face a markedly increased chance of death. According to UNICEF, 13% of children under five years old in the developing world are wasted, and 5% are extremely wasted, an estimated 26 million children (UNICEF 2009, p. 20).

    Underweight. UNICEF estimates that 129 million children under five years old in the developing world are underweight—nearly one in four. Ten percent of children in the developing world are severely underweight. The prevalence of underweight is higher in Asia than in Africa, with rates of 27% and 21%, respectively (UNICEF 2009, p. 17).
8. It is important to distinguish, however, the complexities of this statement. Many of our can's end up in disaster: the threat to the climate is largely the result of the idea that if we can to something, dig something, or suck something out of the ground, then it ought to be done. My point here is made to turn this argument on its head. This is important in a time when people concerned about climate change can feel unable to act.

9. Baba Kamma 32b (New York: Soncino Press, via Davka edition, indexed 2001).
10. Do I understand both the steadiness of the logic of my argument and the practical difficulty of really enacting it? Yes.
11. Hannah Arendt, *The Human Condition* (Chicago: University of Chicago Press, 1958), p. 198.
12. Hannah Arendt, "The Space of Appearing," *Stanford Encyclopedia of Philosophy*, http://plato.stanford.edu/Arendt.
13. Arendt, *The Human Condition*, p. 199.
14. Hannah Arendt, *The Crisis of the Republic* (Rumford, ME: Mainer Press, 1972), p. 151.
15. Arendt, *The Human Condition*.
16. Hannah Arendt, *The Origins of Totalitarianism* (New York: Meridian Books and World Publishing Company, 1958), 270.
17. Hannah Arendt, "We Refugees," in *Hannah Arendt's Jewish Writing* (New York: Schocken Books, 1963).
18. Ibid.
19. Ibid.
20. UN IPCC, *Land Use and Climate Change Report*, 2019.
21. See, for example, *The Ethics of Encounter: A Jewish Perspective on Justice* (Durham: University of North Carolina Press, 1999).
22. See, for example, Jameson in *The Failure of Reason*; Lisabet Kolbert in *The Tipping Point*.
23. Hebrew Scripture, Genesis 42.
24. Quran, Sura 12:88.
25. Emmanuel Levinas, "The Rights of Man and the Right of the Other," in *Outside the Subject* (Palo Alto, CA: Stanford University Press, 1994), p. 117.
26. Bereshit Rabba, 91: 1–6 (New York: Soncino Press, via Davka edition, indexed 2001).
27. Ellenblum. Ronni, in a conversation about our work at Clare Hall, University of Cambridge, in the summer of 2019, when both he and I were writing on climate change. This book is the one I wrote, and his book, *Fragility* was published in Hebrew in 2020, just before his death. His theory of fragility is also described in this work: *The Collapse of the Eastern Mediterranean: Climate Change and the Decline of the East. 950–1072* (Cambridge University Press, 2012).

Chapter 5

1. http://www.charitywater.org/whywater/
2. http://www.charitywater.org/whywater/
3. https://www.who.int/news-room/fact-sheets/detail/cholera
4. https://www.choleraalliance.org/en/ressources/news/cholera-epidemic-yemen-2020-update
5. https://gbvguidelines.org/wp/wp-content/uploads/2020/03/29_Haiti_UNICEF_Briefing_Note_Gender_Cholera.pdf
6. "Gender and Development," United Nations, Vol. 10, 2002.

7. https://earthobservatory.nasa.gov/images/147480/severe-drought-in-south-america#:~:text=Large%20parts%20of%20South%20America,and%20northern%20Argentina%20by%202020.
8. H. E. Dregne, "Desertification of Arid Lands," in *Physics of Desertification*, ed. F. El-Baz and M. H. A. Hassan (Dordrecht, The Netherlands: Martinus, Nijhoff, 1986), 56.
9. Pope Francis, "Laudito Si," 2014.
10. Peter Brewer and James Barry, "Rising Acidity in the Ocean: The *Other* CO_2 Problem," *Scientific American*, September, 2008. Brewer and Barry note: "The planet's seas quickly absorb 25 to 30 percent of humankind's CO_2 emissions and about 85 percent in the long run, as water and air mix at the ocean's surface. We have 'disposed' of 530 billion tons of the gas in this way, and the rate worldwide is now one million tons per hour, faster than experienced on earth for tens of millions of years."
11. Emmanuel Levinas, "The Paradox of Morality: An Interview with Emmanuel Levinas," in *In the Provocation of Levinas: Rethinking the Other*, ed. Robert Bernasconi and David Wood (London: Routledge, 1988), pp. 171, 174.
12. Michael Morgan, *Levinas's Ethical Politics* (Bloomington: Indiana University Press, 2016), p. 352.
13. Morgan, *Levinas's Ethical Politics*, p. 51. Morgan is citing Levinas, in "Diachrony and Representation," *Entre Nous* (1985): 165–168.
14. Likutei Moharan 216:1:1–2ב-א:א:זטר "ליקוטי מוהר"ן.
15. Midrash Rabbah—Deuteronomy VI: 4.
16. Wendy Doniger, in discussion at the University of Chicago.
17. Franz Rosenszweig, *The Star of Redemption* also see the discussion of this idea in Robert *Gibb's Why Ethics? Signs of Responsibility* (Princeton University Press, 2012) and in Zoloth, *Second Texts, Second Opinion*.
18. Pope Francis, "Laudito Si," 2014.
19. Pope Francis, "Laudito Si," 2014.

Chapter 6

1. Bernard William, "Moral Luck," in *Moral Luck* (Cambridge: Cambridge Press, 1981), chapter 2, pp. 1–3.
2. Deuteronomy, 21:1–11. In Sefaria. There is a dispute about the term "harsh" wadi. That is the version used in the Jewish Publication Society translation, while both Briggs Driver Briggs and Sefaria use the term "ever-flowing" to describe the wadi. In other versions, it is described as "hard."
3. Mishnah Sotah 9, 2–3 Sefaria.org.
4. Mishnah Sotah 9, Sefaria.org.
5. Emmanuel Levinas, "The Face," in *Ethics and Infinity*, Conversations with Philip Nemo, trans. Richard Cohen (Pittsburgh: Duquesne University Press, 1985), p. 86.
6. Mishnah Sotah 9, Sefaria.org.
7. Girard, Rene, "Violence and the Sacred," 1979, Bloombury, London, UK.
8. Ibid.

9. There is also a famous comment by Rashi (45:27) that the reason that Jacob understood that the wagons sent from Egypt were from his son was because they were pulled by "egla arufahim," these special calves, and the last thing that the father and son had studied together was this section of the Mishnah before Joseph was sent off—to the field—to see his brothers and show them the coat of many colors. Jacob saw this as a coded message from his son, and so agreed to come to Egypt with the brothers: "All the words of Yoseif. He [Yoseif] gave them as a sign—the subject that he was studying at the time that he left him [Yaakov]—the topic of עֶגְלָה עֲרוּפָה—the heifer whose neck is broken. This is [alluded to by] what is said: "And he saw the wagons [עֲגָלוֹת] that Yoseif had sent" And it does not state, "Which Pharaoh had sent."
10. Mishnah Sotah 9, op cit.
11. Mishnah Sotah 9, op cit.
12. https://www.carbonbrief.org/explainer-nine-tipping-points-that-could-be-triggered-by-climate-change
13. https://www.nature.com/articles/nclimate2964
14. Stefan Rahmstorf, Jason Box, Georg Feulner, Michael Mann, Alexamder Robinson, Scott Rutherford, and Erick Schaffernict, "Exceptional Twentieth-Century Slowdown in Atlantic Ocean Overturning Circulation," *Nature Climate Change* 5, no. 5: 475–480.
15. https://www.sciencedaily.com/releases/2021/02/210225113357.htm
16. https://www.theguardian.com/environment/2021/aug/05/climate-crisis-scientists-spot-warning-signs-of-gulf-stream-collapse
17. L. Caesar, G. D. McCarthy, D. J. R. Thornalley, N. Cahill, and S. Rahmstorf, "Current Atlantic Meridional Overturning Circulation Weakest in Last Millennium," *Nature Geoscience* (2021). DOI: 10.1038/s41561-021-00699-z as cited in L. Caesar, G. D. McCarthy, D. J. R. Thornalley, N. Cahill, and S. Rahmstorf, "Current Atlantic Meridional Overturning Circulation Weakest in Last Millennium," Nature Geoscience (2021). DOI: 10.1038/s41561-021-00699-z.
18. https://www.pbs.org/wgbh/nova/article/warm-water-found-beneath-thwaites-glacier-antarctica/
19. "Scary" is something you really do not want to hear a scientist say.
20. https://www.pbs.org/wgbh/nova/article/amoc-shutdown-gulf-stream-climate/
21. Natan Z. Levy, paper at the American Academy of Religion, 2014.
22. Margaret Urban Walker, "The Virtues of Impure Agency," in *Moral Luck* (New York: Cambridge University Press, 1981), 235–250, 236.
23. Ibid., p. 238.
24. Ibid., p. 238.
25. Ibid., p. 239.
26. Ibid., p. 242.
27. Hannah Arendt, "Collective Responsibility."
28. Arendt, "Collective Responsibility."
29. Who was this person, Tehina the Pharisee? He is found in the Jewish Encyclopedia as follows: leader of the Zealots. Together with Eleazar Ben Dinai, he is mentioned in the remarkable dictum of Johanan ben Zakkai concerning the Zealots: "Since the murderers have increased, the expiation ceremony of the 'eglah 'arufah [the heifer whose neck is broken for a murder the perpetrator of which is unknown; Deut. xxi.

1–9] has come into abeyance because of the many murders by these only too well-known Zealots. Such murderers are Eleazar ben Dinai and Teḥina, who was formerly called 'the Pharisee' and later on received the name of 'the Murderer'" (Soṭah ix. 9; Sifre, Deut. 205).

This Teḥina has aptly been identified by Derenbourg ("Essai sur l'Histoire et la Géographie de la Palestine d'Après les Thalmuds et les Autres Sources Rabbiniques," i. 279–280, Paris, 1867) with the Abba Teḥina Ḥasida of Eccl. R. ix. 7. Derenbourg, however, takes the epithet "Ḥasid" to be ironical; but he ignores the very nature of the passage to which he refers and which is as follows: "Teḥina the Essene [Ḥasid] with the title Abba [see Kohler, "Abba, Father," in "J. Q. R." xiii. 567–575], returning to his native town on Friday afternoon shortly before the beginning of the Sabbath, and carrying upon his shoulder a bundle containing the provisions for his household for the Sabbath, met a disease-stricken man unable to move, who asked him to have pity on him and bring him into the town, where his wants might receive the necessary attention. This placed Teḥina in a quandary: he was afraid if he left his bundle he might lose all his Sabbath provisions; and if he did not aid the sick man, he (Teḥina) would be accounted as guilty of death. His better impulses proving victorious, he carried the sick man to a safe place, and then went back for his bundle. Meanwhile it had grown dark; and the people, seeing him carry a bundle on Sabbath eve, wondered, saying, 'Is this Abba Teḥina the Pious?' Teḥina himself was in doubt as to whether he had really violated the Sabbath, when a miracle happened: God caused the sun again to shine forth to show that the Sabbath had not yet begun, as it is written (Mal. iii. 20 [A. V. iv. 2]): 'But unto you that fear my name shall the sun of righteousness arise with healing in his wings.'" Later the punctilious Essene became a fierce Zealot (see Zealots).

Eleazar ben Dinai is mentioned by Josephus several times, while Teḥina is not. He has been identified with the Alexander mentioned together with Eleazar b. Dinai by that author (Josephus, "B. J." ii. 12, § 4; see Eleazar Ben Dinai); but Alexander appears to be identical with Amram, cited as companion of Ben Dinai in "Ant." xx. 1, § 1 (comp. Cant. R. iii. 5: "In the days of Amram. [?] and in the days of Ben Dinai they attempted to bring about the Messianic time by violence"; see Grätz, "Gesch." 3d ed., iii. 431), whereas it is quite possible that Teḥina is identical with Ἀννιβας who was executed by order of Fadus (Josephus, "Ant." l.c.; Grätz, l.c. p. 278).

Chapter 7

1. Paul Ricoeur, "Memory and Forgetting," in *Questioning Ethics* (London: Routledge, 1999).
2. Amalaite territory as a geographical entity is mentioned earlier in Genesis 14:7 as a place from which tribes hostile to Abraham are located: "And they returned, and came to Ein-Mishpat, which is Kadesh, and struck all the country of the Amalekites, and also the Amorites, who lived in Hazezon-Tamar."
3. They are both sons of Eliphaz and of Adah.

4. This apparently was what impressed Jethro, according to the rabbinic commentary, and caused him to find the freed slaves and his son-in-law Moses in the desert:

    This is a controversy of Tannaim: Now Jethro, the priest of Midian, heard: 27 what news did he hear that he came and turned a proselyte? R. Joshua said: He heard of the battle with the Amalekites, since this is immediately preceded by, 28 And Joshua discomfited Amalek and his people with the edge of the sword. 29 R. Eleazar of Modim 30 said: He heard of the giving of the Torah and came. (Zevachim 116a)

5. 40 And they rose up early in the morning, and went up to the top of the mountain, saying, Behold, we are here, and will go up to the place of which the Lord has spoken; for we have sinned. 41 And Moses said, Why do you now transgress the commandment of the Lord? But it shall not succeed. 42 Do not go up, for the Lord is not among you; so that you should not be struck before your enemies. 43 For the Amalekites and the Canaanites are there before you, and you shall fall by the sword; because you are turned away from the Lord, therefore the Lord will not be with you. 44 But they presumed to go up to the hill top; nevertheless the ark of the covenant of the Lord, and Moses, departed not from the camp. 45 Then the Amalekites came down, and the Canaanites who lived in that hill, and defeated them, and pursued them, even to Hormah. (Numbers 14:40–45)

6. 10 And the spirit of the Lord came upon him, and he judged Israel, and went out to war; and the Lord delivered Kushan-Rishathaim king of Mesopotamia into his hand; and his hand prevailed against Kushan-Rishathaim. 11 And the land had rest forty years. And Othniel the son of Kenaz died. 12 And the people of Israel did evil again in the sight of the Lord; and the Lord strengthened Eglon the king of Moab against Israel, because they had done evil in the sight of the Lord. 13 And he gathered to him the Ammonites and Amalek, and went and struck Israel, and possessed the city of palm trees. 14 So the people of Israel served Eglon the king of Moab eighteen years. (Judges 3:10–14)

7. 1 And the people of Israel did evil in the sight of the Lord; and the Lord delivered them into the hand of Midian seven years. 2 And the hand of Midian prevailed against Israel; and because of the Midianites the people of Israel made for themselves the tunnels which are in the mountains, and caves, and fortresses. 3 And so it was, when Israel had sown, that the Midianites came up, and the Amalekites, and the people of the east, they came up against them; 4 And they encamped against them, and destroyed the produce of the land, as far as Gaza, and left no sustenance for Israel, neither sheep, nor ox, nor ass. (Judges 6:1–4)

8. 12 Awake, awake, Deborah; awake, awake, utter a song; arise, Barak, and lead away your captives, you son of Abinoam. 13 Then he made him who remains have dominion over the nobles among the people; the Lord made me have dominion over the mighty. 14 Out of Ephraim was there a root of them against Amalek; after you, Benjamin with your tribes; from Machir came down leaders, of Zebulun those who handle the marshal's staff. (Judges 5:12–14)

9. 29 And they said one to another, Who has done this thing? And when they inquired and asked, they said, Gideon the son of Joash has done this thing. 30 Then the men of the city said to Joash, Bring out your son, that he may die; because he has cast down

the altar of Baal, and because he has cut down the Ashera that was by it. 31 And Joash said to all who stood against him, Will you plead for Baal? Will you save him? He who will plead for him, let him be put to death while it is yet morning; if he is a god, let him plead for himself, because one has cast down his altar. 32 Therefore on that day he called him Jerubbaal, saying, Let Baal plead against him, because he has thrown down his altar. 33 Then all the Midianites and the Amalekites and the people of the east were gathered together, and went over, and camped in the valley of Jezreel. (Judges 9:29–33)

9 And it came to pass the same night, that the Lord said to him, Arise, get down to the camp; for I have delivered it into your hand. 10 But if you fear to go down, go with Phurah your servant down to the camp; 11 And you shall hear what they say; and afterwards shall your hands be strengthened to go down to the camp. Then went he down with Phurah his servant to the outside of the armed men who were in the camp. 12 And the Midianites and the Amalekites and all the people of the east lay along in the valley like grasshoppers for multitude; and their camels were without number, as the sand by the seaside for multitude. (Judges 7:9–12)

10 And the people of Israel cried to the Lord, saying, We have sinned against you, because we have forsaken our God, and also served the Baalim. 11 And the Lord said to the people of Israel, Did I not save you from the Egyptians, and from the Amorites, from the Ammonites, and from the Philistines? 12 The Sidonians also, and the Amalekites, and the Maonites, oppressed you; and you cried to me, and I saved you from their hand. 13 Yet you have forsaken me, and served other gods; therefore I will save you no more. (Judges 10:10–13)

11 And after him Elon, a Zebulunite, judged Israel; and he judged Israel ten years. 12 And Elon the Zebulunite died, and was buried in Ayalon in the country of Zebulun. 13 And after him Abdon the son of Hillel, a Pirathonite, judged Israel. 14 And he had forty sons and thirty nephews, who rode on seventy donkeys; and he judged Israel eight years. 15 And Abdon the son of Hillel the Pirathonite died, and was buried in Pirathon in the land of Ephraim, in the mount of the Amalekites. (Judges 12:11–15)

10. I have shortened this by leaving out the many other times Saul blames the people for the problem. It continues: 28 And Samuel said to him, The Lord has torn the kingdom of Israel from you this day, and has given it to a neighbor of yours, who is better than you. 29 And also the Eternal One of Israel will not lie nor change his mind; for he is not a man, that he should change his mind. 30 Then he said, I have sinned; yet honor me now, I beg you, before the elders of my people, and before Israel, and turn again with me, that I may worship the Lord your God. 31 So Samuel turned again after Saul; and Saul worshipped the Lord. 32 Then said Samuel, Bring here to me Agag the king of the Amalekites. And Agag came to him cheerfully. And Agag said, Surely the bitterness of death is past. 33 And Samuel said, As your sword has made women childless, so shall your mother be childless among women. And Samuel cut Agag in pieces before the Lord in Gilgal. 34 Then Samuel went to Ramah; and Saul went up to his house to Gibeah of Saul. 35 And Samuel came no more to see Saul until the day of his death; nevertheless Samuel mourned for Saul; and the Lord repented that he had made Saul king over Israel. (1 Samuel 15:28–35)

11. 13 And David said to him, To whom do you belong? and from where are you? And he said, I am a young man of Egypt, servant to an Amalekite; and my master left me, because three days ago I fell sick. 14 We made a raid upon the Negev of the Kerethites, and upon the territory which belongs to Judah, and upon the Negev of Caleb; and we burned Ziklag with fire. 15 And David said to him, Can you take me to this company? And he said, Swear to me by God, that you will not kill me, nor deliver me to the hands of my master, and I will take you to this company. (1 Samuel 30:13–15)

    1 And it came to pass, when David and his men came to Ziklag on the third day, that the Amalekites had invaded the south, and Ziklag, and struck Ziklag, and burned it with fire; 2 And had taken the women captives, who were there; they did not kill any, either great or small, but carried them away, and went on their way. 3 So David and his men came to the city, and, behold, it was burned with fire; and their wives, and their sons, and their daughters, had been taken captives. 4 Then David and the people who were with him lifted up their voice and wept, until they had no more strength to weep. (1 Samuel 30:1–4)

12. 1 And it came to pass after the death of Saul, when David returned from the slaughter of the Amalekites, and David had stayed two days in Ziklag; 2 It came to pass on the third day, that, behold, a man came from the camp from Saul with his clothes torn and earth upon his head; and so it was, when he came to David, that he fell to the earth, and bowed down. 3 Samuel (saying) As I happened by chance upon Mount Gilboa, behold, Saul leaned upon his spear; and, behold, the chariots and horsemen followed hard after him. 7 And when he looked behind him, he saw me, and called me. And I answered, Here am I. 8 (K) And he said to me, Who are you? And I answered him, I am an Amalekite. 9 And he said to me, Stand, I beg you, upon me, and slay me; for agony has come upon me, and yet I still have life in me. 10 So I stood beside him, and slew him, because I was sure that he could not live after he was fallen; and I took the crown that was upon his head, and the bracelet that was on his arm, and have brought them here to my lord. 11 Then David took hold of his clothes, and tore them; and likewise all the men who were with him; 12 And they mourned, and wept, and fasted until the evening, for Saul, and for Jonathan his son, and for the people of the Lord, and for the house of Israel; because they had fallen by the sword. 13 And David said to the young man who told him, Where are you from? And he answered, I am the son of a stranger, an Amalekite. 14 And David said to him, How were you not afraid to stretch forth your hand to destroy the Lord's anointed? 15 And David called one of the young men, and said, Go near, and fall upon him. And he struck him that he died. 16 (K) And David said to him, Your blood be upon your head; for your mouth has testified against you, saying, I have killed the Lord's anointed. 17 And David lamented with this lamentation over Saul and over Jonathan his son; 18 And he said To teach the sons of Judah the use of the bow; behold, it is written in the book of Jasher. 19 The beauty, O Israel, is slain upon your high places; how are the mighty fallen! (Samuel 2:1–3, 7–19)

13. Chullin 139b:11. Where is Haman indicated in the Torah? In the verse: Is it [hamin] from the tree? This pun refers to The Tree. Sefaria.org.

14. https://www.yutorah.org/lectures/lecture.cfm/790356/rabbi-yoni-levin/the-grandchildren-of-haman-learned-torah-in-bnei-brak/

15. Joshua Koperwas, "Destroying Amalek: Removing Doubt and Insecurity," in Sefaria.org.
16. Hannah Arendt, "On Lying," in *On Lying and Politics* (New York: Penguin Library of America, 2022).
17. Ibid.
18. Finally: is there a duty to forget? Classical Greece: amnesty celebrated at regular intervals: here, citizens had to promise not to recall a past evil event. American law: an end to punishment civil rights restored. However: note the difference between amnesty and amnesia: amnesty is not symmetrical with memory, since amnesty is a going beyond anger and hatred. Justice is the horizon. For Jews: the cities of refuge exist as a place of amnesty. Thinking of Ruth themes: why has Naomi "forgotten" and then remembers a G-d that remembers the people? Think of the injunction to remember and to preserve Shabbat, the re-enactment and retelling of the Pesach narrative and the Shoah memorials.
19. Hannah Arendt, *Responsibility and Judgment* (New York: Schocken Books, 2003), p. 19.
20. Arendt, "Personal Responsibility Under Dictatorship," in ibid., p. 20
21. Arendt, "Collective Responsibility," in ibid., p. 147
22. Naomi Oreskes and Eric Conway, *Merchants of Doubt: How a Handful of Scientists Obscured the Truth on Issues from Tobacco Smoke to Global Warming* (New York: Bloomsbury Press, 2011), p. 6
23. Nathaniel Rich, *Losing Earth: A Recent History* (New York: Farrar, Straus and Giroux, 2019), p. 8
24. https://www.wri.org/blog/2018/09/6-ways-remove-carbon-pollution-sky
25. A tradition that continues to this day. See Mar-a-Lago.
26. https://corporate.exxonmobil.com/about-us/who-we-are/our-history
27. Ibid.
28. https://www1.salary.com/EXXON-MOBIL-CORP-Executive-Salaries.html
29. https://waterwellsforafrica.org/whats-the-cost/
30. Of course, Exxon also paid the executives in the entire upper management huge bonuses as well. And the other companies—Chevron, BP, etc.—matched this salary and these practices without blinking. In total, $22 billion in profits.
31. Rich, *Losing Earth*, p. 48.
32. Ibid.
33. Ibid., p. 49
34. Ibid., p. 132.
35. Ibid., p. 133.
36. https://en.wikipedia.org/wiki/Global_Climate_Coalition#cite_note-13
37. Ibid.
38. https://www.nytimes.com/2019/08/23/opinion/sunday/david-koch-climate-change.html
39. Rich, *Losing Earth*, p. 135.
40. Ibid., p. 136.
41. Ibid., p. 194.
42. https://en.wikipedia.org/wiki/The_Great_Global_Warming_Swindle

242 NOTES

43. Naomi Oreskes and Erik Conway, *Merchant of Doubt: How a Handful of Scientists Obscured the Truth on Issues for Tobacco Smoke to Global Warming* (New York: Bloomsbury, 2011), p. 187.
44. https://www.bas.ac.uk/data/our-data/publication/antarctica-and-climate-change/
45. https://www.campaigncc.org/climate_change/sceptics/hall_of_shame
46. https://www.aap.com.au/factcheck/geologist-misleads-with-climate-change-proof-claim/
47. https://www.theguardian.com/environment/2011/oct/21/lord-lawson-global-warming-errors
48. https://www.carbonbrief.org/what-the-new-ipcc-report-says-about-sea-level-rise

Chapter 8

1. IPCC, *Climate Change 2013: The Physical Science Basis. Contribution of Working Group I to the Fifth Assessment Report of the Intergovernmental Panel on Climate Change*, ed. T. F. Stocker, D. Qin, G.-K. Plattner, M. Tignor, S. K. Allen, J. Boschung, A. Nauels, Y. Xia, V. Bex, and P. M. Midgley (Cambridge: Cambridge University Press).
2. Richard Alley, "Earth, Climate and Integrity," Duquesne University, Creation and Integrity Presidential Conference, October 2015.
3. Ludwig Wittgenstein, *Philosophical Investigations* (Oxford: Blackwell, 1973).
4. Walter Benjamin, "Theses on the Philosophy of History," https://seansturm.files.wordpress.com/2012/06/benjamin-theses-on-the-philosophy-of-history.pdf
5. Ibid.
6. https://www.nytimes.com/2019/08/15/climate/coal-adani-india-australia.html
7. Ibid.
8. Ibid.
9. https://www.esrl.noaa.gov/gmd/news/7074.html. Before the Industrial Revolution in the nineteenth century, global average CO_2 was about 280 ppm. During the last 800,000 years, CO_2 fluctuated between about 180 ppm during ice ages and 280 ppm during interglacial warm periods. Today's rate of increase is more than 100 times faster than the increase that occurred when the last ice age ended.
10. Hannah Arendt, *The Promise of Politics* (New York: Schocken Books, 2005).
11. Arendt, Hannah, "Reflections on Civil Disobedience" New Yorker Magazine, September 4, 1970
12. IPCC, *Climate Change 2013*.
13. Justin Gillis, "U.N. Panel Issues Its Starkest Warning Yet on Global Warming," *New York Times*, November 2, 2014. http://www.nytimes.com/2014/11/03/world/europe/global-warming-un-intergovernmental-panel-on-climate-change.html?
14. We make a living by struggling to understand the truth of the world, speaking *parrhesia*. And here it is important to note that we like hard inquiry, and we believe in skepticism—but we do not believe in ignorance and we don't support the denial of data.

15. The moral gesture of teaching and of working at a university is not an innocent gesture, for we still live as Americans, using three times the resources of most, we still get to fly to San Diego and take it over, living in hotels far above the beggars, eating and drinking, and swimming in what we call work, but is laughably more than the dreams of most people of the world (just ask the women who cleans the toilets in your department, or the man who sweeps the sidewalk of your pretty campus). And we will fly home, leaving the white trail of our carbon streaking and crossing the sky, filling it up this much more.
16. Gillis, "U.N. Panel Issues Its Starkest Warning Yet on Global Warming."
17. Not the whole semester—you can still do exegesis, I told them, or describe the lived religious practices of the Brooklyn Catholics, or translate the last rare copy of the fifteenth-century Viennese manuscript, but make corners in your field, in our field of scholarship: a time tithe, ten minutes of attention about the very real need to think about our climate. Tithe one week a semester, or tithe four hours from weekly email to read one IPCC report, one book about the issue. Study the science, teach the consequences. Tithing could be an ongoing part of our annual meeting, making the AAR a transformative community. We could each take two hours off of our meeting and leave a project in our wake, one garden, even new trees. We can and we must do far better; we could plant trees every place we have been.

Conclusion

1. I am not giving my friends real name nor the name of the Institute where he works, because we really are friends.
2. Of course, you might think I make my living that way as well, but I have full-time job teaching about religion or bioethics and writing about that topic, and climate change research is not exactly seen, alas, as central to bioethical discourse.
3. Here is one slide he sent in 2019:
   - Carbon dioxide is not "carbon."
   - It is not a "pollutant."
   - A certain minimum atmospheric concentration is necessary for life itself.
   - Water vapor and clouds are responsible for 65–85 percent of the radiative properties of the troposphere.
   - Does anyone call water vapor a "pollutant"?
   - Why not? Because ocean evaporation is natural?
4. Published reviews of the scientific literature by Mörner and Etiope (2002) and Kerrick (2001) report a range of emission of 65 to 319 million tons of CO_2 per year. Counterclaims that volcanoes, especially submarine volcanoes, produce vastly greater amounts of CO_2 than these estimates are not supported by any papers published by the scientists who study the subject. https://climate.nasa.gov/faq/42/what-do-volcanoes-have-to-do-with-climate-change/#:~:text=Volcanic%20eruptions%20are%20often%20discussed,volcanoes%20in%20the%20world%20%2D%20combined.

5. https://volcanoes.usgs.gov/vhp/gas.html
6. https://skepticalscience.com/volcanoes-and-global-warming.htm
7. From the personal power points of my interlocutor.
8. https://www.nasa.gov/press-release/2018-fourth-warmest-year-in-continued-warming-trend-according-to-nasa-noaa
9. https://skepticalscience.com/hurricanes-global-warming.htm
10. Ibid., list compiled.
11. https://www.nasa.gov/feature/goddard/2016/carbon-dioxide-fertilization-greening-earth
12. https://www.carbonbrief.org/amazon-rainforest-is-taking-up-a-third-less-carbon-than-a-decade-ago
13. https://www.carbonbrief.org/amazon-rainforest-is-taking-up-a-third-less-carbon-than-a-decade-ago
14. https://www.yaleclimateconnections.org/2019/04/did-climate-change-cause-midwest-flooding/
15. https://skepticalscience.com/climate
16. I actually have two more responses. To this one: "Asteroid impacts, mass volcanic eruptions, powerful earthquakes, tsunamis, mass contagion, terrorist use of bioweaponry, nuclear war, gamma ray storms, massive crop failures, *ad infinitum*. Should we spend 1–2 percent of annual GDP on each of them?" I can say that we should research some things like volcanos and earthquakes and tsunamis and see if we can establish warning systems for evacuation, and we do in fact fund such research. We also fund and have in place a number of responses to mass contagion, including stocks of medicine and antivirals. We spend money on emergency food storage as well. My friend may or my not know about all of this. We spend a lot on antiterrorist threats and on preventing nuclear war. Some things, like a meteor hit or a gamma ray storm, we cannot prevent at all. That is the condition of the creature. But climate change is not some rare event or random local occurrence. It is happening and will keep happening unless we try to stop putting greenhouse gases into the air.

    He also wants to use nuclear energy. That has good potentional and should be explored. Major problems need to be addressed, and storage of waste is the main one.
17. Talmud Bavli, Berakot 16b.
18. http://www.meetinghouse.info/uploads/1/9/4/1/19410913/a_minute_against_slavery.pdf
19. Jill Lapore, *These Truths: History of the United States*. W.W. Norton & Company, New York, September, 2018, 2019.
20. And of course, the human toll on the slaves was incalculable. The war ended the practice but not, of course, the oppression and racist ideology that kept Black Americans poor and disenfranchised for generations.
21. I know how very difficult this can be. For example, could not convince my own family to protest the war in Vietnam at first; and in the case of climate change, I cannot convince my very own family to give up meat, or stop flying for vacations. No turkey on Thanksgiving? Unthinkable! .
22. chrome-extension://efaidnbmnnnibpcajpcglclefindmkaj/https://www.whitehouse.gov/wp-content/uploads/2022/08/OMB-Analysis-Inflation-Reduction-Act.pdf
23. "The Long Hot Summer," in "Science and Technology," *The Economist*, July 28, 2018, pp. 59–60.

Index

For the benefit of digital users, indexed terms that span two pages (e.g., 52–53) may, on occasion, appear on only one of those pages.

Abel, 49–50, 60–61
Abraham
    covenant with God of, 54–55
    "Here I Am" response of, 9–10
    hospitality of, 102
    interruption and, 185–86
    nomadic life of, 51, 83
    Sodom and Gomorrah's destruction and, 54–55
Adam, 9, 48–51, 64
Adani Group, 191–92
Adorno, Theodor, 73–74, 78
Advancement of Sound Science Coalition, 173
Agag, 157–58
Agassiz, Louis, 15, 225n.4
aggadah (narrative), 39–40
AIDS, 13
Amalek. *See also* Amalekites
    ancestors of, 150, 152–53, 160
    as archetypal enemy, 150, 151–52, 159, 160–62
    gematria and, 161
    God's protection of the Jews from, 149, 156, 160
Amalekites
    David's attack on, 158–59
    grandchildren of, 151–52
    Israel attacked by, 151, 156–57
    Israelites' experience of doubt and, 155, 161
    Jews fleeing Egypt attacked by, 149, 152, 153–54, 156, 157, 163
    Jews' victory at Rephidim over, 153–54
    memory and, 149–50, 151–52, 154, 156, 163
    Moses and, 149, 153–55
    Nazis compared to, 149, 151–52, 161
    Negev settlement of, 155
    postbiblical accounts of, 159–61
    Romans compared to, 149, 161
    Saul's attack against, 157–58
Amazon rainforest, 142–43, 144, 209
American Academy of Religion (AAR), 180, 181–82, 203–5
American Forest and Paper Association, 171
American Petroleum Institute (API), 170–71
Americans for Prosperity, 172
Amidah prayer, 120–21
Antarctica, 69, 142–43, 219
Aquinas, Thomas, 7–8, 34–35
Arab Spring, 64–65, 98–99
Arendt, Hannah
    Benjamin's death and, 106
    on citizenship and public action, 96–98, 194–96
    exile and loss experienced by, 95–96, 99
    on forgiveness and promising, 162
    on inner dialogue of thinking, 146–47, 190
    on Jews' lack of legal status, 99
    on loss of community, 98
    on necessity of judgment, 162–63
    on power and legitimacy, 97
    responsibility and the Other in the work of, 4
    on the Shoah and inaction, 147
Argentina, 109
Aristotle, 12–13, 34–35, 58–59, 96, 151
Arrhenius, Svante, 17–19, 21
Ashkenazi community, 188
Assad, Bashar, 89

Atlantic Meridional Overturning
    Circulation (AMOC), 142–44
Australia, 67–68, 191–92
Averroes, 58–59
Avodah Zorah, 53–54
Ayres, Matthew, 66

Baden, Jacob, 73–74
Bahamas hurricane (2022), 223–24
Bali climate treaty (2007), 167
bal tashchit (command against wanton
    destruction), 44–45, 75
Bangladesh, 89
Ban Ki-moon, 199
Basser, Herbert, 4–5
Bayle, Pierre, 71–72
Benjamin, Walter, 49, 73–74, 98, 106,
    189–90
Bernstein, Jeremy, 36, 46–47
Biden, Joe, 25–26, 167, 221–22
bioethics
    climate change and, 181–82
    clinical encounters and, 11
    COVID-19 pandemic and, 14
    Heideggerian ideas of preliterate past
        and, 123
    humans' relationship with the
        environment and, 13
    methodologies of, 44
Boers, Niklas, 143–44
Bolivia, 109
Bouazizi, Tarek el-Tayeb Mohamed, 64–65
Boyarin, Daniel, 4–5, 41
BP, 171
Brazil, 31, 84, 109
Buddhism, 30–31, 87, 202, 217
Bush, George H.W., 24, 165–67
Bush, George W., 173, 184

Cain, 9, 49–50, 54, 64
California
    agriculture and farming in, 82–83,
        129–30
    droughts in, 129–30, 181
    wildfires (2017-22) in, 10, 67,
        181, 224
Callendar, Guy, 18–20
carbon dating, 20

carbon dioxide (CO2) emissions.
    See also greenhouse gasses
    carbon sequestration technologies and,
        167–68, 212, 214–15
    climate change and, 23, 64, 179, 210
    fossil fuel use and, 18–19, 170, 174,
        178–79, 207
    global warming and, 11–12, 13, 18–19,
        20–21, 64, 173, 193, 207, 210–11
    "greening effect" and, 209
    industrialization and, 13, 18–21, 170,
        193
    Keeling curve and, 21–22
    monitoring efforts established (1957)
        for, 21–22
    nineteenth-century experiments
        regarding, 16–18
    ocean absorption hypothesis and, 20–21
    Paris Climate Accord and, 167
    population growth and, 19, 25–26
    volcanoes and, 206–7
    Western consumer habits and, 30
Carter, Jimmy, 22–23
Castellanos, Edwin, 91–92
Chernobyl nuclear disaster (1986), 28
Chevron, 169–70
Chicago (Illinois), 2–3, 10, 11–12, 31
China, 31, 109, 168–69, 223
Christianity
    exploitation of nature and, 33–34, 84
    hospitality and, 100
    Lent and, 217–18
    obligation to charity and, 92
    origins of, 217
    tithing and, 7–8
Chronicles, Book of, 159, 161
Cities of Refuge, 93–94, 141
Citizens for the Environment, 173
citizenship
    argument and, 41
    equality before the law and, 123–24
    obligation to the Other and, 90, 95
    participation and, 195
    public action and, 96–98, 194–96
    theological warrants and, 29–30
civil disobedience, 193–95
climate change. *See also* global warming
    the afterlife and, 200–1

INDEX

biodiversity loss and, 64, 178–79
carbon dioxide emissions and, 23, 64, 179, 210
COVID-19 pandemic compared to, 2–3, 6
denialism and, 2–3, 6–7, 173–75, 206–7, 210–11, 212
disease and, 27–28, 31, 100, 111, 208–9
drought and water scarcity resulting from, 64–65, 66–67, 91–92, 107–8, 110, 111, 126, 164, 178, 181, 208–9
energy extraction companies' responsibility for, 141, 164–66, 168, 170, 175–77, 179, 212–13
exile and, 58, 63–64, 85–86
fires and, 141, 178, 208–9
flooding and, 64–65, 178, 197, 208, 210
food insecurity and, 64–65, 100, 101, 111–12, 144, 200
gender and impact of, 107–8, 109–10
hospitality as response to, 83, 87, 101, 128
human understanding of, 74, 93, 181–82, 199, 211–12
as hyperobject, 86–87, 141, 212
individual action and, 60–62, 193–95, 196
interruption and, 86–87, 192, 197, 199–200
ontological error and, 84
partisan beliefs and, 211–12
refugees and, 89–92, 100, 109, 118, 164, 178
renewable energy and, 214
sacrifice as means of addressing, 6–7, 61–62, 83, 106, 118, 175–76, 196, 203, 211, 214, 221
tipping points and, 141–44
vulnerable populations at greatest risk from, 6–7, 65, 89, 126, 140, 144, 175, 201
Clinton, Bill, 167
coal, 17–19, 191–92. *See also* fossil fuels
Cohen, Nathan, 59–60
Cold War, 19–21, 28, 216
Colorado River, 208–9
Conway, Eric, 174
Copenhagen climate summit (2009), 167

COVID-19 pandemic
American Association of Religion and, 205
bioethics and, 14
carbon dioxide emissions levels during, 25–26, 179
climate change compared to, 2–3, 6
as hyperobject, 6
sacrifice and public health measures to contain, 6–7
vaccines and, 122
vulnerability of natural world exposed by, 83–84
Cuba, 164

Daughters of Zelephophad, 185–86
David, 117, 158–59
Davies, Humphrey, 16–17
D-Day invasion (1944), 19
democracy
global threats to, 127
pluralistic discourse and, 96
public action and, 97, 195
rules about private choices and, 218
D'Entreves, Alessandro Passerin, 97
derekh eretz (way of the land), 30–31
Deuteronomy
abandoned corpse story in, 132–33, 137
Amalekites and, 149, 151, 156
productive cycle of the land and, 57, 222–23
Dorff, Elliot, 35–36

Earth Day (1970), 22
East Siberian Shelf, 208–9
Eden. *See also* Paradise (Eden)
America as, 35, 59–60, 65–66
exile from, 48–51, 64, 85–86, 176
The Fall in, 47–51
Tree of Knowledge in, 47–48
Edison Electric, 171
Edomites, 152–53
Egypt
Arab Spring protests (2011) in, 89
Genesis and Quran accounts of famine in, 101, 103–4
Jews' exile in, 51
Jews' flight from, 114, 149, 152, 155, 156, 157, 163

Eisen, Arnold, 48–50, 52, 53–54, 64
Eizenstat, Stuart, 22
Eliezer (servant of Abraham), 112–13
Eliezer ben Dinai, 148
Ellenblum, Ronni, 104
El Niño, 142–43, 210
Emanuel, Kerry, 208
Endangered Species Act (United States), 22
energy extraction companies. *See also specific companies*
　climate science research funded by, 165–66, 170–72
　deceptive practices by, 141, 171, 173, 174, 175–76
　economic power of, 168–70, 175–76, 212–13
　fidelity and, 215–16
　responsibility for climate change of, 141, 164–66, 168, 170, 175–77, 179, 212–13
England. *See* United Kingdom
The Enlightenment, 54, 61–62, 73, 84–85
Environmental Protection Agency (EPA), 22, 165
Esau, 50, 150, 152–53
Esther, 160–61
Eve, 47–51, 64
exile
　climate change and, 58, 63–64, 85–86
　cultivation of land and, 56–58
　duty and, 58
　Eden and, 48–51, 64, 85–86, 176
　in Egypt, 51
　as ethical ontology, 46–51, 52
　in Europe, 54, 57–58, 73–74, 78–80, 81–82
　Exodus and, 51
　golah and, 42–43, 57–58
　hospitality and, 82, 83
　Messianic Era and, 50–51, 53
　precarity and, 31
　responsibility to the Other and, 42–43
　Roman Empire's expulsion of Jews from Israel and, 51–52, 53–54
　The Shoah and, 54, 99, 106
　Zionism and, 54
Exodus
　Amalek and, 149, 151, 153–54
　command against wanton destruction in, 44–45
　exile and, 51
　Golden Calf and, 137
　trees in, 45
ExxonMobil, 169–71. *See also* Standard Oil

The Fall, 48–51
feminism
　"ancient wisdom" and, 122
　climate change and, 107–8, 109–10, 111, 128
　distributive justice and, 111
　eco-feminism and, 34
　gendered notions of nature and, 120–21
　Jewish ethics and, 120
　reproductive rights and, 109–10
　sustainability and, 124
fires in the American West, 10, 27–28, 32, 67, 164, 181, 224
First Great Awakening, 220–21
First World Climate Conference (1979), 166–67
Flagler, Henry, 168–69
Fleming, James Rodger, 21
Florida, 32, 164, 168, 181
Fonrobert, Charlotte, 37
Foote, Eunice Newton, 15–17
fossil fuels
　carbon dioxide emissions from burning of, 18–19, 170, 174, 178–79, 207
　health consequences of burning, 14
　industrialization and, 18–19
　proposed restrictions on use of, 171, 172, 213–14
Fourier, Joseph, 14–15
Francis (pope), 30–31, 110–11, 125–26, 127, 215

Gaia, 121, 123
Gemara, 37, 139–40
gematria (Hebrew numbering system), 161
Gemorah, 4, 53, 78–79, 94

Genesis
　Amlek and, 152–53
　contradictory theologies of creation in, 75
　cultivation of land in, 53–54
　ecological readings of, 32–33
　Egyptian famine in, 101, 103
　The Fall and, 48–51
　God's reflections in, 197–98
　Jews' migrations recounted in, 31
　water and well stories in, 112–15
Germany, 31, 181
Ghosh, Anand, 86–87, 212
Gilgamesh, 198
Girard, Rene, 136
Glasgow climate summit (2021), 168
Global Climate Coalition (GCC), 171–73
global warming. *See also* climate change
　carbon dioxide emissions and, 11–12, 13, 18–19, 20–21, 64, 173, 193, 207, 210–11
　Foote's experiments (1856) and, 16
　heat waves and, 64
　hurricanes and, 74–75
　industrialization and, 64
　longitudinal data regarding, 207
　melting glaciers and, 219
　ocean temperatures and, 208
　Plass experiments (1953) and, 21
　public health consequences of, 14, 208–9
Gobi Desert, 109, 223
Godda (India), 191–92
golah (exiled population), 42–43, 57–58
Golden Calf, 137
Gomorrah, 54–55
Gordon, A.D., 75–76
Gore, Al, 167
Great Awakenings, 220–21
Great Flood texts, 185–86, 197–99
Greece, 67–68, 223–24
greenhouse gasses. *See also* carbon dioxide (CO2) emissions
　climate change and, 23, 178–79, 210
　global warming and, 14–15, 118, 181, 207–8
　Kyoto Protocol (1997) and, 167
　melting glaciers and, 69
　Paris Climate Accord (2015) and, 221–22
　Western consumer habits and, 118
Group of Seven countries, 167

Guatemala, 91–92, 100, 108–9
Gulf Stream, 142
Guterres, António, 179

Haiti, 13, 108
halachah (system of legal behavior), 5, 38–40, 46, 52–53
Haman, 152, 160–61
Hansen, James, 11–12, 170, 171, 173
Heidegger, Martin, 123
Henry, John, 16
Hirsch, Samuel Raphael, 42
Hitler, Adolf, 151–52, 161–62, 163
Horowitz, Elliot, 149
hospitality
　ethics of, 75–76, 86–87
　exile and, 82, 83
　interruption and, 190–91
　Job and, 85–86
　Joseph and, 102, 104
　limits and, 83–84
　as response to climate change, 83, 87, 101, 128
　sustainability contrasted with, 82–83, 87
　universal availability of, 83
　water and, 112, 113, 116, 117–18
Humble Oil, 170
hurricanes
　Atlantic hurricane season and, 10, 164, 223–24
　climate change and, 27–28
　global warming and, 74–75
　great flood literature and, 197
　Hurricane Katrina (2005) and, 184
　ocean temperatures and, 208

India, 191–92
industrialization
　air pollution and, 26
　carbon dioxide emissions and, 13, 18–21, 170, 193
　fossil fuels and, 18–19
　global warming and, 64
　Industrial Revolution in eighteenth-century Great Britain and, 17, 215
　religious belief and, 215
Inflation Reduction Act (United States, 2022), 3, 221–22

Information Council on the Environment, 173
The Inquisition, 72–73, 78, 81–82, 85, 161
Intergovernmental Panel on Climate Change (IPCC)
    establishment (1988), 24–25, 166
    mission statement of, 25
    reports on risk of changing climate by, 178–79, 180–81, 197, 199–200
    Rio Earth Summit (1992) and, 25
    Syrian drought and, 89–90
International Geophysical Year (1957), 21, 226n.14
interruption
    civil disobedience and, 194–95
    climate change and, 86–87, 192, 197, 199–200
    earthquakes and, 75–76, 79
    God's call and, 184
    Great Flood stories and, 185–86
    Great Interruption story and, 186–88
    hospitality and, 190–91
    The Messiah and, 190
    the poor and, 187–88
    power of the Other over your being and, 189
    sabbatical year and, 185
    Shabbat and, 185, 186
    sustainability and, 125
    The Talmud and, 186
Intertropical Convergence Zone (ITCZ), 142–43
Ireland, 213
Isaiah 58, 8–9
Islam, 100, 217. *See also* The Quran
Israel (antiquity)
    Amalekites' involvement in attacks on, 151, 156–57
    blood of the innocent and, 137–38, 140, 146
    earthquakes as divine retribution in, 76–78, 84
    famine in, 101–4
    Roman Empire's control over, 51–52, 53–54
Israel (modern state), 30–31, 54, 60

Jacob
    angel wrestled by, 152–53
    Esau and, 50, 152–53
    famines and, 51, 101, 103–4
    Rachel and, 114, 118
Jaffee, Martin, 37
Jamieson, Dale, 212
January 6 insurrection (United States, 2021), 123, 125–26
Jeremiah, 55, 62–64
Jesuits, 71–72, 81
Jewish ethics
    deontology and casuisticism in, 37–40
    dietary laws and, 217–18
    discursive method and, 40–41, 70
    duty to the Other and, 55–58, 62–63
    evil and, 43–44, 62
    feminism and, 120
    hospitality and, 82, 100–1
    limiting human desire and, 55–56
    manipulation of the land and, 61
    methods of, 44–46
    nature and, 35–36, 75, 120–21, 124
    obligation and, 55–56, 61–62, 92
    the poor and, 57–58, 62
    tithing and, 7–8
Job, 85–86, 232n.11
Johanon b. Zakkai, 8
John, Gospel of, 115–16
Johnson, Lyndon, 22
Joseph
    coat of, 50
    exile of, 51
    famine in Egypt and, 101–4
    grain given to father by, 137
    hospitality of, 102, 104
Joshua, 79–80, 154
Jubilee year, 42
Judges, Book of, 156–57

Kant, Immanuel, 71–72, 150, 216
Keeling, Charles David, 21–22
Keenen, James, 34–35
Kentucky, 181
King Jr., Martin Luther, 183
Koch Industries, 171–72
Korten, David, 60
Kyoto Protocol (1997), 167, 173

La Niña, 210
Laudito Si' (*In Praise of Creation*, Pope Francis), 30–31
Lawson, Nigel, 175
Levinas, Emmanuel
  on asymmetry of encounters with the Other, 102
  on Cities of Refuge, 93, 141
  on "the danger of premature good conscience," 5–6
  "entrance of the third" and, 119
  on ethics as the vision of God, 9
  on exegesis, 5
  on the face and the Other, 135, 140
  on femininity and Judaism, 121
  on interrupting life with the ethical, 8–9
  on justice and discourse, 83
  on justice and the Other, 118
  on responsibility and the Other, 4–5, 8, 42–43, 126, 127, 190
  on "the scent of paradise," 42
  on urban planning, 86
LeVine, Duane, 171
Leviticus, 6–8, 161
Levy, Natan, 75
Libya, 89
Lisbon earthquake (1755)
  philosophical and theological explanations of, 71–73, 78, 79–80, 84, 85, 86
  Portuguese Jews and, 73–74, 78, 81–82
  Portuguese royal family and, 71, 74, 80
  rebuilding after, 84–85
  scientific explanations of, 80, 85
  scope of physical destruction from, 70–71
Locke, John, 7, 35–36, 57–58, 59–60, 65–66
Los Angeles (California)
  author's family history and, 59–60
  fires near, 32, 67, 164, 224
  homeless populations in, 94
  increasing average temperatures in, 66

Maduro, Otto, 190
Maimonides, 12–13, 31, 58–60, 217–18
Malagrida, Gabriel, 79–81
Marshall Institute, 173–74

Marx, Karl, 125–26
Maxwell, Kenneth, 80–81
Meribah, 153, 161
Meslmani, Yousef, 89–90
met mitvah (duty to care for the remains of the dead), 138–39
minhag (customs), 38
The Mishnah. *See also* rabbinic texts
  abandoned corpse story in, 132–36, 137–39, 147–48
  Gemara and, 37
  sacred imaginary in, 52–53
  special blessing over earthquakes and, 78–79
  on trees, 45–46
mitzvot (divine commandments that direct moral behavior), 38–39
Monbiot, George, 174
Mongolia, 66
moral luck, 130, 145–48
Morgan, Michael, 118–19, 127
Morton, Timothy, 86–87, 212
Moses
  Amalekites and, 149, 153–55
  flight from Egypt of, 114–15, 117
  Joshua and, 154
  prophecy of despair by, 51
Mount Moana Lea (Hawaii), 21–22
Murray-Darling Basin, 208–9

Nachmanides, 55
Nagel, Thomas, 145–46
Naomi, 137
National Academy of Sciences and Engineering (NAS), 21–23
National Coal Association, 171
National Park system, 35, 218–19
National Petroleum Council, 171
natural law, 34–35, 121
Nazism, 95–96, 149, 161
Newcomen, Thomas, 17
New Testament
  discursive format of, 185–86
  obligation to charity discussed in, 92
  water and wells described in, 112, 115–18
Nigeria, 123
Nixon, Richard, 22

Noah, 9, 198
Numbers, Book of, 155–56
Nussbaum, Martha, 145–46

olam haba (the afterlife), 200–1
Oreskes, Naomi, 174
Orpah, 137

Pakistan floods (2022), 181
Paradise (California), 67, 181
Paradise (Eden), 49, 50–51, 216.
    See also Eden
Paraguay, 109
Paris Climate Accord (2015), 167–68, 221–22
parrhesia (public truth), 95–96, 106, 195–96
The Philippines, 197
Phillips, Oliver, 209
Phillips Petroleum, 171
Pirke Avot (The Ethics of the Fathers), 46, 120–21
Plass, Gilbert, 21
Plato, 146–47, 198
Plimer, Ian, 174
Pogrom of 1905 (Ukraine), 59–60
Pombal, Marquês de (Sebastião José de Carvalho e Mello), 80–82, 84
the poor
    homelessness among, 94, 130
    hospitality and, 83
    in India, 192
    interruption and, 187–88
    tithing and, 7–8
Pope, Alexander, 72
Portugal. *See* Lisbon earthquake (1755)
Priestly, Joseph, 16–17
Psalm 83, 159
Purim, 161

Quash, Benjamin, 4
The Quran
    discursive format of, 185–86
    Joseph and the Egyptian famine story told in, 101, 102
    Noah and the Flood story told in, 198
    obligation to charity discussed in, 92
    water and wells described in, 112, 114–15, 117–18

rabbinic texts. *See also* The Talmud
    Great Interruption and, 186–88
    Rabbi Akiva and, 133, 135–36
    Rabbi Ben Jacob and, 136
    Rabbi Eliezer and, 133, 135–36, 216
    Rabbi Gamaliel and, 186–88
    Rabbi Jose and, 159–60
    Rabbi Joshua and, 187–88
    Rabbi Judah and, 78, 133
    Rabbi Kattina and, 79, 81–82
    Rabbi Nehorai, 159–60
    Rabbi Papa, 94
    Rabbi Samuel b. Isaac and, 93
Rachel, 114–15, 118
Rashi, 154, 185–86
Rav Kook, 75–76
Reagan, Ronald, 23
Rebekah, 112–13
refugees
    climate change and, 89–92, 100, 109, 118, 164, 178
    The Shoah and, 99
    Syria and, 64–65, 89, 100, 111–12
renewable energy, 214
Revelle, Roger, 21, 180
Ribeiro Sanches, António Nunes, 79–81, 85
Rich, Nathaniel, 25–26, 166–67
Ricoeur, Paul, 151
Rio Earth Summit (1992), 25, 166
Robinson, David A., 66
Rockefeller, John D., 168–70, 191–93
Rodell, Matthew, 109
Roman Empire
    Amalekites compared to rulers of, 149, 161
    Christianity and, 217
    Edomites and, 152–53
    exile of Jews from Israel under, 51–52, 53–54
    Gemorah on the injustices of, 53
    Israel under control of, 8, 41–42, 47, 51–52
    Second Temple's destruction and, 8, 41–42, 186
Romania, 66
Rosenszweig, Franz, 124–25
Rousseau, Jean-Jacques, 71–72
Ruth, 7–8, 31, 137

Sabbath. *See* Shabbat
Sabbatical year, 185, 198–99, 203–5
Samaritan woman (Gospel of John), 115–17
Samuel, Book of, 76–78, 157–59
Santa Ana winds, 224
Sarah, 51
Saudi Aramco, 171
Saul, 157–58
Schlesinger, Jim, 22
Schmidt, Gavin, 21, 207
sea-level rise
　biodiversity threatened by, 74–75
　climate change denialism and, 175
　Florida and, 168, 181
　human understanding of, 11–12, 27–28
　hurricanes and, 208
　longitudinal data regarding, 175
　melting glaciers and, 69, 74–75, 143, 170, 197, 219
　ocean circulation patterns and, 142
Second Great Awakening, 220–21
Second Temple, destruction of, 8, 41–42, 186
Semachot, 138–39
Shabbat
　Amidah prayer and, 120–21
　command to keep, 57
　interruption and, 185, 186, 198–99
　lo shabbato (not Shabbat) and, 198–99
　retreat from production and consumption on, 42, 198–99
　specific acts prohibited on, 52–53
Shell, 171
Sherman Act, 169
Sh'ma prayer, 56–57, 222
Shmita year (sabbatical year), 185
The Shoah, 31, 43, 54, 73–74, 98, 147–48
Singer, Fred, 173
slavery
　civil disobedience and, 194
　interruption and, 190
　Jews in Egypt and, 51
　Jews' liberation from, 5–6, 42, 152
　United States and, 35, 194, 220–21
Smith, Adam, 57–58
Socrates, 146–47, 194–96
Sodom, 54–55, 195–96

Soteh, 139–40
Soviet Union, 29–30
Stalin, Josef, 149
Standard Oil, 168–69. *See also* ExxonMobil
Steitz, Fred, 173
Stern, Josef, 149
Stott, Peter, 223–24
Sudarshan, Anant, 192
Suess, Hans, 21
sustainability
　existing inequalities and, 82–83, 125
　feminism and, 124
　hospitality contrasted with, 82–83, 87
　interruption and, 125
　nostalgic views of the past and, 121–22
Syria
　civil war (2011–) in, 89, 108–9, 111–12
　drought in, 88–89, 101, 108–9, 111–12, 223
　refugee crisis and, 64–65, 89, 100, 111–12

The Talmud. *See also* rabbinic texts
　Babba Kama 32b and, 93–94
　Bavli and, 132
　building codes in, 218
　as colonialized text, 52
　discursive process and, 40
　interruption and, 186
　minhag and, 38
　period of writing (200 BCE–600CE) of, 39–40
　on responsibility for accidental killing, 93–94
　sacrifice and, 7–8
　tzedakah and, 8
　vulnerable populations and, 5
Tehina the Pharisee, 148, 236–37n.29
Teller, Edward, 170
The Temple, first destruction of, 43, 51–52, 53–55. *See also* Second Temple, destruction of
Texaco, 171
Thatcher, Margaret, 24–25
theodicy, 78
theology of interruption. *See* interruption
Thoreau, Henry David, 194

Three Mile Island nuclear accident (1979), 28
Thwaites Glacier, 143
Tisha b'Av, 63
tithing, 7–8, 203
tobacco companies, 165–66, 174, 217, 220
Trump, Donald, 25–26, 167
tsuvah (return and repair after sin), 43–44
Tu b'Shevat, 63
Tunisia, 64–65, 89
Tyndall, John, 16–17
tzedakah (charity), 8, 57, 222–23, 228n.23
tzedek (justice), 57, 222–23

United Kingdom, 2, 17, 27
United Nations
  Intergovernmental Panel on Climate Change (IPCC), 24–25, 89–90, 166, 178–79, 180–81, 197, 199–200
  Stockholm meeting on the environment (1972) and, 22
  United Nations Environment Programme (UNEP) and, 24–25
United States
  Civil War in, 220–21
  individualism and consumer habits in, 7, 211
  migration to, 91–92, 98–99, 100
  privilege and obligation in, 90–91
  rising average temperatures in, 66
  sacrifice and, 7
  slavery in, 35, 194, 220–21
  US Capitol insurrection (2021) in, 123, 125–26
United States Chamber of Commerce, 171

Venezuela, 109
Vietnam War, 216, 219–20
volcanoes, 165, 174, 206–7

Voltaire, 71–73
Voting Rights Act, 220–21

Walker, Margaret Urban, 145–46
Waskow, Arthur, 75–76
water access
  agricultural practices as threat to, 110
  children and, 107–8
  climate change as threat to, 64–65, 66–67, 91–92, 107–8, 110, 111, 126, 164, 178, 181, 208–9
  Genesis and, 112–15
  health threats due to lack of, 107–8
  hospitality and, 112, 113, 116, 117–18
  as human right, 110
  women and, 107–8, 112, 113–14, 115–18, 126
Weber, Max, 54–55
West Antarctic ice sheet, 69–70, 142–43, 219
White, Lynn, 32–36
wildfires. *See* fires in the American West
Williams, Bernard, 130, 145–47
Wimpfhiemer, Barry, 39–40
Winston, David, 4–5
Wittgenstein, Ludwig, 184
Woods, Darren, 169–70
Woolsey Fire (California, 2018), 224
World Meteorological Organization (WMO), 24–25
World War II, 6–7, 14–15, 19

Yemen, 108
Yom Kippur, 43–44, 76

Zika virus, 111, 223
Zimbabwe, 123
Zionism, 54, 59–60

The manufacturer's authorised representative in the EU for product safety is Oxford
University Press España S.A. of El Parque Empresarial San Fernando de Henares,
Avenida de Castilla, 2 – 28830 Madrid (www.oup.es/en or product.safety@oup.com).
OUP España S.A. also acts as importer into Spain of products made by the manufacturer.

Printed in the USA/Agawam, MA
May 2, 2025

886845.002